Save the Family, Save the Child

*WHAT
WE CAN
DO TO
HELP
CHILDREN
AT RISK*

Save the Family, Save the Child

BY

Vincent J. Fontana, M.D.

AND Valerie Moolman

A DUTTON BOOK

DUTTON
Published by the Penguin Group
Penguin Books USA Inc., 375 Hudson Street,
New York, New York 10014, U.S.A.
Penguin Books Ltd, 27 Wrights Lane,
London W8 5TZ, England
Penguin Books Australia Ltd, Ringwood,
Victoria, Australia
Penguin Books Canada Ltd, 2801 John Street,
Markham, Ontario, Canada L3R 1B4
Penguin Books (N.Z.) Ltd, 182-190 Wairau Road,
Auckland 10, New Zealand

Penguin Books Ltd, Registered Offices:
Harmondsworth, Middlesex, England

First published by Dutton, an imprint of New American Library,
a division of Penguin Books USA Inc.
Distributed in Canada by McClelland & Stewart Inc.

First Printing, May, 1991
10 9 8 7 6 5 4 3 2 1

 REGISTERED TRADEMARK—MARCA REGISTRADA

Library of Congress Cataloging-in-Publication Data

Fontana, Vincent J.
    Save the family, save the child : inside child abuse today / by
Vincent J. Fontana with Valerie Moolman.
        p.   cm.
    Includes index.
    ISBN 0-525-24989-3
    1. Child abuse—United States. I. Moolman, Valerie. II. Title.
HV6626.5.F66 1991
362.7'6'0973—dc20   90-21796
                                                                          CIP

Printed in the United States of America
Set in Janson
Designed by Eve L. Kirch

Some of the names of children, parents and other nonprofessional participants in the case histories have been changed and/or are fictitious. Situations in some cases have been disguised to protect the children involved. However, all of the facts are true.

Dedicated to the memory of:

Ursula Sunshine Assaid *5 years*
Keiko Aylor *5 weeks*
Michael Anthony Baker *10 months*
Dayna Lorae Broussard *8 years*
Jessica Cortez *5 years*
Eli Creekmore *3 years*
Jose DeJesus *17 months*
Michael W. "Bubba" Dickinson *3 years*
Roxanne Felumero *3 years*
Maya Figueroa *3 years*
Tamika Greene *5 years*
Doris Ann Holden *2 years*
Paula Houston *15 years*
Dyneeka Johnson *5 years*
Dennis Jurgens *4 years*
Maurice Kittelberger *2 years*
Lisa Launders ("Steinberg") *6 years*
Johnny Lindquist *6 years*
Bradley McGee *2 years*
Lattie McGee *5 years*
Quintin McKenzie *3 years*
Shawn McKeon *3 years*
Tess Maye *2 years*
Andrew Mitchell *3 years*
Sarah Ann Rairdon *14 years*
Ryan Reed *3 years*
Rachel Sanchez *2 years*
Joseph Anthony Sanders *17 months*
Eugene Shahine *1 year*
Julian Shamoon *4 months*
Barbara Smith *2 years*
Phenix Smith *5 years*
Donna Anne Stern *9 years*
Christopher Sumpter *3 years*
Wendall Two Bears *14 months*
. . . and Joshua DeShaney

(And all the thousands more, whose names we do not know)

91-34479

CONTENTS

ACKNOWLEDGMENTS

I have written this book to acknowledge the existence of the horror of child abuse and awaken society to the many atrocities that have disintegrated our families and numbed our senses.

There is no way I can do justice to the many individuals that have entered my life and helped me in fighting the battle against child abuse in the few hundred words provided here. What I can do is give credit to those who contributed to the making of this book.

First and foremost, there is Alexia Dorszynski, my editor. She has guided me and been a source of ideas. Her friendly manner and professional competence have been an inspiration.

I owe a special debt of gratitude to my associates who gave generously of their time and knowledge, Dr. Esther Robison, and Clair Yaffa; my literary agent, Jane Dystel; and my secretary, Eleanor Atkins. Sincere thanks also go to Sr. Cecilia Schneider and Sr. Helen Murphy for their leadership, friendship, and support in the development of the child abuse treatment and prevention programs described throughout the book.

Deep appreciation to the staffs of Covenant House and the Fortune Society for the opportunity to hear and speak with the victims of child abuse about their experiences.

A personal tribute to the late Francis Cardinal Spellman, who in 1962 appointed me to the position of medical director of the

New York Foundling Hospital, where I first observed the horror of child abuse in the eyes and on the bodies of the hundreds of abandoned children in our nurseries.

Finally, I thank God for the inspired energies and the time given to me to care for and speak for these, the least of his brethren— the children.

"Do you understand gentlemen, that all the horror is in just this: that there is no horror."

—Aleksandr Koprin

Prologue: Another Small White Coffin

New York City, March 25, 1969. Three-year-old Roxanne Felumero, reported missing, is found at the bottom of the East River with rocks in her pockets to weigh down her beaten body and her head swollen to the size of a birthday balloon. A few months earlier she had been removed from the care of loving foster parents and returned to the custody of two heroin addicts—her mother, Marie, and her stepfather, George Poplis.

Do you remember this story? I can never forget it. What gets to me, every time, is the terror of the dying child.

"I hit her lots of times," Poplis said later, totally without remorse. "She was always wetting the bed." Poplis was charged with murder. Marie, herself a battered wife, testified against him.

The case was a lurid, front-page sensation. Witness after witness described visiting the Poplis apartment within the ten days preceding the little girl's death. Several of those testifying were drug addicts who were accustomed to using the apartment as a shooting gallery. George would let them use the place to get high, they explained, in exchange for a fix for himself.

For days, the visitors testified, the child cowered in the bathroom. Her face and body were black and blue and her head was swollen—"two feet wide, you could hardly see her eyes," according to testimony.

Then she was lying on the floor in the bedroom. One witness

tried to get into the room to see her, but Poplis appeared to be blocking her way. Then, as the woman edged around him, "He threw a blanket over the baby. Only one hand was sticking out. It moved a little."

This must have been close to the moment of Roxanne's death, for it was the next day that she was reported missing and the search began.

At least eight people had seen her during the days of her dying— supposedly concerned neighbors as well as addicts—and none reported what they saw to any agency. Perhaps it would have made no difference; Roxanne was already "in the system," and that hadn't helped her. A Family Court judge, lacking full details of her case, had summarily removed her from a loving foster home and sent her back to her mother and stepfather, in spite of the fact that her foster parents had reported that the child was being beaten every time she visited George and Marie Poplis. Roxanne's case was familiar to the Bureau of Child Welfare and to the Family Court, where she had her own law guardian—and yet no one followed up on her case or made a watchdog visit to the Poplis home. Perhaps it was assumed that somebody else was doing something about keeping an eye on her. But nobody was.

Poplis was convicted and sentenced to twenty years. Marie, the silent, unindicted partner in the abuse, vanished from public view, free to form other liaisons and birth other children.

The report of the Judiciary Relations Committee of the Appellate Court on the handling of the case stated: "A fair appraisal of blame for this tragedy must focus on the lack of resources within the Family Court complex and the lack of coordination and communication among the various agencies and disciplines involved in the case."

The brutal murder of Roxanne, coupled with public revelations of faulty communications between and even within agencies, brought about passionate outcries for change, action, and reform. We vowed that never again would we, as individuals, fail to report the telltale signs that a child was being abused. Never again would we let our child protective agencies get away with slipshod work and callousness and lack of follow-through. If these agencies needed revamping, streamlining, shaking up, and cleaning out, so be it. We would make structural changes, pass new laws, spend more money, educate the public, revolutionize our creaky institutions, become crusaders for our children and our future.

Child advocates of all disciplines were galvanized into action. When the outrage had simmered down I wrote a book, *Somewhere a Child Is Crying*, telling the stories of many Roxannes. As chairman of the Mayor's Task Force on Child Abuse and Neglect and also as Medical Director of The New York Foundling Hospital, I had many such tragic tales to tell. I wrote, too, of the changes that had already been implemented, and I made a number of recommendations for further improvements in our child protective system. Some of them have since been implemented: New York and other states have set up central registries of case files, and most states have hotlines to handle crisis calls; screening for potential foster and adoptive parents as well as day care workers has been tightened up; all states now have mandatory reporting laws for child abuse and neglect, and more people have been required by law to report.

With the memory of Roxanne to spur us on, we had the passion of crusaders. This time, we thought, we were really getting somewhere. And we did, indeed, educate the public and become crusaders for our children. But we did not realize at the time that most of our great plans were little more than patchwork, short-term remedies. Our laws remained largely unchanged, the structural fixes were minimal, and our creaky institutions went right on creaking.

Eighteen years later. On Sunday night, November 1, 1987, and into the early morning hours of November 2, another child lay dying on the floor of a New York City apartment. She was six-year-old Elizabeth, called Lisa.

The littered Greenwich Village apartment was occupied by an affluent middle-class lawyer named Joel Steinberg, his female lover-companion Hedda Nussbaum—once a writer and editor of children's books—and their two supposedly adopted children, Lisa, aged six, and Mitchell, aged sixteen months.

Earlier that day a visitor might have observed a sort of Sunday afternoon serenity in the place. The apartment was dirty and in disarray, and the only piece of children's furniture in sight was the broken playpen in which Mitchell both played and slept, but there was something homy about the way Joel and Hedda were chopping vegetables together in the kitchen, helped by Lisa with her own little knife and watched by baby Mitchell from his makeshift crib. It was in fact a travesty of domestic contentment, for Hedda Nuss-

baum had been battered almost to the point of death and Lisa was
a frightened, bruised, neglected little girl, but no one was there to
see the family as it really was. No one ever came to the apartment
anymore.

By seven o'clock that evening, according to Hedda Nussbaum's
testimony at Joel Steinberg's trial, the apparent idyll had been
shattered. So had Lisa. She lay undressed and unconscious on the
bathroom floor, water and chewed vegetables dribbling from the
corners of her mouth. There were new bruises on her head, one
of them—as the medical evidence revealed later—caused by a blow
so savage that her brain shifted inside her skull, resulting in a
massive subdural hematoma. Steinberg had gone out to dinner,
leaving instructions with Nussbaum to get "in harmony" with the
child, but do nothing until he came home. Nussbaum, a destroyed
wretch of a woman whose smashed face, multiple broken ribs, and
ulcerated, gangrenous legs reflected only a small part of the abuse
she herself had endured, tried ineffectually to arouse Lisa, allegedly
believing that Joel would "raise up and cure" the little girl when
he came back. It was only at about 6:30 on Monday morning that
the rescue squad was finally called and the comatose child taken
to St. Vincent's Hospital.

The whole incredible story started breaking within the next couple of days and has not yet been completely told. What is most
likely, though no one outside that household really knows, is that
when Joel came back from dinner that night, he and Hedda free-
based cocaine, as they had done almost every night for the previous
three months; that he had beaten Lisa several times, the last time
fatally, for "staring hypnotically" at him; and that he had brain-
washed Hedda into believing that she was the tool of a hypnotic
cult that was out to get him. What is certain is that at no time did
he exhibit remorse or sorrow for the battered child. Indeed, in the
hospital emergency room, he smiled and made a joke when told
by a physician, while Lisa was in a coma, that she was permanently
brain-damaged.

Three days after Lisa entered the hospital she was detached from
life-saving equipment and allowed to die.

As the story unfolded, bits and pieces of Lisa's life with
Steinberg and Nussbaum began to fall into place, forming a bitter
pattern.

Neither Lisa nor Mitchell had been legally adopted; both had been stolen children and should never have been in the Steinberg home.

Neighbors and business associates (mostly drug-dealer clients) of Joel Steinberg had seen evidence of abuse but did nothing about it. When the case broke the neighbors claimed they had called various agencies "hundreds of times," but later scaled their claims down to a couple of reports of domestic quarrels and one or two reports of possible child abuse.

Social workers from the city's Special Services for Children (SSC) had visited the Steinberg apartment in 1984 after Hedda had been treated at Bellevue Hospital for a beating. Although the abuse of Lisa had already started, they found nothing amiss, and made no recommendation for follow-up investigation.

Responding to a neighbor's report of suspected child abuse in the Steinberg household, a different team of SSC caseworkers had made an inspection and judged the allegation "unfounded."

Police had responded to a complaint of domestic abuse at the Steinberg apartment a few weeks before Lisa's death and saw nothing worthy of report.

Several teachers and aides at Lisa's school noted her frequent absences, disheveled appearance, and bruises but made no report, except to each other.

At the school Halloween party a student's mother and a magazine photographer took pictures of Lisa, uncombed, disheveled, in ill-fitting clothes, forlorn and badly bruised. They were apparently unconcerned, and made no report.

A teenage neighbor and her mother testified at the trial that Lisa came to their place almost every day after school to play, and that in the month preceding her death she had been bruised and dejected, her hair was matted and on occasion torn out in clumps, and she was wearing clothes she had long outgrown. They said nothing to the supposed parents, nor did they convey their observations to any agency.

This pattern is familiar to all of us involved with child protection.

I dwell on Lisa's story because it is the Roxanne case of our time, today's symbol of child abuse. We who responded so energetically to the tragedy and the challenge of Roxanne's death have again been galvanized into reviewing and renewing our efforts. The headlined death and burial of yet another child are not only terrible events in themselves but eye-openers to those among us who may have forgotten that these horrors exist. It would appear that we rediscover child abuse whenever an abused child's death makes headlines. This, our reawakening, is Lisa's legacy. But the Steinberg case is also important for a number of other reasons, some of them contradictory yet all worthy of contemplation:

• In many of its aspects, the Steinberg case is characteristic of child abuse cases ending in murder, as well as many of those that do not.

• Although it is an aberration, a case so peculiar in its bizarre details that it cannot be seen as typical, it points up the fact that child abuse can cut across all boundaries of socioeconomic level, race, ethnic heritage, and religious faith.

• The shared reluctance of all the witnesses to intervene on Lisa's behalf suggests that the social status of Joel Steinberg and Hedda Nussbaum helped shelter them from investigation.

• As a televised trial of more than usual high drama, the case suggests that Steinberg and Nussbaum achieved stardom because the public expects more of affluent middle-class people than of the lowlifes we assume to be committing these crimes.

• The story leads many observers to assume that child abusers are all depraved monsters who should be boiled in oil. In fact, what must *not* be one of the lessons of the Steinberg case and similar tales of horror is that child abusers are necessarily sadistic brutes. Most of them are decent, troubled parents who know a cry of pain when they hear one and need help to cope with the stresses of their lives—*most*, but obviously not all.

Those of us who attempt to serve the cause of children were surprised when the public reacted with such incredulity to the murder of little Lisa. New York City alone has an average of two child murders a week. During the year in which Lisa Steinberg was battered and killed, 102 other children in New York were also abused to death. These—and I pull cases from my files at random—are some of them:

• In the last weeks of her life, five-year-old Tamiya Reade was repeatedly whipped with an electric cord, forced to stuff herself with food until she threw up, and finally poisoned. Her stepfather was convicted of murdering her and also of smothering his infant son by a woman companion.

• Three-year-old Shawn McKeon died after being given a tub bath by his mother. She had plunged him into scalding water because he had been driving her crazy with his crying and because she felt he needed discipline.

• Infant Donny B., two of whose siblings had been abused, died of battered child syndrome and malnutrition. The father had recently been released from prison after serving a sentence for severely beating one of the older children.

• Julian Mansour, five years old, died of internal bleeding and multiple abrasions after being beaten with a baseball bat for interrupting his father's chess game.

• Ramon DeJesus, seventeen months old, died of ruptured intestines after being struck with a fist or a blunt object. Previously he had been hospitalized with lacerations, bruises, and contusions around the mouth suggesting a gag.

• Baby M., four months old, was admitted to hospital with a broken leg after reportedly having fallen from a bed. A few days subsequent to release she was taken to another hospital, dead on arrival as the result of a fractured skull.

• There was no suspicion of homicide when five-week-old Laika Naylor stopped breathing in her crib, but autopsy tests revealed a skull fracture and hemorrhaging in the skull. Her nineteen-year-old father said he had clapped her ears because she would not stop crying.

Sifting through my notes, I see that what these—and other—examples of child murder in 1987 have in common is that every single family involved was already well known to at least one city agency.

In 1988, 127 New York children died of abuse and neglect—a near-record for the '80s. Again, fully half the families involved were previously known to some unit of the city's child protective agency or to Family Court or to an emergency ward or a police precinct or some other public or private agency directly or indirectly concerned with the welfare of children—none of which shared its knowledge with any other agency.

Roxanne was known; Lisa was known. What good did that do them?

Perhaps it seems that I am concerned only with New York City and only with fatalities. This is not the case. I speak from a New York base and with outrage at the ultimate crime, but my scope is much larger. I believe it is not going too far out on a limb to say that New York City suffers from all the nation's ills and suffers them all to a monumental degree; I believe, too, that it is the child abuse and neglect capital of the world. The child protection problems in New York City are generic to the rest of the nation. This is a sorry claim, yet the magnitude of our crisis demands that we concentrate our most skillful and dynamic efforts on finding a solution.

It seems to me that this city has galloped downhill, completely out of control. It is a city filled with unrelenting violence, a place where the bizarre is becoming a way of life. In 1990, we had 2,000 murders. Kids are afraid of other kids in the schools, and teachers are afraid of the kids. Drugs are peddled and used openly on street corners and in playgrounds. Babies are being sold by drug addicts to support their filthy habit. Houses burn down because crack smokers or drug dealers turn uglier than usual. Stray shots hit innocent kids and decent people minding their own business in their own homes.

Look at this city—a prototype of the American megalopolis—and you see cramped, ridiculously overpriced apartments for those who can afford them, subways and city sidewalks strewn with homeless people, despair-breeding welfare hotels, poverty, unemployment, and the stress that goes with it. Look at the people and you'll see an ongoing epidemic of family chaos, with divorces and separations and domestic violence. Babies are having babies, unprepared for single parenthood. Infants are born drug-addicted or already dying of AIDS. Adolescents are running away or being thrown out of their homes and are selling their bodies for survival in the streets.

All these elements combine to make New York a model for the

psychodynamics of child abuse. It isn't the only city with this glut of problems, but it is the city with the worst and the most. Whatever is wrong anywhere is wrong here. It looks to be beyond redemption.

And yet I don't believe it is—any more than I believe that kids and stressed-out parents and families can't be saved.

Just as we lead in the horror statistics, so do we lead the campaign against the horror. And as leaders in the field of child abuse prevention, we *must* find solutions in our own community. Further, it is our obligation to create a model for the prevention of child abuse throughout the nation.

Nationwide, the child abuse death toll has gone as high as 4,000 *known cases* a year. Yet no more than 2 to 3 percent of child abuse cases throughout the country end in death. Coast to coast, more than 2 million cases of child maltreatment are reported annually, covering the spectrum of poor parenting from neglect and emotional abuse to physical injury and sexual molestation. We are horrified by the murders, and rightly so, but there are hundreds of thousands of other children leading wretched lives and somehow surviving—seriously scarred, for the most part, and likely to have grim futures as unhappy or seriously disturbed adults. These are the victims who are overshadowed by the shocking fatality reports; these are the victims suffering lingering deaths.

Our job as child advocates is to spot the danger signals *before* both parent and child are damaged beyond repair. And even if we do not care about other people and other people's children, we have to realize that unless we help the survivors we are threatened by them, because among them are the abusers, the addicts, and the criminals of tomorrow.

Such selfish considerations aside, our indifferent public attitude toward the loss of our children is a national disgrace. In any civilized nation the children are supposed to come first; isn't that what civilization is about? But in our country they apparently matter so little that child welfare is seldom so much as mentioned as a major concern by our national leaders, who not only seem incapable of recognizing the roots of crime and violence but appear unable to grasp the pain of the present.

And so we stumble along with neither national policy nor leadership to guide us, not to mention the necessary funding. Despite our horror at the Roxannes and Lisas, we have not overhauled our system of child care. In fact we have never even installed a comprehensive system. No matter what stopgap measures we have tried in the past, we witness the same old story: children falling through the cracks of a hydra-headed system, being lost because of poor communication between agencies that are supposed to safeguard them and professionals who do not talk to each other. One hand still doesn't know what the other is doing. That is the nature of our clumsy bureaucracy. But we can't pin everything on the beleaguered bureaucracy. In the last two decades, something has happened to our sense of community and to our sense of family. We have lost our props, and we have endangered ourselves.

"When you talk about child abuse," says Matilda Cuomo, child advocate and wife of the governor of New York State, "you talk about family breakdown." The fact is that the glue that held the American family together for so many years has come unstuck, and the basic family structure has unraveled. Absentee parents or single-parent homes with visiting lovers offer no support systems for the child; and with the gradual disappearance of the extended family, the usual bailouts—such as grandparents, aunts, and uncles—have also disappeared.

As a result of broken families, drugs, stress, and despair, youngsters have given up on their parents and on the future. Teenage suicide, often drug- or alcohol-related, is at an all-time high; it has doubled in the last ten years and is now one of the leading causes of death among young people. Half a million youths run away from home every year; and every year a million or more teenage pregnancies occur, many of them culminating in births to mothers with no parenting experience and no means of support. These mothers are children bringing up children; they expect the impossible of their babies and become enraged when their expectations are not met. Often these child-mothers are drug- or alcohol-addicted; sometimes their babies are born drug-addicted or with fetal alcohol syndrome.

It is an ugly, depressing picture, but my message is not one of despair. It is one of hope, offering concrete solutions, bold approaches. In my view, there is no longer any room for the handwringing and mud-slinging that goes on whenever a new and shocking case bursts into the headlines. It is time for some real action. We have the means of revolutionary change, we have the know-how to educate, we have the technology for instant communication—we have all the resources.

Any proposal for change must integrate all agencies, encompass all concerned human beings, address itself to the fault lines in every aspect of the child protective system and spell out the means of repairing them. We can no longer attack the disease of child maltreatment with the same old Band-Aids—we can no longer rely on a little retraining here and a little more money there and ringing proclamations about children's rights. We need new strategies and a total, integrated plan.

It is my intention to present such a plan. I will analyze the situations and stories of abusers and victims, then dissect and examine the present child welfare system to show exactly where each agency has fallen down in the past and permitted a child to slip through the faults in the system. Finally, I will demonstrate what must be done and can be done to change the system radically. In spite of the failures of the past, I am convinced that

• There are ways to identify families and children at risk.

• There are ways to effect early intervention.

• There are ways to strengthen the family and save the children at the same time.

• There are ways to provide instant help in crisis situations.

• There are ways to coordinate the efforts of all the child welfare agencies and make them work.

• The federal government can and must do certain things to effect that coordination and provide the impetus—as well as some of the funds—for a nationwide plan of action.

Somewhere out there, children are still crying—hundreds and thousands of them—in pain from their injuries and in terror of their parents. Think, if you can stand it, of their fear and helplessness; think of them being alternately neglected and beaten by the adults who are their only protectors. It does not bear imagining, but it is happening. We cannot turn our backs. We *must* think about it. And we must take immediate action.

*   *   *

Dr. Karl Augustus Menninger, one of the nation's foremost psychiatrists, died on July 18, 1990. He was a few days short of his ninety-seventh birthday. In the later years of his life he had become increasingly critical of American society. In November 1989, he spoke to a convocation in New York and said:

"Most of my life has been spent in treating persons one by one. But as I become increasingly aware of the extent of misery and hopelessness in our society, I think more of preventing unnecessary suffering at the source, before individuals take—or are forced to take—the wrong road."

That is what we hope to do: to find the right road, and prevent unnecessary suffering at its source: the family.

1 / America the Beautiful

A Bronx mother was charged with murder yesterday
for allegedly throwing her 2-year-old daughter out
of a fifth-floor window after the girl accidentally
knocked an air conditioner out the window while
two other children watched.

Having made the observation that people who maltreat their children are not usually monsters or seriously deranged individuals, but rather parents deserving of help, I am compelled to say that some abusers do not command sympathy. We can blame "the system" for a lot of our ills, but the fact is that there are criminally negligent and even evil people among us. We tend to say they're crazy, as if that explains their actions. But not all "crazy" people are evil, not all evil people are crazy—and not all parents who abuse or neglect their children are "bad." Most of them are not. We have an extraordinary variety of child abusers in our country, ranging from the overstressed and ignorant to the just plain stupid and negligent to the—let's face it—monstrous.

The very, very small percentage of truly monstrous abusers skews the public attitude toward people who mistreat their children, even those who do it unwittingly or under unbearable pressure. Many of us still believe that *all* child abusers are some sort of monsters, better off on a desert island or in prison. I believe that one of the greatest obstacles keeping us from making substantial progress against child abuse and neglect is the ignorance and prejudice in our country toward the very people who need our help most and whose children have the most to gain by it.

This ignorance, this lack of awareness and understanding, has caused many of us to feel that all child abusers are beyond help, too worthless and depressing to think about. What is *really* depressing is the fact that so many of us cannot see or will not face up to the reality of child abuse and its consequences. We, as a society, have been choosing to see only a small part of what constitutes abuse; with a little more understanding and acceptance of what child maltreatment is all about, we would recognize—and demand action on—more. I believe that lack of involvement on the part of any individual diminishes us as a society and as a country.

She threw her baby out the window. This is the stuff of our times: a common, ugly, mindless child-murder. The mother is a handsome if dead-eyed woman; two weeks earlier, she had been seen by neighbors to throw a puppy and two kittens out of that same window. (The neighbors, of course, did not report this event until after the murder of the child.) The father, a brutish, dull-looking fellow who was said to be asleep at the time of the incident, was charged with endangering the girl's welfare and assaulting the couple's two other toddlers.

Every day of the week, every week of the year, a horrific scenario like this is enacted somewhere in the United States. It is not a typical case of child abuse but neither is it atypical; indeed, it occurs frequently enough to have become a stereotype. People living outside the major cities tend to think it doesn't happen in their backyard, but it does; it happens in everybody's backyard. If the perpetrator is not the mother, it is the father, the stepfather, the stepmother, the "boyfriend," the foster parent, the adoptive parent, an older sibling, the baby-sitter, or the kindly person who works in some sort of child care facility—although some of these people are more likely to indulge in sexual abuse than in murder. Not all the hurtful crimes against children result in their early death: some inflict a long, slow death-in-life, and others are so insidious and subtle that even the victim is unaware of having been abused. But it is the cruel, needless, ugly, and often sudden death of children that evokes our most passionate response.

When the first state-by-state study of injury-related childhood deaths was reported early in 1989, readers were appalled to learn that injury is the leading cause of childhood death and that *homicide* is the leading cause of injury-related death among children younger than one year old. Some child advocates leapt to the conclusion that homicide is the leading cause of death among children. This is not the case: auto accidents, accidental suffocation, house fires, falls, and drowning are other leading causes of injury-related deaths. But within the group of injury-related deaths, murder is the primary cause. And the murder of children is primarily due to abuse and neglect.

In the 1989 survey of public health officials in all fifty states and the District of Columbia, which was conducted by the National Committee for Prevention of Child Abuse, forty-one states and the District together reported 2.2 million cases of child abuse, a 3 percent increase over the year before. The total for thirty-six states was 1,225 child abuse fatalities, a 5 percent increase since 1987 and a *35 percent* increase since 1985.

It should be emphasized that the fatality figure represents only the *reported* cases in the reporting states. Not all states have data available; and even when they do, precise figures are impossible to obtain. It is alarmingly easy to disguise or conceal the death of a child, and obviously the perpetrators often feel it is in their best interests to do exactly that. Deaths of children by abuse and neglect are often misclassified as accidental, or due to natural causes or to Sudden Infant Death Syndrome. Some deaths may be overlooked completely; if the existence of a child is not known outside the family, it is not particularly difficult to remove it from existence altogether and erase the traces. In my opinion—but not only in mine—a more realistic fatality figure per annum in the U.S. is closer to 4,000. Possibly even 5,000.

Nonetheless, even the reported figures keep escalating. In New York State, reports of abuse and neglect increased approximately 15 percent in 1988: in 1987 there were 104,572 reports involving 171,952 children compared to 122,917 reports involving 199,878 children for 1988. Of the 1,225 child abuse and neglect fatalities reported nationally in 1988, 206 involved children in New York State—almost 17 percent of the nationwide total.

Is New York—with 39.4 reports of abuse per thousand children—the scapegrace of the U.S.? No. A report released in mid-1989 by a California group called Children Now, an assemblage of prominent Californians, indicates very strongly that in the race to be the worst, the Golden State—the richest and most populous in the nation—has even less to brag about than does the Empire State. California, with its 7.6 million children—one of every nine in the United States—generates 50.8 reports per thousand children. Only two states have more. Are Californians more diligent about reporting? Possibly. Are Californian children more likely to be abused? That too, perhaps.

In some states, among them Pennsylvania, Maryland, Texas, and Tennessee, the phenomenon of child abuse and neglect is apparently not a major issue, although it is by no means unknown. This is not the case in Illinois, whose Department of Children and Family Services investigated 93,347 reports of child abuse and neglect during the 1988 fiscal year. During that period, 98 children died as a result of abuse, neglect, and parental negligence, a large number of them showing brain damage with skull fracture and internal hemorrhaging. Illinois, perhaps coincidentally, has a very active child abuse hotline. Reportedly, it is so busy that it requires relays of recorded voices that put the caller on hold between pressing buttons on the touch-tone telephone—an overloaded system that must surely discourage the most well-meaning and patient of callers.

So it goes around the nation. No community is immune.

In our horror at the physical batterings resulting in death we tend to ignore less drastic, more commonly accepted forms of corporal punishment and underestimate the more insidious and long-term effects of the non-battering forms of child maltreatment. When a child is beaten to death, we are all appalled and outraged. Many observers understandably believe that active abuse is more serious than neglect; and in its ultimate expression, it often is. But others are convinced that the rate of injury or impairment is greater in neglect cases than in abuse cases. One major survey has shown that two-thirds of all serious maltreatment injuries or impairments occur in cases of neglect or negligence, rather than in cases of physical battering, and the effects of such damage can be as long-lasting as those of the cases of outright abuse. In fact, more children die of physical neglect than of physical abuse. Top that off with sexual molestation, emotional abuse, educational neglect, bizarre forms of discipline, and other manifestations of weird or ignorant parental or caretaker behavior, and the lasting effects of *non*-battering maltreatment may be far more devastating than most deliberate physical abuse. And such maltreatment occurs throughout our land of liberty all the time.

We are dealing with facts and with children's lives.

Here are scenes of everyday life from all over the United States:

Denver, Colorado. Five-year-old Phenix Smith chokes after allegedly being force-fed a ginger cake and dies in Children's Hospital. Police report she apparently "choked to death on a large amount of food" and also showed signs of possible sexual abuse. Her stepmother, thirty-one-year-old Beverly Smith, stands accused of force-feeding the little girl as a punishment for sampling a ginger cake without permission. Three siblings are removed to foster homes. The circumstances suggest that death was not the intended result, but that the child nonetheless died of the adult's anger. Is it possible that the woman, parent of four children, could not have realized the danger? Somehow I doubt it.

Salem, Virginia. A woman is sentenced to twelve years in prison for force-feeding her adopted four-year-old daughter a fatal dose of table salt as punishment for stealing sugar. Testifying in her own behalf, Beth Riggs claimed she had no idea that the salt would prove fatal; on a previous occasion she had punished the child by forcing her to eat pepper, and the child had not died of that. One wonders, among other things, why a four-year-old has to "steal" sugar—and then die for it.

Albany, New York. An irate father allegedly ties a belt around his thirteen-year-old daughter's neck and forces her to crawl down the street and bark like a dog after coming home unacceptably late that night. Neighbors disturbed by the racket call the police. Joseph A. Dickson, forty-two, is released on $1,000 bail following arraignment on charges of third-degree assault and endangering the welfare of a child. "Apparently he considered it a form of discipline for his daughter," a police sergeant observes.

Jersey City, New Jersey. A twenty-six-year-old Jersey City housewife slashes her two-month-old daughter to death with a kitchen knife and is charged with murder. Baby Melanie, an only child, was in her crib at the time. The husband was asleep in the couple's apartment when the baby's screams awakened him at about 10:30 P.M. When he tried to intervene, his wife turned from the crib and stabbed him a number of times. He ran for help and she followed him to the hallway outside the apartment, where they struggled together until the police came. By that time the baby was dead in a bath of blood. This woman had no prior history of psychiatric disorder or drug use. Lacking any other clues, one can only speculate that she may have been suffering from postpartum depression.

Markham, Illinois. A popular community activist and clergyman from Chicago's South Side is convicted of sexually abusing a teen-age foster son. The Cook County jury returned the verdict against the Reverend Paul Hall, a licensed foster parent and founder of a boys' club. He was found guilty of two counts of criminal sexual assault and five counts of aggravated criminal sexual abuse. Hall was also indicted last year for repeated sexual assaults against two boys who lived at his home in South Holland. The trial involved only one of the youths, who said he was molested over a period of nineteen months. The pastor denied the charges.

Cases like this, and regrettably there are many of them, highlight two important points: One, that a respectable front as a champion of children is often no more than that—just a front; and, two, that foster homes are not necessarily safe havens. After a case of child abuse or neglect is discovered there is often a knee-jerk reaction to yank the child out of the home and hurry him into foster care, but this can prove to be a very grave mistake.

Port Angeles, Washington. A lawyer who adopted at least sixteen children, mostly from Asia and Central America, has been charged with sexual abuse amid indications of what a county prosecutor described as "wanton sexual activity" in his home. A twelve-year-old blind girl told investigators she was molested repeatedly by the forty-six-year-old lawyer, his adopted thirty-year-old son, a former reserve sheriff's deputy, and at least one juvenile in the residence, according to documents filed in Clallam County Superior Court. Police are also investigating claims of sexual abuse by several children in the household.

In recent years there has been an extraordinary increase in the number of reported sex abuse cases. In gathering a random sampling of maltreatment episodes from around the country I find a disproportionate number that involve sexual offenses against the child, and the vast majority of them occur within the family. This does not mean, however, that the seductive stranger with candy or the dirty old man is no longer with us. He is.

Pittsburgh, Pennsylvania. A fifty-seven-year-old man who admitted setting up bogus federal programs to entice young children to participate in so-called scientific experiments was convicted of twelve counts of sexually abusing children. The defendant told the court that he had videotaped and photographed hundreds of encounters with children and stashed the tapes and pictures under the floorboards of his house "for my own sexual pleasure." An

Allegheny County jury found Eugene Allen, high school dropout and traveling salesman, guilty of all charges, including sexual abuse of children, indecent assault, and corrupting the morals of a minor.

Of course, the kids should never have gone with that dirty old man, and we wonder why they did. Were they too young to know better? Or were they missing attention at home, where they should have been with their parents or a trusted baby-sitter?

New York, New York. A couple who reported their seven-year-old son missing have been charged with child abuse after the bruised and malnourished boy was found on a subway car with cigarette burns and black eyes, police said. Rene Samacarit, twenty-eight, and Zorida Maldonado, thirty-one, of Brooklyn were charged with second-degree assault and endangering the welfare of a minor. The couple reported the boy missing at 2:30 P.M. Less than half an hour later, Transit Police found the battered and undersized child on a subway in Manhattan. He had run away from home. Taken to St. Vincent's Hospital, he was found to have multiple injuries, cigarette burns, bruises, and a black eye. He was also suffering from a throat infection and malnutrition. Transit police officers said, "He was pretty tight-lipped until we got him a candy bar and a can of soda, and then he told us his mother gave him the black eye. Every time we found a scar or an old burn mark, we'd ask him who did this, and he'd say his mother."

Fort Lauderdale, Florida. A woman accused of forcing her two children to drink windshield wiper fluid has been sentenced to four months in jail. Judge Robert W. Tyson Jr. on Tuesday also placed Benita Wege, thirty-six, on probation for five years on her no-contest plea to two counts of child abuse. Her children, Brent, eight, and Brigitte, seven, were hospitalized in critical condition along with their mother after drinking the fluid. All three recovered. The fluid contained methyl alcohol, which can cause blindness or death. The woman and her husband were obtaining a divorce and had just fought when she and the children checked into a Coral Springs hotel, where she gave them a mixture of wiper fluid and fruit juice. Brent told police his mother had threatened to "pour the blue stuff down our throats" if they didn't drink it. Granted, this case is extreme, but it does illustrate how children can get caught in the cross fire of ugly divorce cases.

Aberdeen, South Dakota. The mother of a fourteen-month-old boy who died after being left in a hot car with the windows closed pleads innocent to a charge of felony child abuse. Leola Bull Bear, thirty-two, is accused of knowingly placing her son, Wendall Two Bears, in the custody of an individual who was intoxicated and incapable of caring for him. That individual, her friend Timothy Two Hearts, pleaded innocent to second-degree manslaughter, felony child abuse, and drunken driving. Authorities said the child was left in the car for about two hours while Two Hearts took his four older brothers swimming. Bull Bear discovered her son's body when Two Hearts and the other children returned from the swimming trip.

St. Paul, Minnesota. An occupational therapist is charged with assault after doctors secretly videotape her smothering her one-year-old son in his hospital bed and then reviving him. The child had been hospitalized eight times since he was seven weeks old for what authorities had thought were respiratory attacks. The mother, thirty-six, has been charged with third-degree assault for blocking the breathing of her son until he lost consciousness. Hospital officials had become suspicious of her when the boy was brought in for the eighth time, and commenced video surveillance that showed the woman pressing her son's nose and mouth against her chest while he slept, then calling for help and giving the little boy mouth-to-mouth resuscitation.

Sarasota, Florida. A jury convicts a Christian Science couple of murder and child abuse in the death of their seven-year-old daughter for relying on spiritual practitioners to cure her diabetes. William Hermanson, forty-two, and his wife Christine, thirty-eight, were charged with third-degree murder and felony child abuse. Their daughter, Amy, died of diabetes in 1986, after the couple tried to heal her with prayer instead of medical treatment. Church authorities say that there are no church sanctions for followers who seek medical aid, and a Christian Science nurse who tended Amy testified that when she saw prayer wasn't working she urged a spiritual healer to summon an ambulance. At the trial a state witness testified that both parents had sought medical treatment for themselves on occasion but had not done so for their daughter.

Oregon City, Oregon. Children at a rural commune billed as an athletic camp for ghetto youngsters are found to have been ritualistically beaten, left to go hungry, and forced to watch as an eight-year-old girl was flogged to death. Neighbors had complained about the group, which called itself the Ecclesia Athletic Association, since it took over the farmhouse thirty miles east of Portland the summer before. They said they were concerned about the number of people they saw coming and going and their secretive, regimented nature—and about the rigorously disciplined routine of athletics that the children were being put through. But nothing was done at the time by state or local authorities, until four adults showed up at the Clackamas County firehouse with the body of Dayna Lorae Broussard, the daughter of Eldridge J. Broussard, founder of the group and also its authority figure.

Officers obtained an emergency search warrant and went out to the farmhouse with a bus. They found fifty-three children, ranging in age from three months to sixteen years, crammed inside the unfurnished four-bedroom house. Most of them were malnourished and had been severely beaten. They had been sleeping on bare floors and in shared sleeping bags in the unheated rooms. The windows were sealed shut. The only food found in the house were a few tomatoes and a head of lettuce. The children, confused and compliant, were taken to a county shelter while arrangements for temporary custody were being made.

According to a court petition, some of the children were beaten eight hundred strokes at a time while others were forced to watch and keep count. The floggings were systematic and administered by staff using such devices as paddles and electrical cords. The child Dayna had died from injuries to the head and chest; her torment and its conclusion had been witnessed by the other children. The Oregon Children's Services had initially been asked to investigate; they had not done so, they explained, because there was no clearcut evidence of child abuse. But the neighbors had thought there was such evidence. They had seen children who never laughed, never talked, never played—children, they said, who were like zombies. Yet the authorities didn't listen to the neighbors, not even to make one quick, visual check on conditions in the broken-down farmhouse; and the children continued to suffer.

It may be observed that these examples are not "typical" child maltreatment cases, in that they are nearly all extremely serious and seemingly a little offbeat. I don't happen to think they are in any way unusual. My own belief is that most abuse is of a less sensational variety—lower-keyed, more mundane—but that there are infinite variations on the textbook scenario and that the above scenes are among them. Not one of them is unique. Each event represents countless examples of what happens with awful frequency in our very own America. To those who have made these things happen, they are not even out of the ordinary. They merit only fleeting mentions in our newspapers; they don't make headlines. Hundreds of thousands of other stories, perhaps less dramatic but often equally chilling, get no mention at all. They bore the jaded public. Yet many of them are on record in the files of the various child protective agencies, proving that there are no limits to what some adults do to children . . . except their own boundless imagination and the specificity of their tastes.

The Oregon City case is unusual, I admit, although it recalls for me the Jonestown cult and its captive souls. What is particularly interesting to me is that the Oregon camp seems to have started as something with healthy potential that went completely off the track under the guidance of a charismatic figure who—probably unwittingly—sacrificed his own daughter to his own distorted principles. Yet strange as this story is, it contains very familiar elements: the neighbors reporting that something is wrong, the children's service agency saying there is insufficient evidence to investigate, the death that reveals a scorpion's nest of child maltreatment, and a picture of private institutional abuse at what must surely be its worst. Or maybe not.

I have tried to present an assortment of vignettes in an attempt to demonstrate that child abuse touches all races and socioeconomic classes; that it occurs in rural areas as well as in cities; that there are no guarantees of safety in adoption or foster care or in institutions designed for the rescue of children; that it appears in many forms—psychological, emotional, and sexual as well as physical; that neglect can be as deadly as battering; and that not all maltreating parents are brutish subhumans. What I have not yet said with sufficient emphasis is that abusive parents are, nearly always, people who themselves have suffered great torment and who continue to suffer even as they perpetuate a pattern of pain and abuse. The following is an illustration of what it is like to be the other victim of abuse, the abusing parent, expressed in the kind of anguished letter I get often and that always wrings my heart.

It comes from Louisiana, and it says:

Dear Dr. Fontana,

I am presently twenty-nine years old, white, female, married, and the mother of two children: Warren, age seven, and Dawn, age five. I live in a middle-class neighborhood and have all the conveniences available to a modern-day housewife. I do not work outside the home, preferring to stay behind closed doors where it is safe. In all respects I should be a happily married woman and proud mother of two beautiful children. Unfortunately, this is not the case. To my neighbors I appear to be a well-balanced person, whom they are pleased to have living in their neighborhood.

To my husband, I am an uncommunicative, frigid wife who has no desire to socialize or be sexually active with him. To my children, I am someone who barely tolerates their presence; who walks around with the belt in the hand, using it every time they step out of line, which is any time they are in my way or not being quiet; who constantly is verbally condemning them for something trivial they may have done; who violently attacks them, using my fists and wire kitchen whisks and kicking with my feet and then leaving them where they lay, crumpled in pain and misery, to wonder what they could have done to warrant such punishment. Seeing in their eyes the question that I asked myself when I was in their position, "How can you do this to me?" I ask myself that same question when I look upon their sleeping faces. "How can I do that to them if I love them?" But how can I love them and hate to be around them at the same time?

I promised God that I would never treat my children the way that I was treated. Yet the violent cycle continues. Why can't I stop the wheel of abuse? I do not know. I have tried. Once I went to a Parents Anonymous meeting in a nearby city. But my husband became violently enraged when I told him, and threatened to blow all their heads off if I ever went back. He does not want anyone to know. I have tried Christian counseling, I have tried alcohol and drugs, I have twice tried suicide. I could not even succeed in that.

I do not understand why my children must suffer for my inadequacies, but suffer they do, even to the point of hospitalization. Perhaps my past and heritage will shed some light on my incapacities as a wife and mother.

I was born at New Orleans Charity Hospital, the third child after two brothers. My parents were having marital difficulties and were divorced three months later. My mother became institutionalized as a paranoid schizophrenic with little chance of recovery, and my brothers and I were sent to my grandparents. When I was three my mother was released after being diagnosed as not being harmful to herself or anyone else; she married a man she had met in the institution. He also was released, having been deemed free of the sickness for which he was admitted. This sickness was child molestation. Because he was gainfully employed and married to my mother, the courts ruled that my grandparents had to release me and my brothers to my mother and new stepfather.

As for what happened to me between the ages of three and thirteen, I have no knowledge. Those years are blank, as if they were erased by an eraser. I do not know why. My Christian counselor suggested that I may be suffering from intentional amnesia, that something so horrible happened to me that my mind closed that part of my life for my own protection.

From the age of thirteen to the age of eighteen I was physically and sexually abused by both my mother and stepfather, and physically and sexually abused by both of my brothers, who were physically and emotionally abused also.

So, with my family history of mental illness and abuse, perhaps I not only learned to act violently with children but even received violent tendencies through genetic inheritance. Still, I do not excuse my actions. What I do is a grievous crime and a sin. I hate my violent actions and myself. I know what I do is wrong but I cannot control it.

How has my childhood affected my adulthood? It has deformed me. Not physically; the broken bones, cuts, and bruises have mended, the gunshot wounds have healed, leaving behind only small scars that I can cover up. It is the inner wounds that are still unhealed, visible by my inability to make friends, inability to form a close bond with my husband, and worst of all, unable to love my children in the way they were meant to be loved. For one can only teach what one has been taught, one can only give what one has been given. I was given only pain expressed in silent anger and depraved actions. Is this all I have to give to my children and my husband? I would gladly lay down my life in order to secure happiness for them. They are the innocent ones.

And this woman, I feel, is also one of the innocent ones. She suffered as a child and as an adult; she is suffering endlessly. She could have been and should have been helped. To me, she epitomizes the abuser/abusee who inflicts her pain behind closed doors and shuttered windows and hates herself and her life. To the world, she is a nice, middle-class, stable parent. But we can see her through her own words as something very different. What an unhappy family. What a miserably unhappy woman.

It is axiomatic that the stresses brought on by poverty, unemployment, premature parenthood, and emotional disturbance increase the likelihood of abuse. But we also know that the more privileged classes are not immune to inflicting abuse; they just happen to be insured, for the most part, against its being made public. Their doctors don't tell, the neighbors don't call the police, they don't have social workers nosing around, and nobody would believe it of them anyway.

But believe it. Something is happening on your block. Something is happening in a family you know. In a house nearby there is a young man so withdrawn from the world that you never see him and you never *will* see him; he was abused as a child. Or a child is being belted and emotionally abused by a mother or father who expects too much and will wind up with nothing. Somewhere, close by, a kid or a parent needs help and doesn't know where to turn; somewhere, among the people you talk to on the telephone or the people you correspond with, someone is crying to be heard.

Knock on any door and there will be somebody behind that door who was victimized as a child or knows someone who was. Something happened to them or their sister or their brother or their husband or an in-law or one of their best friends—something the victims couldn't talk about at the time because they were afraid or ashamed or needed their abuser or all of the above, but that has to be aired out before the victim suffocates. Or before there are more victims.

Some of today's child advocates claim to believe that there has been no genuine increase in the annual child abuse rate—in spite of the evidence provided by the drug explosion—but rather an increase in reporting and in fact overreporting. I will observe that a report that does not immediately prove true or provide sufficient evidence of maltreatment is not necessarily a false report. But I will not argue the point at this stage, except to say with passion— Don't be fooled by these claims! We're looking at that proverbial iceberg's tip again, and we should not delude ourselves that what is not on public record doesn't exist. Nor should we feel smugly reassured when we are told that the majority of maltreatment cases involve forms of neglectful and emotionally abusive treatment that pose no serious physical danger to the child. Are we back to the days when only broken bones and death were measures of abuse? I hope not. We have made no great forward strides; I hope we have not slipped several paces back.

Notwithstanding the alarming fatality statistics and the growing catalog of bizarre abuse and neglect cases, only twelve states responding to the 1989 survey by the National Committee for the Prevention of Child Abuse reported an increase in their child abuse prevention budget, and those increases were primarily cost-of-living adjustments. More crimes against children are being committed, more reports are being made and followed up by child protective services, more needs are being uncovered, and yet the funding for these services has not kept pace with the responsibility of protecting our children.

Why this seeming imbalance between numbers of child victims and dollars spent? Child advocates search vainly for an answer.

Meanwhile, the questions raised by the fatality and abuse/neglect reports are multitudinous: questions about the adequacy and efficiency of the child protective systems in the various states; about the national child protective system, which, incredibly, does not exist; about whether any or most or all of the crimes against children could have been avoided by more efficient systems or more alert and responsible observers; about what initial and additional preventive actions could have been taken along the child protection chain; and about what life-saving lessons we can learn from hindsight.

We ask ourselves why and how people can do such dreadful things to children. We have some answers, but they do not tell us everything. Acceptance of public violence has much to do with it. Drug use, of course, has introduced horrendous ramifications. Drugs and alcohol have been a factor in crimes against children for a very long time. But since the early 1980s, substance abuse looms as an increasingly important element in child abuse cases. More than two-thirds of the states responding to the national survey report drug abuse as a dominant factor in abusing families. And until and unless we find a way to neutralize crack and crank and ice—the latest wrinkles on the drug scene, with perhaps many variants to follow—the inner-city drug syndrome is going to keep on bleeding out into the outer city and the outer suburbs and into the small towns, too.

The search for the control or cure of AIDS, drug addiction, cancer, and heart disease must go on. But our biggest challenge is simply preserving and properly caring for our young. That is the surest way to save the most lives. And most experts agree that we have sufficient resources and know-how to end this tragedy confronting humanity—if we would just get on with the job.

We have failed for so long to address ourselves to the national disease of child maltreatment that we have placed ourselves at critical risk of being engulfed by its complications. What are we to do about drug-addicted mothers and babies dying of AIDS and uneducated kids running wild with guns? We don't know, because we haven't thought these things through. We haven't seen the connections. We like our evils sanitary and, if possible, remote. Starving children in Biafra, apartheid in South Africa—these are massive ills that most self-respecting humans can work up their bile about. But this other thing known as child abuse revolts us. It's too dirty. It's too close to home. It's like talking about . . . well, excrement. But we are talking about *our lives*.

2 / Crack: The Ultimate Betrayal

It is an unutterably desolate scene I see before me on this always desolate island, even more dreary than usual today under unfriendly skies. Rain slants down upon row after stacked row of little pine coffins, none much bigger than a shoebox, unpainted and unmarked but for pink paper labels—like disposable packing slips—bearing names, dates of death, and the names of the hospitals in which the tiny occupants died.

The place is Potter's Field on Hart Island, burial ground for the unwanted and forgotten of New York City. Convicts on grave-digging detail from a nearby prison take the boxes from the rows of stacks and place them with unwonted care into a common grave.

There is no one here to pray or shed a tear for the lost babies. A priest comes by occasionally, but he is not here today. The only mourners are the diggers; the prison inmates shoveling dirt into the pit, and their grief is fleeting pity that will be gone by the time they get back to their cells. Perhaps they were born under circumstances hardly more fortuitous, circumstances that let them live to be what they have become. I feel pain as I watch the damp earth cover the tiny boxes, but I do not grieve over untimely death, for these deaths were not untimely. I am a physician and my directive is to save lives; these lives could not have been saved even if the children had lived.

The grave is the traditional six feet deep but its other dimensions are vast: thirty feet wide by one hundred feet long as it grows to accommodate its allotment. Previous consignments have almost fully occupied it already. Forty dead babies are being added to it today. The job takes less than twenty minutes. There are one thousand little bodies in the grave by the time the day's work is finished, and the mass grave is complete. One headstone, with only a number on it, will mark them all. There are no white coffins for these castoffs. No one has ever cared for them, not even for a moment—nor ever will.

Some distance away, at the side of a little-used road, a battered monument stands. "Cry not for us," it says. "We are at peace."

I hope so.

Hundreds of thousands of paupers and other abandoned people have been buried on Hart Island in the last 120 years. Babies have always been among them, but until recent years there was a steady decline. Now the number of outcast newborns has soared to epidemic proportions. In 1986 the baby body count was 1,128. By 1988 the number had risen to 1,489—an increase of 32 percent—and in 1989 it reached 1,606.

The reason? Crack and AIDS.

The babies are virtually born dead: conceived in sickness and delivered on the point of death by women themselves ravaged by one or both of the twin killers. These babies are the latest manifestation of child maltreatment: prenatal abuse. And in many cases, those who die are better off than the living dead.

Americans are no strangers to the misuse of substances, nor is prenatal abuse a new phenomenon. But the present extent of the abuse is alarming and astounding.

In the beginning, there was alcohol—wine and beer. Wine has been with us in some form ever since the first ripe berries fell from a tree, fermented on the ground, and made the local wildlife very happy aeons ago. Today, in a rainbow variety of taste treats and potency, alcohol is easily available, inexpensive, and highly potable in comparison with the crystals, leaves, and powders of other drugs. To the majority of users it is pleasant and innocuous. To others, it is addictive and deadly dangerous.

In 1981 the Surgeon General of the United States issued a health advisory recommending that women who were pregnant or who were considering pregnancy should abstain from using alcoholic beverages because of the possible harm to unborn babies. Young women were widely warned of the possibility of Fetal Alcohol Syndrome, or FAS—a cluster of mental and physical defects including prenatal and postnatal growth deficiency, facial and other physical abnormalities, central nervous system dysfunction, learning disabilities, and varying degrees of major organ system malformation—occurring in babies born to women who drink heavily during pregnancy.

Apparently the message was received by a skeptical or uninterested public, because a 1989 survey found that only four out of ten adults had any idea of what is meant by the term "fetal alcohol syndrome," and less than 3 percent of the total number surveyed seemed aware of maternal alcohol use as a potential health hazard to unborn babies. This is dangerous ignorance: FAS is now recognized as the leading known cause of mental retardation in the Western world, and one that is totally preventable.

I suppose it is because the drug constitutes such a well-established social amenity that we let ourselves forget—in spite of warning signs and labels—that alcohol is not only an addictive but a baby-damaging drug. Some scoff at this concept or don't want to believe it or don't care. But the truth is that it need not require excessive alcohol intake during pregnancy to produce a child with fetal alcohol syndrome and a future almost as grim as a crack baby's. And most addicts have more than one addiction, with alcohol nearly always being one of them. A round of drinks goes nicely with a round of pipes.

Even "social" drinkers and smokers—those who indulge in booze plus nicotine—run the risk of birthing incomplete babies, and these are the ones we should be able to reach. It's too bad we can't take them all to an Indian reservation, the semi-rural, middle-America equivalent of the inner city. On some reservations, whose inhabitants are notoriously alcohol-allergic and addicted, from 5 to 25 percent of the youngsters suffer from fetal alcohol syndrome. In varying degrees, the children are retarded, malformed about the head and ears, hyperactive, difficult to raise, and even more difficult to educate. They don't look normal; their thought processes are not normal. Something has been taken away from them—mainly, their capacity to think.

Having said that, I can't go along with the scare stories pushing the premise that as little as one drink or an occasional glass of wine during pregnancy is likely to damage the fetus. There is no research nor any other reason to support this notion. There is research, however, that demonstrates that prolonged excess intake by the drinking male may cause the liver to break down testosterone, resulting in abnormal sperm production or even impotence and atrophy of the testicles. Prenatal care is not only female business. It may seem so, because birth is so uniquely a female function, but where there is a damaged baby there is almost inevitably not one but two irresponsible people involved.

After alcohol, the big drug problem was—and to some extent, still is—heroin. In the '50s, '60s, and '70s it was not unusual for heroin-addicted babies to be born to addicted mothers. The agony of their withdrawal is a terrible thing, and long after recovery they exhibit a number of repeat symptoms and behavioral disorders.

But when I say the baby heroin junkie was "not unusual," I do not mean to suggest that it was an everyday occurrence. Women have never been as attracted to heroin as men. Even when the main male in the household was a user, the woman very often was not. Seemingly, the most intense and speediest rush comes from using a needle to skin-pop or muscle or mainline the stuff, rather than from snuffing it up the nose; and many women have a distinct aversion to sticking needles into their bodies. It's not just that they don't like the needle; more likely, they can kid themselves that they are not really junkies if they don't inject. Besides that, the first effects of heroin in any form are not always pleasurable, which tends to make women pause before indulging. Finally, in the prime years of shooting up, the cost of regular hits of heroin was prohibitive for women who put home and family needs first. Thus, during the reign of heroin, women were still the strong, functional adults in the family.

And then affordable crack came along, with its neat little water pipes and instant, rapturous highs, and all the drawbacks of the Big H were swept aside. The new stuff was irresistible. For the price of a couple of bad movies, here was instant escape to paradise. And without the needles.

But it was not paradise for babies in the womb.

There is no reason to search for the cause of the gigantic leap in infant mortality rates in cities like New York and Washington, D.C. No doubt emphasis and use will soon shift to some other drug or combination of drugs—crank (inhalable methamphetamine), perhaps, or ice (smokable meth with a prolonged high)—but right now the problem is crack.

In New York City in 1985, drug addiction was reported as a major problem in 11 percent of fatalities attributed to child abuse. In 1987 this figure, swollen by crack, rose to 73 percent. It is still rising. And the number of cases of abuse and neglect by parents under the influence of drugs tripled between 1986 and 1988. Crack cocaine was the main contributor.

In all inner cities, crack has vastly accelerated the destruction of families. Nothing in recent memory has contributed more to the rapidly increased breakdown of families in poor urban neighborhoods than crack. And the loss of women, in one sense or another, is clearly an important factor in the collapse of poor families. For years, the popular understanding—and a correct one—was that it is the women, the mothers and the grandmothers, who have held the families together. But the protectors have lately joined the destroyers, and in some areas more women than men now use crack. A recent Justice Department report states that crack-related arrests of women were exceeding those of men in New York City; Washington, D.C.; Kansas City, Missouri; and Portland, Oregon.

When females become users, the first effect on the family is the abdication of the women from their traditional duties. They no longer raise their families; they're busy doing crack. They want money for the drug, and that is all they want. They prostitute themselves, or they send the younger females in the family out to sell sex and raise the money for them. Young pregnant mothers and not-yet pregnant girls endanger their lives to get the drug in crack houses or on the street, and seriously endanger the children they are carrying or will soon conceive.

Heroin was bad enough, but it affected relatively few newborns; we didn't see a great deal of it in pregnant women. But we do see crack. We see thousands of cases of pregnant women on crack, and cocaine is infinitely more devastating to the fetus than heroin. And the most saddening, frustrating part of it is that by the time we see the crack mothers, it is often too late to do very much to help the child.

In New York City, an estimated 5 percent of infants in the black communities of the inner city are exposed to cocaine in the womb. For comparable communities in our nation's capital, the estimate is 15 percent. And this catastrophic situation is not restricted to inner-city communities. Throughout the country the disease is encroaching and metastasizing like some awful alien growth. Take Cincinnati, for example: in 1985, 2 cocaine babies were born in that city; University Hospital there expects 150 in 1989. And Philadelphia: at the Hospital of the University of Pennsylvania, an incredible 30 percent of the 3,500 babies born in 1988 were born to crack-using mothers. In a survey of eight other Philadelphia hospitals, the Philadelphia Perinatal Society reported that an average of 16.3 percent of their babies were born to cocaine-using mothers. Then there's the state of Illinois: during the last half of 1988, the number of cocaine babies rose to 978, a 78.8 percent increase over the same period a year earlier. And Florida: Dr. Charles Mahan, a Florida state public health officer in Tallahassee, observes that one in every fifteen newborns in Florida is born to a woman who used crack during pregnancy. "We have coke babies from nearly every little tiny town in the state," he says.

Clearly, the phenomenon is not limited to cities or states notorious for their social problems. Cocaine-exposed babies are cropping up in some of the most unlikely places: Boise, Idaho; Medford, Oregon; and Peoria, Illinois.

Yes, even in Peoria.

Obviously, the figures available are based only on recorded cases. The private use of cocaine in any of its forms, and its effects on babies, is largely undocumented outside seriously afflicted communities. When the epidemic is concentrated in a particular area it becomes a threat to the afflicted community and it becomes public knowledge. But so-called recreational users of the middle class are not clustered in large, visible communities and are not known to the network of protective services. They can hide their problem—if they even recognize that they have a problem—and their financial and other resources can protect both them and their children, to some extent, before, during, and after the birth.

But cocaine is hell on babies. It is a most insidious type of child abuse, one that is taking its toll of lives and leaving us with thousands of horribly damaged children.

Cocaine can affect a pregnant woman and her fetus in many ways, none of them desirable. It can cause miscarriage, intrauterine death, and premature birth. The latter is no problem for some mothers-to-be; these women have learned that smoking crack induces faster, less painful deliveries, and they have made crack the drug of choice for inducing labor. That the preemies are likely to be critically underweight infants with undersized heads is apparently of little concern to them. Virtually all maternal feeling and all self-respect have been smoked away and replaced by a passion for crack.

Mothers' use of cocaine during pregnancy can cause even more frightful damage to babies in the womb: deformed hearts and lungs, abnormal genital and intestinal organs, permanent neurological impairment, paralysis, seizures, strokes, and irrevocable brain damage. Some of these babies are born literally without a brain. At the very least, cocaine babies come into the world undersized and addicted, suffering the terrible agony of cocaine withdrawal. And they do suffer terribly. They cannot be held or even fed properly because they are so fragile and extremely sensitive to the touch; some just keep flailing their limbs around to find a little relief.

One would think that no woman could fail to be moved and even somewhat remorseful at the sight of damaged, painfully unhappy babies. Giving birth to a single such child should surely be enough, especially for those in which maternal instinct is totally lacking. But it is easy for some women to make babies, so easy that they just keep having them, no matter how deformed or tortured the child may be. Hospitals and courts today frequently see women who have given birth to their second, third, fourth, and even fifth drug-afflicted baby. I have myself seen many such women and their suffering infants.

The mothers never seem to learn; they seldom seem to care. Their lives are dominated by the drug. I am reminded of the story, reported by the Associated Press, of the young woman who left her ten-month-old baby girl with a male friend after midnight one night while she went off to buy more crack. When she hadn't returned by eight in the morning the friend left the baby with a woman known both to him and to the mother. This woman kept the child until around noon, at which time she passed her along to another woman. The second woman abandoned the baby within the half hour, leaving her parked in her carriage behind a building in the Bronx. The child had just been handed around until somebody dropped her. Is the mother going to have another baby? Probably. Will that baby be better cared for than the first? Probably not.

Perhaps some of the repeaters think they'll have better luck next time; they swear they'll get off the drug as soon as they know they're pregnant. But that is likely to be too late; the damage may be done even before a woman realizes she is pregnant. Studies have shown that most of the worst effects of cocaine—whether or not in the form of crack—occur during the first three months of pregnancy, when the infant's organs are forming.

Many users are apparently under the impression that the placenta shields the fetus from harmful substances. But this is not the case. The placenta acts like a sponge; the drug is absorbed through it and goes directly into the womb, where it lingers and continues to damage the child for days after it has left the user's system.

Even the occasional user is not immune. God alone knows why in some sectors of the middle class and upwardly mobile it is still considered chic or fun to snort coke—and if the sniffer is a woman and is unaware that she is pregnant she is in great danger of producing a damaged child. Dr. Ira J. Chasnoff, director of the Perinatal Center for Chemical Dependency at Northwestern Memorial Hospital in Chicago, conducted studies among 115 pregnant women at 36 hospitals around the country and found that 11 percent, on average, had exposed or were exposing their unborn babies to illegal drugs, more often than not cocaine, without thought of the consequences. Apparently most were under the impression that an occasional little "treat" surely couldn't do any harm, and that if they stopped using or used the drug only intermittently during pregnancy, everything would be all right. Dr. Chasnoff concluded that this was not the case, that recreational use of cocaine is extremely likely to produce babies with physical or behavioral problems, and that almost no cocaine-exposed baby completely escapes the drug's effects.

Chasnoff tells the story of a suburban couple who had been recreational users of cocaine for a number of years, snorting once in a while as the mood moved them. The woman stopped when she discovered that she was in her second month of pregnancy, and remained drug-free until she was almost ready to give birth. Then, to celebrate an anniversary, she took five grams of cocaine. True to form, the drug acted instantly and precipitated labor. The baby boy was born prematurely and with limited use of an arm and a leg. Other damage would become apparent later. He had suffered a cocaine-induced stroke just before he was born, and a large segment of his brain was damaged. It's not clear whether the damage was done to the fetus by the first or the second hit, but Dr. Chasnoff's research strongly suggests that *any* single use during pregnancy can cause lasting fetal damage.

Even in the less extreme cases, the babies exposed to cocaine have been subjected to intrauterine growth retardation and are slow to develop. Furthermore, a chemical by-product lingers in the system, so that even as they grow they are subjected to continuing stresses. Respiratory problems are common. Crack babies are at enormously greater than normal risk of "crib death," or Sudden Infant Death Syndrome (SIDS); they stop breathing for abnormally long periods, and ultimately they stop breathing altogether.

Crack babies are fragile; their nervous systems are overloaded and underfunctioning; they tend to be hypersensitive and irritable. They scream at the least provocation, which does not endear them to mothers who are uninterested in caring for them in the first place. And they are almost invariably battered and neglected by crack-crazed parents caught up in their own survival problems.

Neonatal clinics and their intensive care units are bursting at the seams with the epidemic of crack babies. "It is impossible to work, you can't even turn around," says a neonatalist at Bronx-Lebanon Hospital Center. She adds: "This is our next generation. What kind of generation can it be?"

Doctors in these clinics never cease to be appalled by the behavior of the addicted women. Most crack mothers-to-be have no concept of the importance of prenatal care for their high-risk babies and little interest in finding out. If they do show up for examination they leave it until very late in the pregnancy. More often than not they see a doctor in barely enough time to give birth. And then, more often than not, they don't give a damn about the baby. I don't know which is the worse fate for the child: to go home with the mother to an impossible home situation, where neglect and probably abuse are likely to take the place of loving care, or instant abandonment in the hospital and a life among busy strangers.

I hear this kind of thing from health professionals every day, and I see it proved before my eyes: "These mothers don't care about their children, and they don't care about themselves. They're not feeding their kids. They're selling their food stamps. They're selling their souls. They're selling their bodies. They are destroying their lives and they are destroying their kids. They are like the walking dead."

Dead babies wind up on Hart Island. Live babies wind up in limbo. If crack babies are to thrive at all, they need loving attention and special care. But who is going to give it to them? Mother? Crack mothers abandon live babies as well. They give birth, then disappear to feed their hunger for more crack. "We don't know where the mothers are," says Lorraine Hale, executive director at Harlem's Hale House. "They walk in the front door, they walk out the back door, and we don't see them again."

Kids of disappearing mothers become somebody else's responsibility—boarder babies in hospitals and temporary homes, lodgers with foster parents, often permanent wards of the child welfare system because they are not adoptable. Sometimes they die in hospitals after years of malfunctioning. Often they are discovered to have AIDS, endowed by a mother who is still out there someplace sharing needles and trading sex for drugs.

Then of course there are those parents who are able to persuade social workers and courts that they have truly and forever reformed and who demand to have their children back. Sometimes their yearning for their babies is not so much because they love them but because they want to regard them as possessions. Children who are possessions are inevitably abused, and the more so when their neurological problems make parenting even more than usually difficult for parents who are already stressed. In a drug-abusing household, love alone is not enough to provide the child with a stable, nurturing environment.

In the overall picture of child maltreatment, far more damaging than physical or emotional abuse is the harm caused by the intrauterine exposure of a fetus to drugs. In both the short term and the long term, the impact on families and on society is devastating. Babies born with less than a full deck because of a mother's addiction start out with a greater disadvantage than that endured by most physically abused children; their learning difficulties are often profound, and they become a drain on the school system and ultimately on the community. Those who endure extreme trauma and yet survive are probably the most costly to society because they must be professionally tended as long as they live, and yet no amount of care and treatment can ever restore them. They are, in a sense, a new race of mutants: brain-damaged, permanently deprived mutants with no real future.

Many factors precipitate child abuse; today, crack cocaine is the main villain. It is galloping around unchecked; it is ruining millions of lives.

Why is addiction so widespread? Because the drug exists and because it is inexpensive—it is ubiquitous, finally becoming a constant need. Because people lust for it and lose themselves to it. Because adolescents and adults who themselves were molested or physically abused or rejected need a way to shield themselves from their despair and self-hatred. Many of these people have already been through the child protective system or the juvenile justice system as kids, and it didn't help them much because nothing in these systems provided them with a sense of personal value and self-respect—a home of sorts, yes, but very often no more than that. Now they are perpetuating their problems in the most destructive way with their own children. They cannot help themselves. They are caught up in a terrible sickness for which no cure has yet been found.

In searching for solutions to the problem of crack-inflicted child abuse, people have come up with some extreme notions. One is to round up all pregnant drug users and put them into detention centers to receive enforced care until their babies are delivered. This has not happened yet. Other people talk passionately but impractically about sterilization. Prosecution on the basis of fetus rights is yet another approach; several cases have already come into the legal system.

In May 1989, in Rockford, Illinois, the mother of a baby whose death was linked to the woman's abuse of cocaine during pregnancy was charged with involuntary manslaughter and delivery of a controlled substance to a minor, a charge usually used against drug dealers. According to the county coroner, cocaine was found in Melanie Green's system and in the body of her two-day-old daughter, Bianca. The drug had been carried through the placenta to the fetus, causing oxygen deprivation and resulting in brain damage. A grand jury, however, refused to indict the twenty-four-year-old mother on any charge.

In July 1989, a judge in Sanford, Florida, found a cocaine-addicted mother guilty of delivering drugs to her two children through their umbilical cords at birth. In effect, he was ruling that the mother was a drug pusher. Rejecting defense arguments that the law under which the woman was tried was meant only for criminals engaged in illegal drug deals, Circuit Judge O. H. Eaton, Jr., said he regarded the children of Jennifer Johnson as victims.

"These children had no ability to control what was being intro-duced into their bodies," he said at the end of the nonjury trial. "The defendant had that ability." The mother faced a thirty-year sentence, but the prosecutor said he would recommend that she complete the drug program she was undergoing and then serve a lengthy probation period.

Other cases have been pursued in Illinois, Florida, California, Maryland, New Jersey, New York, Texas, Massachusetts, South Carolina, and Virginia. We can anticipate a rash of them. Those who support prosecution urge that the rights of the fetus must be recognized, and that punishing drug-using mothers will place addicts on notice that they have a responsibility to seek treatment. Yet I find it hard to believe that prosecuting and jailing drug-using mothers will have any deterrent or curative effect. If prosecution becomes a major trend, the courts will soon become as over-whelmed with drug-baby cases as the neonatal clinics are right now. Addict-mothers will undoubtedly be sentenced to treatment as part of their penalty, but the question of prenatal abuse will not have been addressed. Neither will prison authorities be eager to take on responsibility for addicted, pregnant women. Furthermore, I suspect that bringing criminal charges against addicted women may prove to be an effective way of driving cocaine-abusing moth-ers underground and preventing them from seeking help with either addiction or pregnancy. At the same time, I applaud a New York court's decision that the presence of neonatal narcotic with-drawal symptoms is prima facie evidence of child neglect. When prenatal maternal conduct is injurious to the fetus, that is both abuse and neglect. Courts have affirmed that "justice requires rec-ognition that a child has a legal right to begin life with a sound body and mind." This means that a child in the womb *must* be protected from drugs and continue to be protected after birth.

The question is: how?

In the present crisis situation we have to address the issue of drug-abused infants long before it gets to the courts. We have not been doing this. We saw the crack explosion coming, and we did nothing to prepare for it. Preventive services are grossly inadequate. Follow-up and long-term rehabilitative treatment for parents on drugs is minimal. The placement program for crack-affected infants is chaotic. We have no comprehensive, multidisciplinary system in place to address the needs of pregnant addicts or their children. There is little or no coordination, cooperation, or even communication among the drug treatment clinics, the prenatal centers, the child protective agencies, and the criminal justice system. Child and family often get lost in the shuffle between agencies.

Of course, this lack of coordination or even a workable agenda is true of the entire child abuse question and the child protective system in general, but if we can get our act together by using the drug explosion as a springboard by all means let us do so.

These must be our priorities: We must launch a high-powered nationwide campaign to pound home the message that doing drugs is suicidal and doing drugs while pregnant amounts to child abuse and maybe murder. Incredible as it may seem, a great many young women are not convinced that the drug they use while pregnant—whether it be cocaine or alcohol—can possibly harm their babies. Somebody else's child, perhaps; not theirs. *They* have to be convinced that they and their children are in imminent danger. *We* have to make a committed attack against drug abuse as well as a major effort to prevent drug abusers from becoming pregnant. I can't believe this is not possible. We all know what appropriate advertising can achieve. This campaign should be led by the Surgeon General in partnership with the Secretary for Health and Human Services—although neither office has ever shown itself to be interested in anything relating to child abuse. (That amazes me. If it's not their business, whose is it? The combination of drug and child abuse is one of our country's major health problems today. *Where have they been?*)

Government at all levels—federal, state, city, county, borough, whatever—and community leaders and social activists, institutions from schools to churches to hospitals, private enterprises such as pharmaceutical companies and advertising agencies and publishing companies, and individuals such as doctors, writers, teachers, artists, rock stars, sports figures, and actors, must energize and multiply existing efforts to spread the word about drugs and pregnancy and child abuse. It is not enough to suggest delicately that if a mother wants to have a perfect baby she'd be better off not doing drugs. We've got to get the message across: *Drugs kill and cripple babies!*

If there is any question about why anyone should be interested in contributing valuable expertise to such a crusade, it is only necessary to look around at our own streets and see where our self-interest lies. We do not want to breed another generation of violent, drug-addicted street people who threaten our lives as well as destroying their own.

One way or another, we must identify mothers and children at risk. This means that we must develop innovative approaches that will encourage drug-addicted mothers to come in for prenatal care and treatment of their drug addiction. At least twenty countries have infant mortality rates lower than ours. We in America pour our baby dollars into the salvation of ailing preemies and other low-birth-weight babies, whereas other countries apply their best medicine early in pregnancy rather than after birth.

Dr. C. Everett Koop, former Surgeon General of the United States and often referred to as the Medical Moses of the twentieth century, has for years advocated and preached for the adoption of preventive health measures. He has stated: "If we spent one-third of the effort on preventing things from happening that we do on trying to cure or repair them, we would be way ahead. Estimates say that of the years you gain, the premature deaths that you postpone, you get about 70 percent of those from prevention and about 15 percent from repair."

In countries with low infant mortality rates, timely and intensive care is given to all pregnant women. We are only beginning to consider the basic concept that all pregnant women and all women contemplating pregnancy are equally entitled to prenatal care. We had better move fast to make prenatal care compulsory, if for no other reason than that it will be cheaper for all of us in the long run. And of course we will have healthier babies and mothers who are better prepared for parenthood. Some people have a problem with "mandating" such care. But can compulsory health care be more offensive than compulsory income tax payments? If all women have equal incentive and equal access to prenatal as well as postnatal care, there can be no stigma attached to seeking timely and comprehensive medical attention.

The most frequently cited stumbling block to universal access to prenatal care is the difficulty of persuading pregnant drug addicts to come into a prenatal clinic and keep coming back until their babies are born healthy and their lives are stabilized. This is indeed difficult, but it is not impossible. New York's Harlem Hospital Center, one of the first clinics in the country to care exclusively for drug-using pregnant women, is flooded with women seeking help. The clinic encourages them to. It is bright and friendly, and nourishing breakfasts are served. Initially, a lot of women come for the free meal, if for nothing else, and then they keep coming back because the clinic's counselors offer them help with a whole galaxy of problems. Most are poor, and ignorant of social services to which they are entitled; many are frightened and homeless.

"I often say the medical problems we address here are almost secondary," says Dr. Janet Mitchell, the obstetrician who runs the clinic. "Homelessness takes a heavy toll." But there is a plus side to this. Young homeless women desperately need the sense of home and family that they find in the center. As Dr. Mitchell says, "The women tend to bond to us. They even come back after delivery with their gynecological problems, because they know they will be paid attention to."

How do they find out about the clinic in the first place? Word gets around. The women say, "The people there, they care. They don't lecture. They feed you and they care." "When I see a woman whose life is the street, the whole idea is to let her know that I understand her situation, that I care," says Brenda Williams, a drug counselor at the clinic. "The whole idea is to help them get some self-esteem in their lives. With that, you can sometimes get them into the clinic. With a lot more work, you can keep them coming back."

This is a model clinic, and there should be many more like it. But it is staffed largely by professionals who have volunteered their time and skills, and it operates on a skimpy budget. How long can they go on? How long can programs like this be run by selfless volunteers? This is a national concern. We must establish programs for the early intervention and treatment of crack babies and their mothers. These programs must be put in place *now*. There is no more time to waste. Yes, there are costs involved. The short-term and long-term costs get higher the longer we wait. Think! The results of our failures are going to be out on the streets in the time it takes to reach adolescence, if not sooner, and they are not likely to become admirable citizens.

We must expand or create new intensive care nurseries for the treatment of drug-addicted newborns and enable hospitals to continue to care for these babies until they are medically and socially ready for discharge. By "enabling" I mean empowering the hospitals with both the legal authority and the financial resources necessary to provide such care.

We must put family-oriented drug treatment programs into action: programs that can teach recovering abusers the parenting skills they did not learn in their growing-up years, and programs to reach the children of substance abusers to help them overcome the consequences of early drug exposure. New York City's Lincoln Hospital has a drug treatment clinic that offers pregnant women and parents a spectrum of services that include counseling, acupuncture, employment assistance, and Narcotics Anonymous meetings, with ongoing urine testing to detect drug use relapses. Lincoln's program has proved to be so effective that, to date, five other New York City hospitals have established similar clinics. Other cities, I believe, can do the same.

We must make available extended care facilities for continued follow-up of infants discharged from intensive care nurseries— before release either to the parents or to foster care placement. By the same token, we must make sure that drug-abused children are not returned to and left with drug-addicted parents who are unwilling or unable to care for them. A most significant and often ignored risk factor in the child's safety is the drug use of the mother's partner, which may be even more intense than that of the mother and pose a greater danger in terms of the continuing abuse of the child.

It is essential that we revamp our foster care and adoption system so that endangered children can more easily be removed from the custody of drug-using parents to the custody of qualified, caring substitutes. We have witnessed an explosion in the number of "boarder babies"—at least partly because there is no system that permits early placement of babies with foster parents.

Boarder babies are infants and young children who remain in city hospitals for weeks, months, and even years because their parents have abandoned them or died of AIDS. These little ones do not have problems that require continued hospitalization. Even if they have AIDS, or if they have deficiencies relating to parental crack use or physical abuse, they no longer need medical care. All they need is a loving home, which is surely a child's entitlement.

But the foster care system is in chaos. In New York there are at least another one hundred infants and youngsters living in emergency group care programs operated by the city's child protective agency and volunteer child care agencies. Periodically there is such a dire shortage of placements that some children have slept overnight in city offices because caseworkers have been unable to find any other place for them. Effectively, these children are being warehoused instead of given homes. It would seem better to keep them in hospital.

The trouble with hospitals, however, is that they are geared to give medical care, not family love. They cannot raise children; they can't provide the emotional and intellectual stimulation children need. Kids must be nurtured or they will not thrive, no matter how healthy they are. They deteriorate when kept in hospital wards for a long time. I can look at any pediatrics ward today and see an eleven-month-old baby taking her first few toddling steps in her crib, with no one there to hug and encourage her; or a four-year-old who has cried alone all afternoon because no one has time to read to him or play with him; or a mildly retarded five-year-old who is rocking, rocking, rocking in his wheelchair, doomed to be a vegetable unless he gets hands-on attention; or an AIDS baby who has never known a home and probably never will; or a crack baby who is going to die within weeks.

I see many lost children, and once in a while I do see them taken into someone's home. An eight-year-old who had AIDS died six months after being placed in foster care with a woman who had known his mother and gave him, at least, a decent death, and a crack baby placed in foster care died a month later.

And then I see the lost ones in the Foundling, damaged kids for whom there is no place to go until, somehow, they are repaired; children born with mental defects so severe that no one wants them, or who have grown up too abused to function normally. These lost souls may die without ever having any home but an institution.

3 / Making the Rounds at the Foundling

Foundling: An infant of unknown parents that
has been found abandoned.
                                    —*Webster*

Times change. Eventually, definitions change to keep up with
them, but today's dictionaries do not yet include under the heading
of "foundling" the classic cases of contemporary abandonment:
babies dumped by known parents—or, at least, known mothers—
who quickly disappear. Nor do they include the kinds of cases I
see when I make rounds at the Foundling Hospital. The children
in our special treatment facilities have not been abandoned in the
old-fashioned way. But thrown out is thrown out; unwanted is
unwanted.

I see the abused, the homeless, and the handicapped, and it
seems to me the parents have one thought in common: when things
get tough, throw out the kid.

And things do get tough in dysfunctional families.

There are several differences between the children we treat at
the Foundling today and the traditional newborn foundling—or the
deserted crack baby. All our kids have known identities. They
have all been brought to us for extended, specialized care. And
they have all been in contact with some city agency or hospital,
which provides us with whatever information is available. So we
know something of their history and background—often a great
deal. The fact is, of course, that they are here *because* of their
history and background. They are the cast-off products of misfor-
tune, violence, abuse, and neglect. Most of them are not babies

anymore, which allows us to see what their babyhood has done to them and then gives us the opportunity to try to repair the damage.

The Foundling has two major programs for the care and treatment of damaged children. I am not including here our Crisis Nursery, which is in a category of its own; I am discussing only the nitty-gritty of our working day, in which we see how child maltreatment affects children on their way to adolescence and adulthood.

We call one of our programs Blaine Hall, as if it were some fancy private school. In reality, it is a live-in diagnostic center for troubled, acting-out preadolescents whose psyches have been so mutilated that their parents or other caregivers have given up on them. We try to give these kids some semblance of a normal life, which includes schooling, discipline, and counseling. The other program resides in the Skilled Nursing Facility, which attempts to alleviate the unhappy lot of severely handicapped children who promise such scant hope of improvement that their parents want little if anything to do with them. Sometimes we actually succeed in making life more bearable, even hopeful, for them.

Let me introduce you to Carl, acting-up preadolescent in Blaine Hall. Carl is eight years old and was placed with us because of severe behavioral problems at school and at home. His teachers describe him as a bright child with a short attention span. They say he was constantly involved in fights with other children and refused to obey any requests, pleas, or commands to conform with normal standards of behavior for an eight-year-old. In short, he would not *listen*. More than a few parents are probably familiar with this attitude, but most have not encountered the extremes which Carl presented. This boy, small for eight, was rebellious and disobedient to an intense degree.

Carl's school gave up on him. His mother already had. When Carl was admitted to the Foundling's preadolescent program, his mother stated that she had often been beaten up by her husband, sometimes severely enough to require hospitalization during her pregnancies. After one of these beatings she was hospitalized and gave birth prematurely to Carl. By her own account, she soon began to physically abuse the boy, supposedly to punish him for his "badness." And he *was* "bad"—as bad as his brief life experience had made him.

About a year before coming to the Foundling, Carl was hospitalized for such behavioral problems as fire-setting, suicidal threats, and homicidal inclinations. His misbehavior had begun at a very early age: reportedly he started his first fire at the age of eleven months by throwing papers and magazines into a hot oven, nearly burning down the apartment. On another occasion he deliberately set a fire in a garbage can. At the age of two he jumped out of a second-floor window. According to his mother, he would often jump out of a car while it was in motion. Once he tried to hurt himself by tying a shoelace around his neck. The record also shows that he tried to suffocate his newborn sister.

After all these episodes, real or alleged, his mother beat him severely. This was of course an inappropriate response—but what else would a battered, ignorant, and frantic mother do to handle so difficult a child? Considering her own background, I would suppose that in hitting Carl she was getting revenge on her own mother for having hit her, while at the same time taking out on the child what the husband was doing to her.

Carl is presently on a psychotropic drug and is doing fairly well. We have some hope that in time his destructive and disturbed behavior will decrease. But he will need long-term psychotherapy and a structured and supervised environment for perhaps several years to come. In the light of the family involvement with the child welfare system and Carl's own colorful history, it is surprising to me that he wasn't brought to us much sooner. Obviously he was a seriously at-risk child. Surely somebody would have been keeping tabs on him. But then, the agencies are very busy.

When I first started making rounds at the Foundling some thirty years ago there were usually about 350 children in the nurseries, ranging in age from a week to four years old. All had been abandoned, one way or another; their parents hadn't left them on the doorstep, but concerned professionals in the child welfare field— caseworkers, clinic physicians, public health nurses, and the like— had referred them to us with broken bones or various other injuries or a variety of persistent childhood ailments. We wondered, often, how so many strange injuries could be caused by the ordinary household accidents that were reported to us, but we were not able to discern a pattern.

Then the term "battered child syndrome" became a byword

among physicians. In a paper published in the July 7, 1962, issue
of the *American Medical Association Journal*, Dr. C. Henry Kempe
described an array of physical symptoms characteristic of children
who were victims of battery and abuse. The phenomenon had been
observed many times before, but not pinpointed and defined, and
the Kempe paper was received with enormous interest in the medical community and by pediatricians in particular.

I think we all looked at our small patients with new eyes and
reevaluated the welts and burns and fractures that we saw. I know
I examined mine with a heightened viewpoint, and with my sharp-
ened sensitivity I saw yet other things: diseases that should not
have been, a pattern of malnourishment, an uncared-for look, a
general lack of nurturing. It was then that I recognized the fact
that many of these children were not only being physically man-
handled but were enduring insidious abuse and neglect. They were
diseased not because they were unlucky but because they had been
neglected. Their skin hygiene was poor, their personalities were
repressed, they were simply failing to thrive even if they had no
physical scars. Some cried too much, some not at all; some cringed
from staff members and visitors alike, while others clung with pitiful eagerness to anyone who reached out for them.

It was clear that we were dealing with more than the battering
of children. What we had been observing, in the battered child,
was really the last phase of a spectrum of maltreatment; severe
physical battering is the end of the line for the child. The more
we looked the more we realized that we were looking at the entire
spectrum: a range of physical abuse from strap marks and bruises
to skull fractures and brain damage, *plus* a range of other parental
inflictions such as physical, medical and emotional neglect, maternal deprivation, verbal and psychological abuse, and sexual molestation of toddlers and even tiny babies. The victims were, literally,
unwanted, abandoned children—for all child maltreatment is in
itself a form of abandonment. And the range of horrors inflicted
on them was a dreadful revelation to me.

But it was only a beginning. I did not realize back in 1963, when
I first described the Maltreatment Syndrome of Children in the
New England Journal of Medicine, that the problem would escalate
throughout the years—almost every year there is a 15 to 20 percent
increase in cases reported—and become so immense that thousands
of children would die of it in this country every year. I had no

inkling then that so many families would become fragmented, that there would be so many teenage pregnancies and juvenile suicides, and so enormous an increase in drug use. And of course I had no idea that we would all, directly or indirectly, be infected by the disease called crack. I saw some of the results of alcohol and heroin use—both substances were popular in abusive families—but there was nothing like the drug use that would mushroom in the early to mid-'80s. I would not have believed that behind 50 to 75 percent of the kids who are dying of maltreatment today is a parent whose life revolves around drugs, or that so many youngsters would be born already damaged by prenatal abuse.

It is not that everything has changed so very much; it is more that it has become intensified. We thought that we were holding back the tide with all our politicking and pilot programs, but while we were diligently keeping our fingers in the dike the tide became a tidal wave.

Now, when I make my rounds, we don't have hundreds of infants and toddlers in huge nursery units as we did before. We have them in special programs geared to their special needs. Those who survived their long-ago abandonment have grown up, and some of the children in our programs now are theirs. Only the children in our crisis nursery program fill me with confidence and hope. They are being rescued before it is too late. But I am not so confident about many of the others: some of the six- to twelve-year-olds in our preadolescent program who are at risk of never developing or functioning normally, and the kids of all ages who are so severely handicapped by mistreatment that I can see no future for them at all.

The children with the greatest damage are in our Skilled Nursing Facility.

Clinical records culled from major medical institutions indicate a history of abuse or neglect in from one-quarter to one-half of children handicapped by mental retardation or cerebral palsy or in treatment for severe psychological disorders. I would say the higher number is the more accurate, and the prognosis poor.

What, for instance, is to become of two-year-old Noah? He was recently admitted after emergency hospitalization in the New York Hospital Burn Unit with second- and third-degree burns received when he allegedly climbed into the kitchen sink at home and turned on the hot water. (We hear a lot of those "accidental" scald stories, and we are extremely skeptical of them.) The child suffered a cardiac arrest while under emergency care but was promptly revived. However, he is not your usual happy two-year-old. Now with us indefinitely, he is being treated for a variety of developmental delays—and he is not being helped by the non-visits of his parents. He keeps asking for "Mommy, Mommy," but I think he is permanently out of her custody. We hope that ultimately he will be well enough to go into a nice foster home, or even be adopted.

The Skilled Nursing Facility is essentially for handicapped children. Noah qualifies because of the severity of his damage, but he is not a typically handicapped child. There are over ninety children here ranging from infancy to twelve years of age, and a substantial number of them have their parents to thank for their condition. They manifest a variety of physical and mental handicaps: deformities or brain damage as a result of drug, alcohol, or nicotine use by the mother during pregnancy; low birth weight and its consequences; birth injuries; congenital problems; cerebral palsy; convulsive disorders; physical disabilities—handicaps beyond measure, many caused by physical bashing but more and more of them the result of substance abuse. Time and time again I see here babies born with half a brain, the other half destroyed by crack, or with the small heads, strange little faces, and retardation of fetal alcohol syndrome.

A number of our handicapped kids were longed-for children, planned and received with joy that turned into pain and sadness, brought into loving homes and nurtured as best their parents could. But over 25 percent of the total suffered some form of parental abuse before being sent to us by social service agencies or other hospitals. Most of these children are so damaged that they will never achieve a semblance of normal human life. Even the better-intentioned parents either cannot or will not take care of them. We work with these mutilated kids in the hope that we can enhance their limited potential enough for them to be put into foster care or be adopted. Meanwhile, some of the parents sometimes visit. Many of them don't. Their kids have nobody but us—doctors, nurses, child care workers, therapists, and foster grandparents—to care for them, play with them, feed them, and wheel them around on outings. We become their family.

This, to me, is really pathetic. How did these children lose the right to have a home and family?

As I check in on these handicapped kids, I review the record on four-year-old Mary. She was admitted when she was nine months old, having been subjected to prenatal abuse and subsequent neglect. The mother had a history of drug abuse and psychiatric problems. Mary was born prematurely; she was not a cute baby, not cute enough at all for a disturbed woman to care for. When she wasn't being slapped for crying she was being ignored. The child is now being given therapy for hydrocephalus, cerebral palsy, and convulsive seizures. She is holding her own, such as it is. Her mother is not at all interested in getting her back, ever, not unless we turn her into a little princess, which we can't.

And here's Lonnie. Now eleven years old, he was first admitted to the Foundling at the age of ten months for convulsive seizures. At that time we found him to be severely retarded. He was discharged after treatment for the seizures but continued to receive supportive psychotherapy, occupational and physical therapy, and medical care on an outpatient basis. In 1987 he was brought to the hospital with a fractured left femur, attributed to abuse, and removed from his biological parents by the child protective agency. Physically he is in good shape, but, unsurprisingly, he is still profoundly retarded. He would seem to be an unlikely candidate for adoption, except by a saint. And although there are a few such people out there, we haven't found many.

Ramon is another eleven-year-old. He has cerebral palsy and is severely developmentally delayed. At the age of two months he was hospitalized at North Central Bronx Hospital for suspected abuse and neglect. He was dehydrated, malnourished, and had a skull fracture with bilateral subdural hematoma and retinal hemorrhages—the classic physical symptoms of the battered child. After spending four months in the intensive care unit he was transferred to New York Foundling with a diagnosis of severe cortical and cerebral atrophy—brain damage. Six months later he was discharged to foster parents, but soon returned to the Foundling because agency caseworkers had determined that the foster parents were not taking adequate care of him. At this point in his life Ramon is suffering from collapsing spine, hearing loss, optic atrophy, and convulsive seizures. Who will take him home?

Do any of these severely damaged children leave here alive? Yes. Tracy may be one of them. Six years old at present, she was admitted to the Skilled Nursing Facility at the age of three after having been severely abused by her parents. She was brought to us with cerebral palsy, subdural hematomas, developmental delays, and convulsive seizures. Incredible as it may seem, she is now in stable condition, as healthy as she can be with all her damage, and freed for adoption—which means we feel she is ready to live in a real person's home, if not lead a normal life. Tracy is waiting for someone to want her and love her.

These are only a sampling of our handicapped kids. Stories of the others are sadly similar. We are in the business of healing and saving, but it is hard not to think that for many of these children a quicker death might be more merciful than a death in life.

The preadolescents, like Carl in the Blaine Hall program, have a somewhat better chance. These are kids who have been abused, but not to the point of extreme bodily harm. They have been maltreated physically, emotionally, or sexually—most of them sexually—and they have been neglected in almost every way, but their presence here is not due directly to abuse. They are here because the people most important in their lives, having abused them, now find it impossible to live with them.

Their long-term handicap is likely to be psychological, possibly severe psychological trauma. In the short run, their behavior is antisocial and aggressive. They don't get along with people. They're not liked. They come to us via social service agencies that try, first, to get them out of unloving homes and into foster homes. Then the agencies discover that they are not doing well in the foster homes, either: they are so hostile, so aggressive, that even kindly and experienced foster parents can't put up with them and so give them back. So the youngsters bounce around from one foster home to another until the agency finally says, "Enough! Let's get them into a program!"

And we have that program. Essentially, what we do is diagnostic placement. The children live here and go to school here until we feel they are ready to move on, which we hope will be within a year. Meanwhile they get intensive psychiatric care and counseling in the hope that we can change or modify their behavior so that they can go into a foster home without disrupting it or perhaps even go back to their own parents should the latter find them acceptable.

Typically, a child comes to us because of "misbehavior" or "adjustment disorder." He or she is, invariably, the product of a chaotic and violent home and the target of varieties of abuse and neglect. What can such a child know about normal life and responses? To the child, what goes on in the home is the way life is, and—unless there is some form of intervention—what he sees and experiences is what he becomes.

This is the case with seven-year-old Linda Sue, who has been taking lessons in delinquent behavior virtually from birth. Her family situation is so chaotic as to defy unraveling. In her own home Linda Sue had been abused and neglected by a wife-beating father and a crack-addicted mother; periodically, she was left with the father's live-in brother. When the household came apart at the seams and the mother, homeless and hopelessly addicted, took to the streets, the little girl was shuttled over to the mother's sister.

Linda Sue's aunt was not very enthusiastic about her, complaining afterward that the child was disobedient and foul-mouthed. School officials said that she was extremely disruptive, picking on other children, cursing, spitting on her teachers. When she went home while living with her aunt, Linda Sue often came home to an empty apartment. The aunt began to leave her unattended as a matter of course, filling her needs for food, shelter, and clothing but supplying no emotional sustenance. When she brought her to us she said that the child had become impossible.

In the program, Linda Sue continues to do her thing. She is uncooperative, she complains about everything, she instigates trouble, and she hits her peers. Once she bit another little girl, explaining that the child had been bothering her. Staff members try to keep her busy with games and toys; but what she really seems to enjoy is being with the other girls, starting trouble and then blaming them.

Linda Sue is of average intelligence and has nothing wrong with her physically or neurologically, but she is suffering the aftereffects of her home environment: like the adults she has lived with, she cannot control her own impulsive behavior. She becomes violent at times without seeming to have any clue that her behavior is unusual or unacceptable—even when we discuss her lapses with her, which we do on a regular basis.

We are considering the possibility of having to send this child to a long-term residential treatment center. At this point, her scars apparently are too deep to allow for any appreciable improvement in a diagnostic center such as ours. We worry about her: if she is an incorrigible seven-year-old, what is she likely to be as an adult?

Janine, at ten, is rather more sophisticated than Linda Sue. She was referred to us because she was keeping late hours and being disruptive in school whenever she chose to attend. School records showed that she had played truant on more than twenty occasions within a year. On some of those occasions she had also run away from home, sometimes staying away for up to four days at a time and afterward refusing to tell her mother where she had been. About a year ago, she disappeared for several days. She was picked up and sexually abused by a man she says was fifty years old—although, to her, anyone over twenty-five is at least fifty—but declined to say where she had met him. However, it was common knowledge that she often stayed on the subway train, riding back and forth for many hours. Then the police would call her mother, or whoever else answered the phone, and take the child home.

"Home" is a household consisting of the mother, mother's boyfriend, six children including Janine, an uncle, and a grandmother. Her mother used heroin and alcohol during her pregnancy with Janine, the youngest, and there is evidence that the child was born with withdrawal symptoms as a result of her mother's drug addiction. Her mother has a long history of repeated incarceration for shoplifting, and the child was raised mainly by her grandmother. Janine tells us that her mother still uses drugs and that the man she calls her father uses needles. Once, she says, he beat her on the head with a stick.

Janine herself admits to having tried beer but denies using any other drugs. She is, however, extremely knowledgeable about all the street drugs, from pot and alcohol to coke and dust. She says she doesn't like crack "because it makes you stupid and turns you dizzy," and she knows so much about how to use it that we wonder if she might not have experienced it herself.

The staff people, who are accustomed to disruptive children, note that Janine is a particularly difficult child to manage. She is stubborn, defiant of authority, and often starts trouble with other girls on the unit. At various times she has considered running away from the program, inciting others to go with her. She has not, however, succeeded in engineering a mass breakout, and does not in fact take advantage of opportunities to run away by herself. When asked to imagine what her life will be like in ten years' time, a question we often ask of our preadolescents, she says: "I'll have a baby and go to work and I'll have a husband and an apartment." Right now she would settle for a bike, five dollars, and a checker game—although she would much rather get pregnant.

With the family drug and alcohol problems and the mother's propensity for pilfering, it would seem that there is little hope that this child will ever find a stable home with her own family. And at this point it is unlikely that she would be an acceptable addition to anyone else's.

Dawn is an eight-year-old recently admitted to the program after living with foster parents for about a year. Her account of her own life is so incoherent that it is impossible to sort out who did what to her, or to which "mommy" or "daddy" she is referring. All that is certain is that she had been sexually abused by her biological father from a very early age; it is probable that she was physically abused by her own alcoholic mother and subsequently by her foster parents. According to the agency report, the foster parents simply didn't like her and wanted to get rid of her.

"My mommy puts me in a corner," she tells us. "She yells at me. My father spanks my butt. He makes me black and blue. Like he wanted me to take a bath real fast and I was too slow and he hit me. He hits a lot. He's got strong hands to hit. He pushes Mommy. He's mean. Mommy doesn't clean the clothes. She stays in her room all day and don't do nothing except throw up sometimes. Daddy, he drinks a lot. If Daddy drinks, he don't do nice things."

Some of the not-nice things are reflected in Dawn's behavior. The child has had episodes of sex play with other children since the age of three or four and a history of excessive masturbation. She cries a lot and is chronically depressed and unhappy; she has little appetite, keeps losing weight, and has frequent nightmares. When she gets angry at nothing in particular she screams and breaks her toys, and when she gets angry at adults she breaks things belonging to them. Sometimes she says she wishes she was dead. There is so much sadness and hostility here that we are finding it very difficult to get through to touch the child within.

Then there is Derrick, a handsome little six-year-old who was admitted to the program because of behavior problems in school and what passes for his home, although he is virtually homeless. He was removed from his mother's care a couple of years ago on charges of neglect by her and possible sex abuse by his mother's live-in boyfriend, and was sent to live with his grandmother. When she died this past year the boy was placed in foster care with a maternal uncle, then removed to yet another relative's casual guardianship when the uncle was charged with misuse of foster care funds. That relative soon complained about Derrick's hyperkinetic behavior, as did his teachers, so now he is with us—tough, defiant, and miserable.

This is an almost stereotypical case of an insecure and sad child who has been plagued by separation and abandonment and who is now attempting to armor himself in aggressive behavior. He has managed to achieve quite a bristly exterior. But he is young and physically healthy, and perhaps his scars are not yet so deep that they cannot be erased. It has been suggested by psychologists and psychiatrists in the program that perhaps this boy could be released and placed with carefully chosen foster parents who can meet his needs for attention and nurturing and see to it that he receives psychotherapy on a weekly basis. The combination of therapy and a caring home should, it is hoped, effectively deal with his feelings of abandonment while strengthening his self-image. We just don't know how he's going to take to another surrogate home.

The police picked up eight-year-old Cindy and her mother in the city's Port Authority Bus Terminal, and the child was brought to us. Reportedly, Cindy's mother was using her for prostitution. The family had been known to various social service agencies, and a history of Cindy was available. She had been sexually abused by her biological father to the point of intercourse and similarly abused by a male friend of the mother's. She was, in effect, sexually experienced on a primitive level even before being used as a money-machine by the mother. How the woman succeeded in eluding the child protective agency net is something I feel the agency ought to be able to explain.

When Cindy came in we found her to be hyper-anxious and unhappy to the core. Her self-esteem was about zero and she thought of herself as ugly even though she was, and is, quite an attractive little girl. In a pathetically pseudosophisticated sort of way she used all her wiles in the attempt to acquaint male staff members with her available charms. We felt that she was not simply acting out her role; she had learned flirtation and promiscuity as a way of life.

In spite of being—as we discovered—learning-disabled and blunted by sadness, she was alert and oriented. During her stay at the Foundling her behavior has slowly changed so that it is much less seductive and more appropriate for her age. She is not nearly so anxious as she was when she entered the program and seems to be much happier than she was. There may be a little vein of resilience here; there may even be something of a success story shaping up. Maybe, with a great deal of caution and tender loving care, followed by appropriate placement, we can help her grow into an approximation of normal adulthood. But what a past to overcome!

Cindy will not have an easy time of it. Although it isn't inevitable and certainly can't be regarded as normal, it is not unusual for children who are the victims of sex abuse to act out the sexual abuse on each other. I think of a boy I don't even know and almost certainly will never meet. Like Cindy, he is eight years old; unlike her, he comes from an apparently respectable home and has not been offered as a prostitute on the street. However, at his tender age he is already a sex offender and his pathetic story has been made much of in the newspapers. Outraged parents at a Greenwich Village school called upon police, as a last resort, to arrest the child on charges of sexually molesting his third-grade classmates. The child was not arrested, but the complaining parents had made their point: their kids were being subjected to a learning experience that definitely was not in the school curriculum. The boy, they said, had grabbed at the genitals of at least half a dozen other boys, exposed himself, repeatedly asked to perform oral sex on them, and drawn explicitly sexual pictures. These acts were obviously offensive and bewildering to the children, but they also suggested very strongly that the boy was himself a victim of sexual abuse. He was not removed from class; the other kids began ostracizing, beating and taunting him. I don't know how this problem is being resolved; when last I heard, school officials were saying it was nobody's damn business what therapy, if any, was being provided for the boy. I would hope it is adequate—because if it isn't he is more than likely to become an adult abuser. And I can't help wondering who did what to him in the first place, and what is happening to them.

At least when our kids come to us, we generally know what happened. Here is a disturbed yet likeable nine-year-old named Troy. At the age of five he was admitted to a hospital with first-degree burns on the buttocks and lower parts of the body, plus various bruises, abrasions, and contusions behind the ear and on the upper body. Also, judging by the marks, someone had apparently used a strap across the child's chest, back, and legs. According to the mother, the child was getting ready to take a bath when he fell into the tub of hot water and scalded himself. She had no explanation for the assortment of scrapes and discolorations he exhibited.

While the case was being investigated, the mother quietly disappeared, thus avoiding the charge of child abuse. Troy was placed with an aunt who, as he later told us, "hit up on him." He became rebellious; she threw him out. In short order Troy went through a series of foster homes and was obstreperous and abused in each. He came to us after a brief spell in a psychiatric center to which he had been sent after starting fires. He is extremely hyperactive and has what the psychologists call an "adjustment disorder"; interestingly, however, he gets along well with the other children on the unit. What seems to bother him most is his mother's abandonment of him and the fact that he doesn't know where she is. He is also sad and angry that his aunt hit him. When asked who he'd like to live with, he says, "Someone who is good to me."

That is all that most of them want or have ever wanted. These kids have lived in deprived and violent homes, in which they have been deprived and subjected to violence. They become troubled, often aggressive and hyperactive, and invite even more abuse. They have never had any sense of being wanted or cared for. Yet they all, still, desperately need to be loved and to be part of a family. One abandoned eleven-year-old, who knows all about crack, needles, reefers, and alcohol but very little about anything else, asks only for what every child should have: "To be with my mother, to go to school, and for us all to be together and have our own house."

But I doubt if that will ever happen. Many of them have no place to go except to a program such as the one we have at the Foundling or to a foster home. All of them are badly damaged, but how badly damaged and how salvageable they are remains to be seen. We don't know yet how successful our kind of intervention is going to prove in the long run. Perhaps if we can reach these youngsters early enough there may be hope for their survival. But what is "early enough"? And is there any realistic hope of helping these children in the sort of program that provides intervention for only several months or perhaps, at most, a year?

If we did not think so, we would not be trying. Experience to date gives us reason to believe that long-term prognosis in approximately 50 percent of this population is poor. Many of these children have been so damaged and so exploited and so exposed to violence in the home that the scars and trauma inflicted on them may be irreversible; in spite of everything, they will survive only to multiply the pain already inflicted on them and turn it on other people.

And then there's the other 50 percent. If we can get that many off to a fresh start—and I think we can, even if the scars remain—what we are doing is worthwhile. But on such a small scale!

It is true that other hospitals scattered throughout the country have similar programs. Put them all together, and the scale is still small. But what is even more alarming than the smallness of the total effort is that there is no national plan and no central direction. We are all fighting separate battles in the joint cause. I believe very strongly in private enterprise and in local community efforts, but I also believe a good effort deserves central planning, leadership, and coordination. Yet that is lacking throughout the child protective system in this country.

A 50 percent failure rate is far too high. We must get to these children much, much earlier; we have to get to the parents even *before* they become parents, and begin preventive strategies even before the beginning. This is not pie-in-the-sky talk, but absolute necessity. It will take a nationwide, concerted effort, but that effort must be made.

The youngsters at the Foundling today represent the consequences of our failure to grapple with the child maltreatment problem we identified over a quarter of a century ago. If we fail to grapple with it now, we may be well and truly lost: our failures, and the hundreds of thousands and millions of kids who get no help at all, are destined to be the adolescent misfits and destructive adults of tomorrow. Surely we have enough of those already. If we don't care about them, surely we must care about ourselves and the quality of our own lives.

I continue to be astounded by the national attitude toward child abuse. I can understand ignorance and apathy. But every other week there is a television drama or documentary exposing the horrors of child abuse, and almost every day there is a headline story or a newsmagazine feature on yesterday's or today's appalling case. Obviously, the public is neither uninformed nor uninterested; the public knows, and the public is fascinated.

But after the fascination—nothing. If it were learned that an infection or virus had been killing several thousand children a year and damaging millions more, there would undoubtedly be a nationwide uproar and calls for a vaccine or medication to stop the spread of the disease. When a similar toll is taken by child maltreatment, there is no such cry for action. I suppose this is because it has become commonplace to read or hear about a child being abused, maimed, killed, or sexually molested—so commonplace that we become inured to instead of incensed by these happenings. But child maltreatment is a disease, and a particularly loathsome one. It is in the same league with pornography and pollution and all the things that are inveighed against as outrageous in our church sermons and editorials and club cars.

Yet child abuse is more than that; it is not something to be ignored when the drama of the moment switches to something else, but a critical problem to be confronted on a personal as well as a national level. To look into the eyes of an abused or neglected child and not *feel* is not even an admission of apathy; it is an admission that you have finally stopped being human.

And what are we doing about it as a nation?

I ask myself this when I look at the broken children who should be our hope for the future and at the disarray of the agencies supposed to be serving them. What *are* we doing?

Virtually nothing.

The tragedy of our failure is what will happen to these kids tomorrow. If today's abused children do not get treatment—or even if they do—what then? Certainly not many of them are going to be our society's most upstanding, well-balanced citizens. Few will be stable, fewer will be happy; some will be a danger to themselves and some will be a danger to others.

4 / Bent Twigs: You Made Me What I Am Today

We have come a long, long way since our recognition of the "battered child." The route has not been pleasant; neither is the place we have arrived at. Every day we find more evidence that there is far more to the maltreatment syndrome than battering and neglect and humiliation of body and psyche, and every day we learn that the cessation of abuse is not necessarily the start of cure. It may be the beginning of a new phase of life that is equally unbearable: a life in an institution, or a life on the streets, or a life of perpetual inner torment; or a life that has no love in it because all recognition of love has been wiped out or permanently frozen inside.

When we look at the kids of yesterday's abuse, what do we observe today? In special programs such as those at the Foundling Hospital, we see damaged children for whom we have only a fifty-fifty hope of release, never mind recovery and a normal life. And if we look at the world outside our seemingly normal homes and schools and city streets, we can see long-term effects of untreated abuse, a situation that is not going to improve unless we somehow manage to rescue the victims before they become dangerous to themselves or others. For as they grow, their inner selves assume twisted shapes that nature never meant them to have.

First in their development as bent little beings comes their own immediate pain. Here, in the jargon of the child care professions, are some of the obvious and everyday consequences of child maltreatment: severe, uncontrollable temper tantrums in infants; extreme withdrawal, rebelliousness, and hostility in older children; impaired aggressive impulse control; diminished ego competency; reduced reality testing; and poor object relationships. What the average layperson observes is a moody, angry, seemingly not very bright and definitely unpleasant young person. These are not fleeting manifestations; the temper tantrums may go but the anger remains, and so does the warping of the psyche and the dulling of the intellect.

In time, many of these children become increasingly violent and aggressive. They may become juvenile delinquents, or develop more slowly into adult criminals. Or they may become self-destructive, killing themselves slowly by their manner of living—or quickly, by sudden suicide. And then again they may live in secret pain for the rest of their lives.

There is a great deal we still do not know about direct cause and specific effect, but over the past quarter-century it has become increasingly obvious that many—though not all—abused and neglected children are far more likely than non-maltreated children to "act out" in society, to become disruptive and violent, and eventually to become inmates of juvenile and adult correctional facilities.

And we, their parents and their keepers, have set them on this road.

She was only ten when her mother remarried and not quite eleven when her stepfather started abusing her sexually. The abuse went on for two years. Eventually she told her mother about it. Her mother refused to believe her. She ran away from home at thirteen. She was waylaid at the bus station in her destination city by a young man who offered her drugs and a job. She took both. The job was prostitution. At fifteen she was murdered by her pimp.

I know the first part of her story because she told it to me. The cops told me the rest of it. It is a common sort of story, one that happens every day in one city or another, except that it doesn't always end in murder. More often, it ends in death by AIDS or drug overdose.

Mitch is fourteen. The only reason he is not in the city's juvenile jail is that the judge dismissed his case when the victim failed to show up in court. Mitch had been charged with second-degree robbery for stealing a bike. In the course of stealing it he had grabbed the teenage bike owner in a choke hold—a technique he had learned from television—and squeezed him until he was unconscious. Mitch rode off on his victim's bike. "I was tired of walking," he explains. He promptly skipped out of the youth program in which he was placed. He talks of going to vocational school and staying with his grandmother, but he is living on the streets; he grabs chains, jumps subway turnstiles, and boosts merchandise from stores. His family is a nest of problems. His father, who beat his mother and once pushed three-year-old Mitch out of a window and permanently damaged his hearing, walked out abruptly several years ago, and Mitch's mother went on welfare to provide for their four children. Only one of them, the oldest child, a girl, is leading a stable life and paying her own way.

Sara is not quite eighteen. She ran away from home for the first time at the age of eleven because she was being physically and sexually abused by her adoptive father. On the surface, her parents were perfectly normal people who lived in a nice middle-class neighborhood and went to church every Sunday. The abuse started when she was about five and continued each time she got dragged back home by the police. She could not bring herself to tell anyone about the abuse; she felt that no one would believe her. At fifteen she left home for good, hanging out with whoever would give her a place to sleep. From time to time she has contemplated suicide. She admits to having been promiscuous but she insists she has never been a prostitute, is no longer into drugs, and is through with the thirty-year-old man with whom she has been living for the past year.

I see these kids on the streets of New York City every day. So do the police. Dropping out and running away from an abusive home situation—even though it seems the only way out of an impossible situation—is often the first step on the road to self-destruction. Many of these ill-used youngsters become part of a lost generation of drug addicts and perverts, prostitutes and petty thieves, killers and other criminals. It is not a foregone conclusion that they will, but they often do.

Some kinds of abuse seem to have more debilitating long-term effects than others. Careless indifference, coldness, neglect, or emotional whiplashings often do more serious damage than physical beatings. Few things are more devastating to the child than being constantly berated and told how unwanted and stupid and worthless he is. Such verbal darts as "I wish you had never been born,"

"I hate you," "I wish you were dead," repeated often enough, are guaranteed to undermine a child at the very core of his being. And sexual molestation, the ultimate violation of the child's self and self-respect, may mutilate the maturing psyche beyond repair.

There has been a lot of talk in professional circles about the cycle of violence, much of it by me. My own gut instinct and personal observation convince me that violence begets violence, that abused children are at great risk of becoming abusers, that neglect breeds neglect. Training for life begins in the home, and no child can fail to be influenced to some degree by the environment in which he grows up and the examples set for him. But it would be simplistic to suggest that the cycle is inevitable or that it involves a neat repetition of a specific form of behavior. An infinite number of variables comes into play.

The fact is that we have limited, imprecise knowledge of the long-term consequences of an abusive home environment. Until recently, research has been anecdotal and retrospective. It tells us, for example, that almost 100 percent of the killers on Death Row at any one time have been the childhood victims of extreme physical or sexual abuse, many of them enduring severe neurological damage. More than 80 percent of the general prison population speak of sexual molestation, icy indifference, or physical slapping around within the home. Some 75 to 80 percent of young runaways who become prostitutes report having been sexually abused by family members. A study of a number of young mothers incarcerated for fatal child abuse has found that all of them had been severely maltreated as children themselves.

The trouble with the hindsighted anecdotal studies is that many subjects are loath to admit that their father or mother or brother abused them, and many others relish the opportunity to explain or justify themselves. They will pour out a tale of abuse that can make your heart bleed—though it may sometimes begin to sound overelaborate after a while. Forthcoming or not, they are all wounded people, and often their perceptions and reactions have become distorted by the things that have happened to them, or their answers influenced by the questions they are asked.

Nevertheless, those studies tell us something useful: parental abuse does not necessarily produce a parent who abuses a child. It may, instead, produce an individual who abuses other individuals—and society—by committing acts of violence or other crimes, or a tormented soul who abuses himself with feelings of self-loathing or depression or masochism or some other form of psychological self-mutilation. The ranks of criminals, alcoholics and drug addicts, prostitutes, and psychiatric patients are filled with adult victims of various forms of child abuse. So are the ranks of those among us who live with festering misery and hurt. I believe that these are the most representative abusees, the silent sufferers who hug their hurts to themselves and never—unless they receive strong emotional support or therapy—become completely whole again.

What the retrospective studies *do not* do is track abuse victims from childhood to adulthood. Recent attempts to do such tracking indicate that about 30 percent of abuse victims become abusing adults, either as parents or as public enemies. This is a significant percentage, but it is much lower than had previously been assumed. This same research further confirms that abuse in childhood increases the likelihood of adult drug abuse, alcoholism, depression, sexual maladjustment, and various forms of psychosis—crimes against the self that spill over and hurt others, though not necessarily by deliberate intent.

Although these tracking studies are flawed and inconclusive, I can't help being slightly cheered by the suggestion that 70 percent of abuse victims do not, as adults, automatically replay the crimes visited upon them, and that an adult life of abuse or crime is not a foregone conclusion for the maltreated child. I am reminded, too, that there are many factors and events in a child's life that can shake up the odds and save him. Indeed, even adult criminals often redeem themselves.

So perhaps the cycle is more easily interrupted than we had thought. Yet I look backward with the street kids that I meet and I know that they were caught in it. And I don't know if it will end with them; obviously, they are not getting all the help they need to avoid the perpetuation of the cycle or even save themselves. In some ways the streets are even more dangerous for them than their homes, and yet we have no more than a flimsy and disconnected system of services with which to rescue them.

I see the stray kids all over the city, but mostly in the Times Square area and down on Fourteenth Street and in the parks and what we call the Village. Some of them live one place one night, another place another night; some drop in on pit-stop shelters run by the city, and not a few of them live for a time in cardboard shanties before they are picked up and moved along to a jail cell or an emergency residential facility operated by a charitable organization. As to those, I admire them, but I have become cynical about their ultimate value. I have known kids, far more cynical than I, to use them as flophouses, working their way from one end of the country to another as if traveling the youth hostel route, and I find it hard to believe that many of these nomads are not simply using "the system" for their own short-term ends. But does it matter if they are? If anything helps them in any way, let it help.

I know these mean streets and their people well, and there is nothing about their squalor and pathos that surprises me. To say that I grew up under similar circumstances would be very far from the truth—the city was a different place when I was a boy, and I was not a troubled kid in an unhappy home—but my family didn't exactly head up the Social Register or clip coupons for a living. We knew what life was like on the streets because we saw it every day. This wasn't extraordinary; times were bad for nearly all of America.

We—my parents, my brother and sister and I—lived in the Williamsburg section of Brooklyn in what was then a largely Jewish neighborhood. We kids were brought up in the Depression, and whatever allowance we got was money we earned from various little jobs we did for neighbors. I used to spend my Friday evenings earning quarters by lighting up the gas stoves for our Orthodox Jewish neighbors, since on Fridays they couldn't do it themselves.

In my high school days I worked summers in a sweater factory to earn the money for books and clothes. The place was literally a sweatshop: There was no air-conditioning, and the heat from the pressers and other machines made the atmosphere close to unbearable. A lot of older people were fainting, but a kid could take it. My job did not require a great deal of physical exertion, but it was intense. I was a button marker and I had to be fast and accurate. I took the sweaters as they came off the machines and made marks corresponding to the buttonholes so that the buttons could be sewn on where I made my little marks. The boss was nearsighted and would peer down over people's shoulders to make sure everyone was working and doing it right. He thought I was pretty good. I made twenty-five cents an hour.

"Forget about school," he used to say to me. "Don't go back to school. I'll teach you how to operate the machines. Stay here, and make your career."

I was tempted, but not very. Instead, I went to college on a scholarship and worked at Macy's Thursday nights and weekends and summers. I worked my way up from stock clerk to salesperson, and I was still getting twenty-five cents an hour. Somehow I could not believe that my future lay in operating sweater-making machines or selling upholstery hardware.

As things turned out, it didn't.

But nothing came easy; I did not come into this world with a silver spoon in my mouth. I met people along the way who had great difficulties, who were really suffering. A lot of the people I grew up with didn't make it. I think my past experience has sensitized me to the problems of those who are suffering. I can relate to hard times and troubles and people on the streets.

The following episodes are a few of today's thousands of street stories. They don't all have unhappy endings; many haven't ended yet. There are hundreds of thousands of thrown-away and runaway kids, most of them not even included in the child abuse statistics, living by their wits and bodies in the dark places of our cities. Yet they are on the streets because they have been abused, and their life today is their response to what their childhood has done to them.

She walks serenely among the plastic bags and broken glass littering the sidewalks of the Great White Way. Lara (her professional name) is twenty-three and works in an after-hours club. It is not the job of her choice; it is the job that was there. "It beats asking for money or sleeping in the park," she says. Her ambition is to earn enough to buy herself a college education. When she decided to leave home at the age of thirteen her mother said, "Fine! Get out!" and drove her to the bus depot.

What had Lara done wrong? Nothing. Her stepbrother, two years older, had been having sex with her, and Lara had told her mother what was happening. Her mother, on the third or fourth of her several unsatisfactory marriages, had always blamed Lara for her own unhappiness, and when Lara told her what was happening, the mother blamed her again. And Lara believed her. She says, "So I left home. I became sexually promiscuous, just as she said I would, and I started doing drugs." Recently, during intensive therapy, she has remembered that her mother herself had molested her sexually until she was perhaps four or five years old. "I was trained at a very early age to be a sexual plaything," she observes. "I'm not going to be one for anyone ever again." I would suggest that she try some other line of work, but she does not take kindly to suggestion. It all seems like criticism to her. Lara doesn't do drugs any more, and right now she's not interested in a close relationship with a man. Her defenses are up and they may never come down. She knows now that her mother was emotionally starved and neglected as a child, but she quite frankly does not give a damn. She does not give a damn about much of anything.

Neither does Felicia. She is nineteen and very angry. She is not about to forgive her mother. "So her father used to hit her—why did she have to take it out on me? My brother raped me from the time I was nine until I ran away at twelve. That's when my mom found out about it, when they dragged me back. She said it was my fault! She blamed it all on me! And then my goddamn stepfather hit me for it. So I ran away again. I would sleep with any man I met on the street just to have a place to stay and something to eat. Sure I'm angry. I will always be angry. I hate my mother more than my brother. What he did was wrong, but she is the one who did this to me by telling me that it was all my fault."

I hear this time and time again: "She blamed me. She said it was all my fault. She said I asked for it." There is an unpleasant picture here: daughter is sexually molested; mother doesn't believe or doesn't care; mother is part of the abuse. And the child is left wounded, betrayed, and untrusting. But *how* does a child "ask for it"? How enticing can a little girl be?

Delores wonders. She is twenty-one, a transplant from the rural South who is in her third year of college and planning to go on for a master's degree. Tense, she smiles a lot with her mouth; and she is obese. Her mother remarried after her father's death. The stepfather battered his wife and sexually abused the child. A social worker determined that Delores should be taken out of the home and put into foster care, apparently because the mother had suggested it wasn't the stepfather's fault. Delores resents this furiously.

Why should she be sent away from her own home when he was the one who did it to her? "I felt dirty," she says. "I felt like I had done something. But I was ten years old in flannel pajamas—how could I be enticing him?"

There came a time when the stepfather died and the mother fell into the depths of drug addiction, and Delores got in with the wrong crowd and experimented with drugs herself. That is how I met her—adrift and homeless, talking about her dreams of the future and her fear of being left alone with older men. She has lost track of her mother and is trying to find her. I am not sure that I fully understand why.

Later I meet Julia and I think I could not see a more classic portrait of wholesome Middle America. She is wearing something neat and pretty in blue and her blue eyes deepen in its reflection. She is dressed to go on a job hunt and she is living in a youth shelter—or she was, until she is asked to leave for the second time for breaking rules about staying out overnight.

She is not quite twenty-one and hails from a comfortably prosperous small town in Illinois. There are four children in her family, of whom she is the second oldest and the only girl. Her father was a successful salesman and an alcoholic; her mother was his companion drinker. Probably that is why the parents were not alert to what was happening in their family. Or maybe they were.

The boys were all athletes, and Julia was not. Hard as she tried, she could not be what her sports-crazy daddy wanted. Nor was she permitted to be a normal little sister. From the age of four until she was twelve, Julia was sexually abused by her older brother. "As a little girl," she says, "I thought that was what love was. But once, when I was ten, my parents saw him touch me. Then I realized that it was wrong, because they slapped me—they blamed *me*."

The abuse stopped when Julia was twelve because she saw the kids in junior high, the girlfriends with their boyfriends, and she knew "love" wasn't like that for her. Still only twelve, she started drinking heavily—hard stuff, like vodka and bourbon—and running away from home. By the age of seventeen she had been expelled from high school and kicked out of the house because of some little escapade with a boyfriend. Shortly afterward her parents were divorced and picked up other partners, and Julia became a floating houseguest with various friends.

There was more, as there always is, but at eighteen Julia hitch-hiked to New York and became involved with new friends who were heavily into drugs. She developed a severe cocaine problem and started sleeping with the drug dealer in exchange for a steady supply of free drugs and a roof over her head. "I was prostituting myself," she says expressionlessly. "It was not the same as the girls on Forty-second Street, but it wasn't all that different, either."

A late-night argument in the home of another "friend" turned into such an ugly scene that she went to the local police precinct house at five o'clock one morning and said she needed shelter. From the precinct she made a call to her estranged—and startled—dad and told him she needed help in getting off drugs. "Basically I had standards," she tells me. "I had values. I had never wanted to do drugs." But now she was hooked. Her father got her into a rehab program, then cut her out of his life altogether. She no longer knows where he is or where her mother is. But she has heard that her brothers are doing just fine.

I ask her what her friend the drug dealer is doing these days.

"Twenty-five to life," she says laconically, and then smiles an engaging smile.

I *think* Julia is going to be all right, but I can't be sure.

Drug use, an almost invariable part of the runaway-delinquency scene, has a lot to do with providing the gratification that is not found in the family in the form of emotional support and guidance. Often, though by no means always, it is the crutch that fills in where the parent should have been.

A lot of the young men I talk to brush aside their drug use as if it were of no importance. It was fun, it was a stupid-kid kind of thing to do, it's over now. Typically they say, "I just let myself go. I'm not going to mess up again."

I wish I could believe it of them. I would find it easier if I did not actually see them dealing in drugs. They are hard-eyed children of seventeen, eighteen, nineteen, products of families in which addictive substances were freely used and kids were routinely slapped around and often sexually molested. The boys put on a tougher act than the girls. They shrug off what has happened to them, though they tend to look for repeat experiences on the street and often earn their bed and board—or bed and drugs—through prostitution or dealing. But to hear them tell it, that's all over now.

In my experience, most of them are manipulative liars, and I pity them. They are what abuse has made them.

For a direct relationship between childhood abuse and later crime, there is no more telling example than the shattering tale of Joseph Wolske. He is seventeen and his life has been a horror. He is a murderer.

When he was ten years old and living in Bay Ridge, Brooklyn, he was sexually assaulted by a sixty-year-old neighbor named Jay Petzold, who was subsequently arrested and charged with abusing Wolske and another boy. The man pleaded guilty to sexual misconduct and was sentenced to three years probation.

Joe's life has never been serene. He was three years old when his father abandoned the family, ten when subjected to sexual molestation, fourteen when his mother committed suicide by jumping from a roof, just over fifteen when his younger brother killed himself. During that time Joe's uncle had become his guardian, but had to give him up when courts put the boy into foster homes because of chronic truancy.

"It bothered Joe that this guy was walking the streets," the uncle said. "He'd see him walking around and that affected him. He couldn't understand how this guy could have committed such a crime and be free."

A resident at a group home on Staten Island, Wolske was hanging out with friends in Bay Ridge when he recognized Petzold's apartment. He knocked on the door and when the man answered, he said: "Remember me?" Inside the apartment, he knocked Petzold to the floor and kicked and stomped on him. Then he went into the kitchen, got a knife, and stabbed the pederast repeatedly in the head and neck until he was dead.

The boy has been charged with murder. His uncle blames child welfare officials, who shuttled Joe from foster home to foster home without providing any psychiatric counseling. "He should have been helped," says the uncle. "Not only was the kid abused by this guy, he has been abused by the system, too. He's never had a break."

Another sad case is Phil Burke. He's probably around forty-five; he doesn't really know exactly. He has done twenty years in the prison system for a roster of crimes, including armed robbery and murder. I am mildly surprised that he is out at all, but he has had some kind of conversion that impressed the parole board. He is working with other ex-convicts now, serving as a sounding board and role model for them.

He was injured by battering parents as a baby and assigned to a foster family. By the time of his first arrest for stealing a car, he had been in eleven foster homes. He has been in almost as many jails since then. That he is leading something like a normal life today is a tribute to some inner core of strength in him.

It isn't easy for him, after all those years in prison, to talk about the life experiences bottled up inside him; as part of his deal with society he goes to support meetings in which he is expected to reveal his innermost self. Initially he felt uncomfortable when he looked around the room and saw it filled with ordinary people who looked a lot more respectable than he felt. But then one day after listening for a while he said to himself: "Everybody in this god-damn room has been abused and sodomized and raped!" And he began to relax and talk about himself.

He talks to me about the people he is trying to help. They are fresh out of jail, jobless and homeless, and everything this side of iron bars is foreign to them. Every one—every single one—has suffered abuse as a child or an adolescent. They say they don't want to talk, but they *do* want to talk. "There is a kind of jagged edge in the guy's voice and in his manner," Phil says, "that makes you feel he can go either way—wind up even tighter and come screaming off that jagged edge, or calm down as you listen to him and just come off gently and let that tension kind of sigh away. For a while there it's really tense but then it starts to come all right."

It makes me think that if someone had listened to them before, things might have been different for them now. But it's not just a question of talking and listening; the problem often is not even knowing that something is wrong. How is a kid supposed to know that something is going on in his or her family that is not going on in other families?

Tony Toler didn't know. His family moved from Puerto Rico to New York in pursuit of the American dream when Tony was a baby. The father, a skilled butcher who could not speak English, couldn't find a job of his choice and was forced to settle for low-paying factory work; the mother went on welfare to supplement his income and provide for the growing family. Her husband's macho pride and self-esteem were deeply hurt. He started drinking heavily, and in his anger and rage he struck out at his wife and children. His drinking and abuse became uncontrollable. Neighbors started calling cops to the home to break up the fights. The cops just took the old man round the block, gave him a pep talk, and went away. The boozing and the banging around increased.

Tony started hanging out in the streets. He was doing well at school but he'd hang around afterward with a bunch of the guys just to get away from the home scene. They drank beer, and then hard liquor, and then moved on to marijuana, and finally heroin. Tony got married very young and beat his wife, just as his father had beaten him and his mother and his brothers. "The way she was raised," Tony says of his wife, "a woman needs a beating when she steps outa line," so she took it for quite a long time. Their baby was born when Tony was eighteen, and a few weeks later Tony was arrested for the first time on a charge of being in possession of a controlled substance—heroin. He was already an alcoholic and a drug addict without being aware that he was hooked.

Arrests—drug possession, burglary, drug possession again—and prison sentences were his life for the next eighteen years, with time in jail interspersed with street brawls over drugs and futile attempts to save his marriage. During his third prison term his wife left him and remarried. He wound up in court for the seventh time and was headed for a five-year sentence when his Legal Aid lawyer— "a woman, did a helluva job for me," he says—persuaded the judge to sentence him to a drug and alcohol program instead.

It took several years and a number of slips, but the Tony of today is drug-free, employed in a human support organization, and happily remarried. He remembers both his parents with sorrow and fondness. His mother, he thinks, was a saint. Indeed, she was a fine woman of the old school, a long-suffering wife and mother. But putting up with spousal and child abuse to keep a dysfunctioning family superficially intact is not enough to save the family or the child. And of Tony and his five siblings, only one has never been in jail.

But neither is it enough for a family to be free of violence and substance abuse, even if the family is God-fearing as well.

Nancy Martinez was the fourth child born into a family that

was all those things—and loving, too. Even that was not enough. "My parents were much older when I was born. I was unexpected; I came out ten years after the last child. I was treated with a lot of love. My father was a minister, a Pentecostal minister. He was a very good man, very humble, very loving. For him, I was the little princess in the house. My mother was very loving, too, but she was very strict. The Pentecostal religion is also very strict."

There was a lot of peer pressure. All Nancy's friends were wearing pants and cutting their hair and wearing nail polish and earrings, and her parents wouldn't let her do any of that. "So," she says, "I started rebelling and doing everything that was a sin!"

By the sixth grade she was drinking beer and smoking cigarettes, and then she "sort of graduated," like Tony, from beer to wine to marijuana and subsequently to hard drugs. One day when she was twelve and playing hookey with a group of friends she saw another girl alone and suddenly said, "Let's rip her off!" And they did. They grabbed her pocketbook and laughed and ran. The girl had nothing but seventeen cents in her wallet. But she recognized one of her assailants and reported the whole lot to the police. Nancy was in official trouble for the first of many, many times. Periodically, she ran away from home.

"I got picked up for shoplifting," she says. "I worked with a gang of women, sometimes three, sometimes six. After a couple of years I had a rash of bad luck. In three months, I had three arrests consecutively. The first time charges were dismissed, the second time I was fined, the third time they gave me a year's probation. At that point I got so scared about going to jail, I couldn't even steal a bar of soap! But as my drinking and drug use progressed I threw fear out the window, because at a certain point I really didn't care. By then I had been married twice, and I had a couple of kids and everything, but still I got mixed up in drug dealing with my husband. We got caught by an undercover cop, and both of us got long sentences."

All this because of strict but loving parents? Because of peer pressure? Because her father had forced her to marry when she was pregnant at fifteen?

No, there was something else. Two or three years ago, while taking a child psychology course in prison, Nancy began to remember. Her sister was twelve years older than she and married to a man then in his thirties. The sexual abuse by this man began when Nancy was about six years old.

"First thing I remembered was asking my mother to sleep with me at night. My sister and her husband were staying over. She had just had a baby, and the baby had died. And the dirty dog molested me! I can still see him standing over the bed and getting in. I remember the fear. That man violated my body. After that, it happened whenever they visited. I told my mother I was afraid to be alone, so she would stay with me at night until I went to sleep. I was so desperate to have her stay all night that once I took a whole bunch of safety pins to bed with me, and while she was laying down with me I pinned her nightgown to the bottom sheet with all those little safety pins so she couldn't get up!" Her laugh is sad.

She still says that her parents were the best parents anyone could want, but adds: "I was very resentful. As a little girl I must have thought that, well, my mother's letting this happen to me. Why is she letting it happen? And I would say that from that experience stems all of my rebellion and drug use and the rest of it. Maybe it wasn't only that. But I'm constantly talking to my children about other people touching them. I don't trust many other people with my children."

I talk to convict Cliff Jones, who is out of jail on a work release program. His story, long and violent but a common one, boils down to this: his mother married young and gave birth at fifteen. West Indian grandparents despised the husband and took the child into their home. The grandparents were extremely strict and forbade all after-school activities with other kids. There was no communication between the adults and the child, no room for self-expression, no room for love. On the other hand, there was much talk of, "You'll never be any good! You're just like your father!" Cliff gets into fights. At sixteen he is accused of stealing, which he denies. The grandparents side with his accuser. He leaves home, becomes involved in one violent situation after another, starts using drugs, gets jailed for drug possession, then for possession of a weapon in a stolen car, then again and again for drug possession; he gets deeper and deeper into drug use.

"My mother died and left some insurance. I used it to buy drugs. That's pretty much the story of my life—drugs, drugs, drugs,

drugs. This time I've been in jail for four and a half years. I've been in a therapeutic program for twenty-three months. But drugs are not my problem and never were my problem. *I* am my problem. But to me there's a pretty clear connection between the nothingness of childhood and something that makes you feel better. The drugs did something to make up for something else I was missing. At least I thought so at the time. But I've been angry, I've been *angry*, since I was a kid."

He is forty-four now and figures he has lost twenty-eight years of his life, maybe more, counting his emotionally sterile childhood.

There is a man named Robert Alton Harris who, as of this writing, is still on Death Row at San Quentin Prison, having been temporarily spared execution for the 1978 murder of two teenagers.

He kidnapped the two boys from the parking lot of a fast food restaurant in San Diego and forced them at gunpoint to drive to a remote area, telling them that he planned to let them loose and use their car as a getaway vehicle in a bank robbery. Instead, he chased them to their deaths in defiance of their pleas and prayers and, having shot them repeatedly, calmly ate the food they had picked up at the restaurant. This was not the killer's first crime; he had recently been let out of prison after serving a term for voluntary manslaughter in the 1975 beating of a neighbor. On that occasion, court records say, he had thrown lighted matches on his victim as the man lay dying.

It is difficult to summon up any sympathy for so callous a criminal. Yet his lawyer has said, "He wasn't born evil; he wasn't born a monster. If anyone had intervened when he was a child, I don't think he would be on Death Row today."

He had been born with fetal alcohol syndrome, the child of an alcoholic mother who delivered him three months prematurely after a battering by his father. The boy's childhood was a horror story of psychological and physical torment by both parents, particularly his father, who routinely beat him within an inch of his life and also choked him until he went into convulsions on occasion. At other times the man would menace him with a gun. Between such episodes, the father exposed his son to displays of violent abuse against the mother.

Neurological tests indicate that Robert Harris was severely brain-damaged by a combination of prenatal abuse and repeated head injuries. Reportedly he suffers, too, from post-traumatic stress disorder as a result of the intense suffering he experienced and witnessed throughout his growing-up years.

His adult crimes are gross. Yet many neuropsychologists and psychiatrists report that they fit the crime pattern of people who were subjected to the kind of violent childhood endured by Harris, and who have suffered injury to certain parts of the brain.

There is not the slightest doubt that his parents made him what he is today.

These are the abused: juvenile delinquents, drug addicts, hustlers, part-time prostitutes, jailbirds, criminals who cannot control their baser impulses. Some have changed their lives for the better and yet still feel unhappy, soiled, and betrayed. They come from problem homes and they have all had encounters with public agencies and clashes with the law. Yet most of them are not unrecognizable people. They could have been our neighbors, or our neighbors' kids; they could have been our own. They grew up misshapen, but that is what happens when twigs are carelessly or roughly bent.

It is a different story when we can get to the twigs when they are still young and malleable, when we can get to the parents before they are beyond all hope.

5 / Rescue of the Innocents: The Crisis Nursery

In 1869 the abandonment of babies reached epidemic porportions in the city of New York. I don't know why that year should have been particularly bad; maybe post–Civil War stress had something to do with the phenomenon. Infants, dead or half-dead or newborn and crying, were found on doorsteps and gutters and in trash cans or bundled in blankets and left in filthy alleys to die. Concerned citizens, newspaper editors among them, finally began to notice what was happening and demand that something be done.

It was not the city government that responded but the Sisters of Charity of New York. In October of that landmark year three Sisters with minuscule funds and enormous dedication opened a foundling home in a small brownstone on East Twelfth Street, put a little crib at the entrance to signal their intentions, and declared the opening of The New York Foundling Hospital. That small but welcoming place was the first and only institution in the city to provide a refuge for abandoned babies.

The ever-vigilant New York press made sure that the public knew of the purpose of the home. From the moment of opening there was scarcely a day that the crib was not occupied with an unwanted child. Each offering was a human tragedy—but not a human sacrifice. The babies left there were alive, although very often near death. They had a tiny chance. Fewer and fewer dead bundles showed up in the city's garbage; more and more throwaway infants turned up on the Foundling's doorstep. Within the first year of its existence, the Foundling had taken in well over a thousand discarded babies and was raising funds for larger quarters in order, as the New York *World* put it, to "rescue the innocents." Wherever the Foundling moved in search of more space and better facilities, babies were left. Some were simply dumped; others came with notes pinned onto their tiny blankets: "Please help me. Help my baby. I love her but I can't look after her."

In time it became something of an informal tradition for despairing or overstressed young mothers to leave babies they could not take care of not only at the Foundling Hospital but at *any* hospital. They considered that a hospital was a place of safety for a child; that in a hospital, people knew how to take care of babies.

But within the last few years, something has changed. Once again, babies are being found in junkyards and dumpsters and in garbage cans and filthy alleyways and in roadside weed patches and in stairwells and in toilet tanks and in shopping carts in parking lots and in cardboard boxes in the woods.

Sometimes someone hears them cry and help may come in time to save them. Other times, they have starved or frozen or become dehydrated by the time they are found, or they have been thrown out of a window to die on impact or maybe many hours later. Not so long ago a panicked schoolgirl tried to flush her unwanted newborn infant down a toilet, and when that failed she slashed him with a razor blade to dispatch him. A recent high school graduate secretly gave birth to a full-term baby boy in the bathtub of her family's home and, fourteen hours later, dumped the body in a lake. A married woman in her twenties, suffering from postpartum depression, drowned her child in a bathtub and hid the body, claiming he'd been kidnapped. Others bottle up their inner turmoil for months or even years, and then strike out and maim or kill. And there is no way they can undo what they've done.

Some don't care until they're caught, but most are anguished and remorseful. These are the mothers who could have been saved, and whose children could have been saved. Because of them, I and a number of like-minded child advocates have felt for many years that the child protective system must provide programs and facilities to help young parents in distress—those to whom a baby looms as an insupportable burden, and those who fear that they are going to hurt the child. Now we do have such services, and we publicly urge overwrought parents to come in and spill their troubles to us without fear of retribution. That is why I was so incensed by the case of a teenage mother named Emmanuelle.

Late one spring night a two-and-a-half-year-old was left in the woman's restroom of King's County Hospital in Brooklyn. Those who found her said she looked cared for and well nourished, although there were some unidentifiable scars on her legs. A note pinned to the child's clothes read:

To Whom It May Concern:
I'm an 18-year-old student and I also work. I can't handle the pressure. I sometimes take it out on her. I love her and would not like to hurt. Please find her a good home where she'll get the love she deserves.

The writer signed the note, "Sincerely Desperate."

By the next day, Emmanuelle Jedonne had had second thoughts. She called the hospital.

"How's my baby?" the young mother asked anxiously.

Keisha had already been taken away by child welfare officials, but hospital officials didn't mention that to the mother. They suggested that she come to the hospital.

When she arrived soon afterward with her older brother she asked to get her child back. "I brought her here because I was depressed and didn't have anyone to talk to," she said, and her brother added that she was a loving mother distraught by the breakup of her marriage—or other relationship—to a twenty-nine-year-old man who had since disappeared. Her family had disapproved of the relationship and given her no support. A mother at sixteen, she was a senior in high school and worked as a cocktail waitress after school hours. Her family had immigrated from Haiti about eight years before. Emmanuelle had recently lost her green card and was unable to find a more suitable job without it. She was distressed and remorseful about leaving her baby and wanted to take her home—even though she had no home to go to, because her sister had told her to leave the apartment they had shared. Her life since the child's father had abandoned them both had been a constant struggle to pay the bills and buy food and clothes for herself and her daughter.

This young mother with no support system needed all the help she could get and had obviously been crying out for it. But instead of getting help, she was arrested and taken to the precinct stationhouse, where she was charged with child abandonment and reckless endangerment and jailed awaiting arraignment.

Now, abandoning a child in a hospital restroom does not exactly qualify a woman as Mother of the Year. Furthermore, scars, possibly burn marks, are suggestive of child abuse. Yet this mother clearly realized she was potentially abusive and wanted the child to be saved. She had not left her in a garbage can or on the street to die; she had left her alive and well, cleanly and comfortably clad, in a nonthreatening environment. She had left her as an act of desperation—and she had come back for her.

Sometimes, when a child is crying, it's the mother who's the child.

What troubled me about the arrest was precisely that the mother was a classic at-risk case who might easily have done away with her youngster, but didn't. She brought it to a hospital. With a little help and counseling she might well be able to care for her daughter, while prosecuting her as a criminal would put one more young woman in jail and another child in the city's already overstretched foster care system.

The larger picture was the disturbing message that the arrest instantly sent out to young parents in similar situations. What we in the parent-help business have been saying is: Don't be afraid to come in for help. We'll take care of you and your child. We're not going to take your baby away from you. We're not going to put you in jail. But the message in the case of Emmanuelle was: Don't you dare come out and ask for help, because you'll be thrown into prison and your baby will be taken away! Stay in your closet and beat up your kid or get rid of her. You'll be safer that way!

If our law enforcers are too insensitive to understand when people are crying out for help and insist on trying to jail parents like this young woman, they risk endangering thousands of other children whose parents will be afraid to come out and ask for help. We want *all* parents in distress, *all* who are on the verge of hurting a child, to come forward to get help. But how can we persuade them to trust us, when we say one thing and the law enforcement agencies say another?

The Crisis Nursery can help mothers exactly like Emmanuelle— but only if they trust us.

*   *   *

"Crisis Nursery" sounds like a contradiction in terms. It isn't. Nor is it an intensive care unit for babies. The Crisis Nursery at New York City's Foundling Hospital is an emergency refuge for children at risk of being damaged by their parents—parents desperately in need of relief from stress. The children brought to the Crisis Nursery seldom need much medical care. What they do need is a respite from their troubled parents, just as their parents need a respite from them.

To me, the Crisis Nursery is a metaphor, some might say a mixed one. But I consider it a metaphor for the national crisis in family care, for the breakdown of the American family, and for what can be done on a practical, everyday level to begin to set it right. That is the importance of the Crisis Nursery program: it is part of the solution.

Thousands of parents in trouble do call us, and we do help.

This is how crisis intervention works—not with a Band-Aid, but with in-depth care. The first thing we do is listen to people who don't usually get listened to.

Several months ago Cheryl James, then twenty, came in to see us, bringing her ten-month-old son. She left him for a brief vacation in the clean, bright rooms of the Crisis Nursery. Cheryl was having a crisis. She is a different person now—not miraculously different, but changed enough so that she can see some hope for getting out of the rut that her life had become.

Cheryl is a typical client in the sense that she fits into the overall profile of the troubled mothers we see. What our clients have in common is an age range usually between twenty and thirty-four, a gamut of family problems, and a partner only sporadically involved in the care of the child. In Cheryl's case, the father of her little boy provides financial help as the spirit moves him but is otherwise indifferent to his accidental offspring. Like 50 percent or more of our parent-clients, Cheryl herself was an abused child.

She and her four brothers and three sisters grew up in what she calls "the projects." Her mother had no time to care for her, though she always seemed to have time for the others. And she did find time to pick on Cheryl, who became the scapegoat of the family. There was a father in the house, but he had no interest in any of them. He was the invisible man in the home.

By Cheryl's account, her mother hit her constantly and kept her home from school so that no one would see the black-and-blue marks on the girl's body. Nobody believed Cheryl when she tried to tell them about her abuse. Today she still has ugly scars on her arms and legs from wounds that didn't heal well, that didn't get needed stitches because her mother wouldn't take her to a doctor.

She is a classic maltreatment case: physically battered, emotionally starved, and verbally abused. Short of murder, the worst thing a parent can do is destroy a child's self-esteem, and Cheryl's mother had done exactly that.

Now that she has started to talk about it, her mother asks her, "If it was so bad, why didn't you leave? Why didn't you just get out?"

I ask her the same question.

"*Where was I gonna go? Where was I gonna go?* I didn't have nobody to go to."

As she grew up she was virtually isolated from anyone who could have helped her because her mother made sure she didn't make friends. And she has no contact with her two grandmothers, one of whom lives in Florida and the other in North Carolina; she hasn't seen either since she was a little girl.

Cheryl's life was further complicated when she gave birth to her first—and, so far, only—child. She was ill-prepared for parenthood.

"He was only ten months old and he was already getting on my nerves," she told me afterward. "I didn't realize he couldn't understand things. I thought he should know more than he did. I didn't understand anything about babies."

From her mother, she had learned to take her frustrations out on somebody else—in this case, another helpless child. But no one had ever explained to her the stages of a child's growth and development. Her mother wouldn't help, and she had nobody else to go to. She used to feed her son when she felt like it, not realizing that even a baby has to eat every day. One day she'd feed him once, and the next day she didn't feed him at all. Nor was she feeding him any solid food, but only bottles of formula.

Small wonder that the child was cranky.

"I didn't mean no harm. I didn't know what scheduled feedings were all about. I used to feel myself wanting to hit him, when he was crying or something. I felt it coming on. I wanted to hit my son—but I didn't 'cause he was so little. I mean, I wanted to hit him for *real*. I did hit him once, not hard, and I felt real guilty. I don't want bruises on my child 'cause I know that they can hurt. I didn't want to hurt my baby. I didn't want to kill him. And I don't want to raise him like I was raised. I don't want him to be like the children are now. They hurt other people, and they hurt themselves. I want him to get everything he can out of life."

Cheryl saw the Crisis Nursery Helpline number on a neighborhood bulletin board one day. She called, and a few hours later came in with the baby she didn't know how to feed and many times wanted to hit.

She was hesitant and nervous at first. But when she saw the bright rooms with their cheerful furniture and the little pantry and the youthful staff she began to relax. This is a common reaction; our clients trust the place. To any eye—including the eye of a child seeing his peers at play—it is a serene, nonthreatening environment.

Cheryl left baby Jay with us for two or three days while she got her act together. She needed a break from Jay and from her own mother; she needed parent training, counseling, financial assistance, and a whole range of services that could put her on the right track. It is a large part of our child abuse preventive work to make sure that parents seeking help make the right connections with the right programs.

Often we can help before something terrible happens.

The impetus for the Crisis Nursery program came in the early part of 1980, when fifty children had already died of parental beatings or neglect that year. Then came the single week in which three toddlers were abused to death. I was chairman of the Mayor's Task Force on Abuse and Neglect at that time, as I still am, and I was boiling with anger that New York City child protective agencies could permit these dreadful things to go on.

It seemed then that in all our years of developing programs to save children we had made no progress at all; we had actually slid back. We were obviously not getting to the families that needed us. We were not getting to the children who were being abused and neglected in secretive homes, and whose plight went undetected, unreported, unprotected until it was too late.

Studying the three cases, I saw certain similarities. None of the parents seemed to be intrinsically bad people. Irresponsible, yes. Lacking in control, pitifully ignorant, and out of their minds with stress, yes. But they were not beyond help, if somebody could have reached them. They should have been helped, and their children should have been saved.

"Why did this have to happen?" I asked myself. "Why don't we have a child protective system in place—one that is truly protective and preventive?" God knows I had been yelling about it for years.

I said all that, and more, when I expressed my despair and pessimism during an interview after the crimes. I was so furious about the glaring failure of our child protective system that I threatened to resign as chairman of the Mayor's Task Force unless the city immediately took emergency measures to stop kids from dying. I also had a plan for something I was determined we should try at once.

I don't know if it was because of my threat, but Mayor Ed Koch expressed his desire to help and set in motion the slow-grinding bureaucratic wheels that ultimately brought the plan to life. With a budget of $200,000 a year from Special Services for Children, the child protective unit of the city's Human Resources Administration, the Crisis Nursery opened its "island of safety" at the New York Foundling Hospital in April 1982.

A twenty-four-hour-a-day, seven-day-a-week Helpline was instantly made available to parents at the end of their rope—depressed, distressed, and touching bottom. Our public awareness program featured posters displaying our phone number and inviting overburdened people to bring their children to us so that we could help to lift their burden from them.

In the beginning cynics said, "You'll never get *them* to come to you! What're you going to do—advertise?"

Right. That's exactly what we are doing.

"For *child abusers?*"

No. Never for child abusers. For strung-out parents.

Periodically, volunteers at the Nursery continue to send out mass mailings to community centers of every variety, from welfare and unemployment offices to laundries and banks. We explain the services we offer and ask harried parents to call us on our Helpline number. Our poster appears on walls and bulletin boards throughout the city: "ARE YOUR KIDS GETTING TO YOU? *Are You Losing Control?* There is an 'Island of Safety' at NY Foundling. Call the Parent Helpline." The number follows.

And the parents do call. We have found that they are eager to use a program such as ours when they know about it. I think many more would call us if they knew where to call, that they would be treated with compassion, and that they wouldn't get a bureaucratic constant busy signal or a tape-recorded message.

When a mother calls with a problem—and more often than not it is the mother—we may be able to advise her on the telephone, or we may suggest that she and the child come in to see us. Then, after making an assessment of the immediate needs of the whole family, we either admit the child or refer the parent to a variety of support services such as a reputable day care center, a parenting education program, a self-help group such as Parents Anonymous, or specialized medical services.

Sometimes we will urge a mother to come in immediately with the child or children. By cab, if necessary, at our expense. We do that when the woman's story or the way she tells it or the tone of her voice indicates an urgent need for hands-on personal attention. Or there may be a background sound of a man's voice raised in anger, a thud, a child screaming in pain or fear. A common theme is that the mother's nerves are worn to shreds and she is ready to boil over at her children. Or that she has already started to boil and needs help with all the things that are driving her nuts before she does something really bad. Or that her boyfriend is hitting the kids.

When the program was set up we anticipated that parents would come in before any abuse or neglect occurred. It hasn't worked out that way. In most cases, some striking out has already started by the time they call. They come in because they're on a roll of anger and they're afraid that it's going to get worse. This came as something of a surprise to us in the beginning, and it points up something that we have had to learn: the fact that many parents cannot bring themselves to reach out for a lifeline until they are already desperately deep in trouble. But it also tells us something else: that even when mothers and fathers are ashamed of what they have done, they *can* ask for help if it is made available in a nonpunitive way in a welcoming place.

There are days when I feel that we are engulfed by the rising tide of child abuse and murder, that all we ever do is make studies and promises and plan paper projects. But then I look around and see the tension fading from the faces of a mother and a child who have found the sanctuary of the Nursery, and I realize again that we have something here that is worth its weight in golden promises—something that does work.

Mrs. Elena Russo calls in great agitation. "I've reached a breaking point. I don't know what to do." Mrs. Russo is the mother of a hearing-impaired daughter and a hyperactive two-year-old whose greatest pleasure is trying to stuff things down the toilet, including the family kitten. Mrs. Russo has handled herself well in spite of family and financial problems, but now everything is getting just too much to bear. Her husband's unemployment checks have stopped, her own mother is ill, the two-year-old has discovered the joys of scrawling in red marking pen all over the living room walls, and the public utility company has cut off gas and electricity.

She comes in, her hands shaking and her eyes red-rimmed with weariness. We swing into action. The Nursery social workers find her a source of emergency funds and straighten things out with the utility company. We enroll the hyperactive boy in a part-time day care and have the little girl examined by a competent physician. We offer Mrs. Russo a program in parenting as well as a whole list of other services available to her. How did she know our number? She saw a poster on the wall of her laundromat.

The Helpline telephone rings in the Operations Room, a large, cheery office full of desks and file cabinets across the hall from the mini-dormitories. The operator on duty, either a social worker or a volunteer, takes verbatim notes on the calls from parents in need or the people who sometimes call on their behalf—a worried relative or friend or neighbor or child care agency worker. We try to get the name, address, and telephone number of whoever calls. Sometimes the caller won't give that information. Most people will. If we feel there is a need for crisis intervention and we don't hear again from the caller, we return the call. We maintain a list of people who need callbacks, and we get back to them on a regular basis. When they don't have telephones, we'll write to them, expressing our concern and urging them to contact us again. We never accuse and we never condemn. We just want to hear from them and give them all the help we can.

The calls come in day after day, night after night, throughout the twenty-four hours. Almost all of them are very specifically stress-related. People don't just say they have a problem handling their children; something else is driving them to despair, and they tell us what it is. They've been evicted and have no place to go. Their welfare checks have stopped coming and they can't reach their caseworker. A jealous child is tormenting the baby. They are fighting with a spouse or a violent lover who won't stay away. Or the problem may be a drug-addicted sister who is neglecting her own family, or a lost job, or an ailing grandmother who needs full-time care, or an amalgam of these problems.

And again and again the callers say that they are afraid they might be taking their frustrations out on the child. They call because they are close to breaking point and hope that for once they have a line on someone who cares.

Rona Nelson, mother of two, calls in. "I'm finding myself flying off the handle more than usual," she says. Both her parents had recently died. She had had a very difficult second pregnancy, and she is sunk into a postpartum depression that leaves her afraid to go out of the house and afraid not to. We ask: Is she worried she might strike out at the child? A pause. The answer: "I've been yelling a lot. I love my kids, I do. But I don't feel I'm in control. I don't want to do anything crazy. Yes, I'm afraid I may hit one of them. Or maybe both."

What she has done instead is call the right number. We tell her we can help her. She says she will come in the next day with her husband and children. The children will stay with us.

Nancy Taylor, twenty-six, comes in with her two girls and a boy: "My husband pulled a knife on my oldest daughter when she was five years old and then he sexually attacked her a few months later. I got an order of protection but that doesn't seem to help me. He is still coming back, aggravating me and my family. I came in here for help to get my children away from my husband while I figure out what to do." The children check in at the Nursery, where they will stay for up to seventy-two hours, and Mrs. Taylor sits down with a volunteer worker who has already started making emergency calls on her behalf.

A father calls and speaks to one of our social workers. He and his wife don't agree on disciplinary action. The father seems to feel that the wife, because she is older and better educated than he, ought to know more about discipline than he does. "But this isn't discipline—it's punishment." He says that his wife makes the boys strip and then strikes them with a belt—which she keeps handy on a doorknob—without leaving a mark. And she makes the two younger children watch.

The present incident has been provoked by the boys stealing some money. The father thinks the woman hits them much too hard. He doesn't think it's effective discipline. All it does is hurt the kids and make them rebellious. And no, she would never agree to come in to the Nursery. Our worker tells the father to call and file a report with the State Central Registry, and she gives him the number. A caseworker from the child protective agency will investigate tomorrow.

Diane Mooney, thirty-one, has five children and unbearable migraine headaches. She says she thinks she's going crazy. "I went to a psychiatrist because I was afraid I was going to hurt my kids. I thought I was going to flip out." The headaches are no better and she feels she is on the verge of "doing something terrible." We talk to her, discuss baby-sitting arrangements, urge her to come in with the two littlest ones, tell her we will have her medically examined for her headache. No transportation? No money? "Get a cab. We'll pay for it."

A distraught young voice says that her eight-month-old boy cries all the time. So far the mother hasn't hit him, but she knows she's on the verge of doing something she will probably regret. She says she read in the paper where a mother put her screaming kid into a scalding bathtub, and that scared her. What should she do? "Bring him in. We can help you."

The mother of a seven-year-old has hit him with a belt buckle. She has left marks, which never happened before. Is that abuse? Now she's worried. "Come see us."

A man calls. His wife drinks and neglects the kids while he's out at work. What to do? We discuss options, suggest a specific agency and other services for him to contact, and ask him to keep in touch. If he doesn't, we'll call him.

Many parents who call the Parent Helpline feel guilty about the way they handle their children and are terrified that one or all of their kids will be taken away from them and put into a foster home. Often a mother who hesitates is afraid of being labeled a child abuser—a monster who may batter or starve her own child to death. She has her pride and her fears, and she does not want to be known as a mother who hits her child.

In a way, child advocates like myself are caught in a dilemma. We have to stigmatize child abuse, to treat it as a major crime against humanity in the hope that it will come to be regarded as the most loathsome of all sins—and we also have to destigmatize volatile acts of striking out so that the mother who raises a hand against her child will not be reluctant to seek help. We talk freely to the parents about "not being able to cope" or "striking out" at their children, but we are very careful not to use the words "child abuse."

The "monster" label unfairly stigmatizes unhappy people who are already cracking under unbearable pressure, making it even harder for them to admit they are mishandling their children. Obviously, mothers or fathers who believe they will be hated and scorned for striking out at their children are unlikely to get on a Hotline or a Helpline and cry out, "Help me!" Yet the fact is the people who answer such calls *want* those parents to call and they understand their turmoil and they *want* them to come in. There *is* help for them. And it is in the early days of their parenthood that we can help them and their children best, rather than when the abuse has become a way of life and death.

The mothers who feel guilty are not monsters, and the cases we see are not the ones that make headlines. The atypical examples of child abusers and child killers are the ones we read about in our newspapers and see on our TV screens. These are the psychotics, drug addicts, alcoholics, sadists, and religious fanatics who make up only about 1 percent of all maltreating parents. The other 99 percent are people who are simply finding it difficult to cope with the stressful situations of everyday living. They want help but they're afraid to ask for it; they fear the stigma of being known as child abusers and they are terrified that we will take their children away from them. That, incidentally, is something that we ourselves never do and very rarely recommend to the city's child protective unit. Rather, we try to help the child by helping the parent. It is not part of our plan to pry youngsters out of the arms of the family to get shuffled around in the foster care system. Once in a great while we have to, but only as a last resort.

The psychodynamics of child abuse involve two victims: the

parent and the child. To help the child, we have to connect with the parents and recognize their suffering. It is pointless to be accusatory; if we are not understanding and compassionate with them we are likely to lose them and the children. The idea is not just to get the kid out of the family; far from it. What we're in business to do is to help *save* the family, so that all the kids and all the adults in it are safe and continue to be safe.

Picking on a child, and ultimately hitting a child, usually happens when parents don't know enough about parenting to handle their children and don't know enough about life to meet their responsibilities. Yet we all have the potential for violence within us. Even good people have dark urges. Imagine yourself in this situation. It is the end of a day of domestic or professional disasters. The kid is crying frantically. You want to cry yourself, or preferably scream. You are being pushed beyond your limits. You feel the volcano within you is about to erupt. You have a moment of craziness. You take it out on the people closest to you, the people you love, the little ones who are driving you nuts. One slap that lands too hard and jerks the head back, one push that slams the toddler against a table edge, and the anguish begins. The child is hurt. "What have I done?"

Why did you do it? And what are you going to do now?

Some parents simply lack information on a child's growth and development, and—themselves immature—expect far too much of a baby. Many young parents don't know that a child of a certain age cannot pick up a glass of milk without spilling it, or that children go through a stage in which it seems natural to decorate the walls with crayons or finger paints; or they don't know at what age a child can be potty trained. They whack the child because they think he or she ought to know better or is just being ornery.

Or they can't cope with an infant's incessant crying. They don't know if the crying is normal, or if the child is hungry or sick or hurting, or if they themselves are unnaturally depressed or abnormally testy. All they can think of is that the yelling *must stop*.

And a lot of parents have learned only one way to supervise— or discipline—their child, and that is to give it a good smack. Why not? Mother always did it to them.

Sometimes the parents' perceptions of discipline and abuse are different from ours. They might come in and say, "I've never abused my kids," and then the social worker will ask how the mother disciplines the children. Often, the mother answers that she hits them with an electric cord, or that she uses a belt on them. But abuse them? Never.

The degree and type of abuse we see is variable. There has often been some hitting beyond the usual whack and slap of the slightly aggravated parent. Sometimes we see welts and bruises, like those inflicted on three-year-old Willie by a stepfather who would just as soon not have him around. Quite often we see cigarette burns, such as those on Darryl's little wrists and tummy, that no one in the family seems able to explain. One woman brings in four-year-old twins, Lydie and Bobby, with sadly undernourished little bodies and closed-in faces; another comes in with a child whose eye is badly swollen. In sum, we see virtually the whole gamut of maltreatment symptoms, short of those requiring hospitalization.

And were the parents whupped themselves as children? They might say oh, sure, Dad always hit them with a belt when they did something bad. But they feel that's normal; everybody got beaten with a belt. They never had to go to a hospital, never had to have any stitches or anything like that, so, no, they weren't abused. We, on the other hand, might consider that they were.

Ironically, in view of their perceptions of abuse as something requiring stitches or hospitalization, more than half of the parents coming in for help will say that they were battered or neglected in their childhood.

This is our opportunity to go right to work on what they are doing to their children.

Our hope is that if the parent leaves the scapegoat child with us for two or three days and nights, it will not only give the child a break but allow the parent a cooling-off period without having that child around to pick on. At the same time we initiate crisis intervention and longer-term treatment for striking-out parents with the purpose of ending, once and for all, the cycle of abuse that persists from generation to generation.

The parents don't always understand this at first. "Why should I have to get treatment," a mother might say, "when what I really need is help with the bills?"

They don't know how easy it is to get into a habit of abuse; they forget, sometimes, how much they went through when they were children. On some basic, deep-down level they know they are carrying on a sort of family tradition, but they don't grasp where it is going. We believe that we can break the cycle of violence breeding violence from one generation to the next, but it is often frustratingly difficult to get our meaning across.

I finally got through to one young mother by telling her that I didn't want to see her grandchildren abused.

"It isn't just a matter of getting you to stop beating your child," I said. "The point is, if you change your behavior, there is a very good chance that your child will not beat up on your grandchildren."

Her eyes widened. After a minute she said "Oh," and that's all she said—but she looked as though she might be looking back at her own past or into her children's future; maybe both.

In effect, the Crisis Nursery is a stand-in for the friends or relatives who are very often absent—deliberately or otherwise—in time of need. Many parents don't have fallbacks or bailouts. They don't have such a thing as an extended family. They don't know where to turn when things go wrong. So we function as the helpful family members they are lacking.

We listen to people as individuals with particular concerns. We sit down with them and tackle their problems one by one, and treat their children as if we were all family. When we find out what their specific problems are and figure out what should be done, we refer them to the human support systems they need in order to do an adequate job of living their lives and raising their children. There are conflicts and complications, but we can nearly always sort things out.

Most of our referrals for counseling and parent education are made to a range of more than 50 private agencies whose services are purchased by the child protective unit. A primary function of these agencies is to help the mother become a better, happier parent and reduce the need for foster care placements.

And while we are setting the support wheels in motion the children are taking a brief break from the tensions of home. They have coloring books and toys, people to hug them when they need hugs, and three square meals a day served from the nursery pantry—all, and more than, the comforts of home without the trauma. Yet almost without exception they want to be with Mommy. They look out the windows of the tall Foundling building and peer down at the people on the sidewalk far below, and they say, "Is that my Mommy coming? Is my Mommy coming now?"

When they leave us, a whole battery of social services goes home with them and their Mommies. We keep track of them and of our referrals by maintaining constant contact not only with the families but with all the agencies involved in caring for them. At least 80 percent of our clients do follow through and become fully engaged in the services offered. So long as we see that they are making genuine efforts on their own behalf we give them all the repeat service they need. If they don't call us, we call them. We don't consider a case closed until a family is either engaged in ongoing services or has graduated out of the system; we stay in touch until the children appear to be safe and the parents content.

There are times when everything goes beautifully, with such wonderful smoothness within our operation and such fantastic cooperation with the families and with other agencies that we come perilously close to congratulating ourselves. Then, inevitably, fate lowers the boom. There are cases where everything seems to go wrong. A bad situation continues to be bad or gets even worse. Or we lose track of somebody. We'll call, the phone has been disconnected; we'll write, there's no response. We'll call the Income Maintenance Office, and the mother hasn't been in to pick up her checks in three weeks; we'll call the child protective agency, and the agency tells us that they never did locate the mother so they closed the case. The family has probably moved, and we will never hear from them again.

Which usually means that yet another child has fallen through the cracks.

It infuriates me when unthinking people say there is no way we can prevent our children from being damaged by incompetent or callous parents. If we say that something can't be done, *it won't be done.* But child abuse and neglect, and death from child abuse, are being prevented right here, in these rooms, in this Crisis Nursery. This one small, purely local, city-supported effort can be multiplied throughout the country to give parents in every community the bailout they need when they know they are losing control and striking out at their children.

We opened in April 1982. As of November 1990, we have had 27,653 Helpline calls. Nearly 100 percent of these calls resulted in supportive action of some kind; 3,810 children from 2,709 families were admitted to the Nursery, and an additional 1,037 children from 504 families were provided with services but not admitted because there was no critical need for their admission.

The Foundling Hospital Crisis Nursery is a model for such centers throughout the country—a front-line, preemptive campaign to help parents in trouble and children in danger.

I see no reason why every large hospital in every major city should not have one of these crisis nurseries. I am sure that many bureaucratic reasons will be presented to me, but I am equally sure they are not valid. Usually they boil down to, "Who's going to pay for the beds?"

Respite nurseries should be in welfare hotels and motels, where child abuse and neglect are endemic; they should be in the housing projects; they should be in shopping malls; they should be in community centers. And they should be publicized and run in such a way that they become as socially acceptable and efficient as McDonald's or Radio Shack or K Mart. It astounds me that, after all these many years and after all we have learned about the prevention of child abuse, there are still only two such centers in New York City and a total of thirty throughout the country.

How many beds is that, I wonder? Three hundred? Four hundred? It is a national tragedy that we have so few. And it is a national disgrace that we have to fight tooth and nail to get such facilities into place, with little if any help from government.

But that is another story. Meanwhile, we have to deal with the flaws in the systems we already have.

Emmanuelle Jedonne, the teenager who left her baby in a hospital restroom, was charged and jailed for doing what she felt at the time was the right thing. She was wrong. There were better ways to handle the problem but apparently she didn't know what they were. In coming forward, even in the way she did, she had taken a positive step. Hospital authorities or the police or the district attorney's office, in their superior adult wisdom, might themselves have taken the even more positive step of getting help for the mother and child. She made a mistake, she tried to correct it, and she wound up in Criminal Court.

I was appalled. With the support of other city medical doctors and child advocates, I held a press conference to let the public know just how inhumane and counterproductive it was to drag the girl into court. Two children die every week in this city from abuse and neglect, often because parents don't recognize when they've reached their breaking point. But *she* knew her daughter was vulnerable; she knew she had to have help. And she didn't get it.

We *want* parents to ask for help! We tell them they will not be punished. We tell them their babies will not be taken away. It is essential that they trust us. Even isolated incidents such as this will drive them underground—and they're going to beat the hell out of their kids without anyone knowing or caring.

Suddenly, the charges were reduced. Emmanuelle's next court appearance was in Family Court. The protective agency abandoned its efforts to place Keisha in a foster home, and the little girl was remanded to her grandmother. The young mother was directed to a family care service called Family Dynamics and found a temporary home with an aunt in New Jersey. She went into counseling and started a series of sessions in infant training. Later she will try to get her general education diploma.

She still has problems—no settled home, no green card, and no job. But she is getting the help she was supposed to have gotten when the system failed in yet another way.

6 | A Search for the Roots of Abuse

Every once in a while we have to remind ourselves what child abuse really is. The horror stories of the tabloids persuade us that it is a phenomenon completely outside ourselves. It is not.

Child maltreatment is many things. It is physical abuse in the form of beatings, scaldings and other burns, strangulation, human bites, and child-bashing of every sort. It is neglect, which is failure to provide the child with such necessities as food, shelter, clothing, medical care, schooling, and a listening ear. It is abandonment. It is emotional abuse and neglect—the insidious attacking and demeaning of a child through constant criticism, insult, and disparagement; or rejection in the form of failure to provide warmth, love, support, or guidance. It is sexual molestation, which ranges from exhibitionism and fondling of the genitals to incest and rape. In whatever form it is damaging to the soul. In its extreme, it is soul murder.

Recognition of child abuse in its many forms is a twentieth-century phenomenon, but the fact of it reaches back to the dawn of human history. Tales of children being maltreated, battered, abandoned, thrown out of the house, or sacrificed to demanding gods are the backbone of folktale, legend, and literature. Such incidents were no mere literary inventions; they happened. Reasons and methods depended on the times. Yet they would all seem to be rooted in the belief that a child was a parental possession, to be dealt with as the parent chose: a nuisance to be discarded, a chattel to be used.

Primitive people, living as nomadic hunter-gatherers, routinely abandoned children to the beasts and elements when they became an encumbrance to the endless journey. Ritual sacrifices of infants and young children to appease the gods and incidentally limit population growth were made in ancient times from Egypt, Greece, and Rome to Mexico. The coming of Christianity brought edicts against abandonment, infanticide, and filicide, but no lessening in these crimes, and the mortality in the institutions created for the throwaways reached such proportions that the establishments themselves had to be abandoned.

The Church in the Middle Ages contributed to child murder by declaring that deformed infants were the product of human liaisons with demons or animals and thus were omens of evil. This position encouraged the common belief that infanticide was no more than a venial sin and that parents had the right and power to decree the life or death of their children. Under the oppressive feudal system the impoverished serfs threw away or drowned the unwanted new mouths in the family, particularly the newborn females, in their own struggle to survive.

Throughout the sixteenth and seventeenth centuries the lives of many children were snuffed out if they were deemed to be not only little bastards but useless ones. Sturdier offspring were forced into apprenticeships with cruel masters or sent to the colonies as indentured servants. A new idea had been born: children could actually be put to some profitable purpose.

And so they continued to be, during the long years of the Industrial Revolution. Mothers and children, together or separately, formed a cheap and obedient labor force for the factory owners. Little boys and girls who were scarcely more than toddlers were chained to their posts for endless hours and beaten to expedite their labors. In the United States, the children of slaves were torn away from them and sold like farm animals to work like farm animals, never to see their parents again.

We assume that the family has its source in man's early history, but we actually know nothing about the where, what, why, or how of its origins. We only have theories developed by social scientists of the nineteenth century who studied primitive tribes, and these are conflicting theories of promiscuity and monogamy, matriarchy and patriarchy. The family as we have known and read of it is a social group sharing the same shelter and consisting of a married couple with children who are either biologically their own or adopted. We know this little unit as the nuclear family. Radiating out from this group, sometimes in contact with it and sometimes not, is the extended family, which includes grandparents, uncles and aunts, cousins and second cousins, nieces and nephews.

In America, the family has been a basic and vital institution since colonial times. Colonists believed that families were a strong and stable core for a developing community, and they placed a high value on the institution of marriage. Couples needed to stay together to survive and be productive, in terms of both reproducing themselves and pulling their weight in the colony, and families needed stable communities in which to thrive. We tend to look back nostalgically to a time when we suppose families to have consisted of several generations all living happily together, or not far from each other, in what we call the extended family. It is true that colonial families were usually somewhat larger than most families of today, but rather because there were more children than there were on-site grandparents. People very often didn't live long enough to *be* grandparents. Mothers often died young after having lost many children; fathers remarried and had more children. The vast majority of families in the past, just as today, were nuclear families. These consisted of a mother, father, and their children—sometimes including step-siblings and half-siblings. This group, not the extended family, was the norm for at least two centuries before industrialization.

It may be that we are nostalgic for something that never was. Yet in earlier times, there was a togetherness. The family in the colonial period functioned as a productive economic unit that depended on the participation of all available hands, as soon as those hands were big enough to help. Whether working on the family farm or in the family store, whether at home where there was cooking and cleaning to be done or in the field, children were expected to pitch in. They paid their way. The fringe benefit was that the youngsters were constantly under the eye of one or both of their parents and other working adults, not necessarily getting a great deal of attention all the time but an integral part of the family scene nonetheless.

The same was true in frontier days, when thousands of families trekked west and put down roots in what they hoped were more promising lands. Those families were not much changed from what they had been in colonial times; they were the heart and core of all rural communities, and every able-bodied adult and child pitched in to do whatever he or she knew how to do.

But the roots of these families were scarcely planted when America began its own industrial revolution, and many of the people who had been drawn to the land were drawn away from it by the new jobs opening up in industry and business. With the shift from villages and farms to industrial centers, the American sense of family and community began to change. The family ceased to be a unit of production, and its fragmented parts were absorbed by the new industrialization.

The husband-father worked, as usual; the women and children of the poorer classes also worked, invariably in low-paying jobs— but they were all working separately. Women of the middle and upper classes, however, stayed home to keep the household comfortable for both the wage-earner and the younger children.

In the late nineteenth century, childhood ended early for the youth of all classes. Some parents arranged apprenticeships for their lads, but many less-fortunate children wound up in backbreaking factory jobs or out on the street as peddlers and newsboys. Boys in their early and middle teens were encouraged to leave home to seek their fortunes or at least learn a useful trade.

Somewhere along the line, a curious duality came into being: on the one hand, children were the most despised and exploited of the labor force, and on the other, they were the object of a new, overtly sentimental interest. In the course of being exploited as little waifs in factories and romanticized as young American heroes, they had become recognized as creatures distinctly different from adults and having distinct needs.

In the middle class, esteem for children began to rise. Parents started looking for ways to equip their youngsters with the skills necessary to find jobs somewhat better than ragpicking. The answer seemed to be formal education in free public schools. And because the learning process was so lengthy, youngsters stayed at home and remained dependent on their parents for a very long time. Children were no longer productive members of a working team or Horatio Alger heroes seeking their fortunes; they were luxuries.

As material luxuries became important to Americans, so did their children: their status continued to rise even though they were not being productive. Their productivity would be delayed until their glorious future, when they would be the support and pride of their aged parents. Meanwhile, they were indulged as never before, treated like adults in terms of being permitted freedom of action and expression while allotted very few responsibilities and burdened with very little parental counsel. European visitors were struck by the precocity of American youth. Something of a youth cult had already come into being.

World War II was the one great catastrophic event that shook up families and changed the American way of life. Generations were torn apart; men and youths were scattered to the far corners of the globe; women once again worked in factories; patterns of community living disintegrated, never to be re-formed, and the strength of the family was seriously eroded. When the nation picked itself up after the war—not as devastated as much of the rest of the world, but traumatized nonetheless—great shifts of population occurred, and the comforting circles of relatives and friends were no longer what they had been. With the loss of young lives in battle, the remaining young people suddenly became doubly regarded as the nation's treasures, and parents had a tough time clinging to any semblance of authority. But there was a sense that people needed togetherness, and with the help of a benign television and its father-knows-best philosophy, families managed for a while.

The postwar period, from the late '40s to the mid-'60s, was a time of tremendous prosperity for Americans and a truly golden age for the concept of family. A wonderful, mythical group of loving, compatible people was widely assumed to be the typical American family, and those who did not fit into the pattern of perfection could only wonder what was wrong with them. As the postwar babies grew up, parents who had known the hardships of the Depression and the War wanted everything for their children that they had not had themselves: lavish amounts of attention and material goods. They gave and gave and gave, finally losing the last shreds of their authority. Their kids, challenging their parents' values and despising their lavishness, turned to each other for love and leadership and inspiration, and to drugs, for the super-sensation that neither parents nor peers could give them. The older generation began to view the younger as some sort of outlandish tribe, impossible for civilized human beings to deal with. These kids were embarrassments—economic liabilities, social disasters, expendable parts of the family who were actively expending themselves.

In the last quarter-century, we have seen yet another twist of the family fortunes: a generation that is sharply divided into the haves and have-nots; an economy that drives two parents back into the workplace, again eroding parental authority and increasing the possibility of child neglect; and a welfare system that saps personal initiative and undermines parental responsibility. The family, and thus children, have once again started slipping their anchors.

It is against this background that we must view child abuse in the United States of America.

People say: "Eliminate poverty, and you'll eliminate child abuse!"

I wish it were true. It would be wonderful if we could eliminate poverty, and God knows it would help to ease a great many of our national ills, including child abuse, but it would not be a cure. Most poor people do not abuse or neglect their children, or commit other crimes. Many well-off people do. Poverty, like other stresses, exacerbates the factors that drive people to mistreat their fellow beings, their children, and their pets, but it is not a primary cause. Is it something in the genes? Maybe, sometimes. Usually not.

Why, then, do people abuse their children?

I suspect that if we could trace our way back to the beginning of human life and the human psyche, and if we could point to the first individual to maltreat a child, we would still not be able to identify the origins or answer *why*. We have an inheritance that we carry around with us, but it is not—with some exceptions—genetic, and it has no single source. Perhaps child maltreatment can better be explained in terms of attitudes that have taken root and been nourished for many, many generations.

A key theme is violence, violence to both body and soul.

Though we are all born with a self-protective mechanism, we

are not born violent or with a disrespect for human life. The will to violence is an acquired attitude; juvenile violence, leading to adult violence, is a learned behavior. We do not all learn it; and even some of us who do manage to, unlearn it.

Although violence begins with the individual and is not an inherited trait or ancestral throwback, there are contributing elements that reach well beyond the individual. We have to reckon with the psychological forces that interweave with the social environment of the times. In different periods of history, the pattern of violence changes, and the factors leading up to it change, too. With reference to the causes of disturbed behavior, Freud, in one of his last writings, observes that "we must not forget to include the influence of civilization." I believe it is not difficult to see what influence *our* civilization has on the developing individual.

My own personal experiences with parents and children over the last three decades have convinced me that much of the physical and emotional abuse that we inflict on our children is an extreme of the violent and self-serving child-rearing practices firmly established in Western culture. These practices are rooted in our cavalier attitude toward children as possessions—often balky ones that have no right to balk—and our own upbringing. We are sickened when a parent scalds a child to death or slams him against a wall with such force that the skull is fractured, but we are well accustomed to the spanking, slapping, yelling, scolding, yanking, ear-pulling, and name-calling practiced on even little kids by our own friends and neighbors—all done under the guise of caring for the child and disciplining him.

Within the definition of the maltreatment syndrome, I can say without question that child abuse in one form or another is taking place in the majority of our American homes today, and the alarming part about it is that it is not being recognized as child abuse. Most parents—yes, *most*—fail to draw the line between discipline and physical punishment. They may not recognize what they are doing, but they are maltreating their kids. If this should be called to their attention, they are astounded. They say, "The kid will only learn if I use the strap! A good paddling never hurt anybody! That's the way I was brought up! There's nothing wrong with me!"

I look at them, and I wonder.

What is really happening is that the parents are replaying an old scene; what they are doing to their children is a variation on what was done to them. In the name of discipline, they themselves were thrashed, manipulated, lied to, deceived, and threatened with the loss of parental love. Now they can do the same. Their children, in turn, are helpless and dependent, easy targets for the owner-adult who has grown up into a position of power. The stored-up hatred and anger of the cruelly treated child-become-parent spills out and engulfs the next generation. Parental cruelty, intentional or otherwise, can take innumerable forms. How satisfying it can be, sometimes, to mock, demean, humiliate, and physically punish even while proclaiming love! And how confusing for a child.

Psychoanalyst and author Alice Miller says: "Beatings, which are only one form of mistreatment, are *always* degrading, because the child not only is unable to defend him- or herself but is also supposed to show gratitude and respect to the parents in return. And along with corporal punishment there is a whole gamut of ingenious measures applied 'for the child's own good' which are difficult for a child to comprehend and which for that very reason often have devastating effects in later life."

One of the devastating effects may be a smoldering but unrecognized hatred that expresses itself in unbridled cruelty.

Never mind that practically every child development expert alive regards corporal punishment as an unacceptable and outdated form of discipline: the habit seems to be ingrained in the American way of life. It is a legacy that travels down the generations, stopping—when? Only when it is consciously, deliberately stopped. I believe the tradition continues to be handed down because of our casual acceptance of violence in general, because of our belief that children are our possessions to do with as we please, and because we feel that parents have the right to raise their children in the manner of their choice. Parents, we believe, have the right to mind their own business. Sadly, what they are likely to achieve is a wary, defensive child with a tendency to lash out at others, maturing into a punitive adult.

Corporal punishment only teaches that it's okay to use violence in solving problems, that it's okay for a powerful person to hurt someone who is less powerful, that hitting is okay if practiced by certain people at certain times. Loving discipline, on the other hand, is an educational, civilizing experience that teaches the child about life and the rules required for getting along with others on terms of mutual respect.

A good many parents, at one time or another, come close to losing control and lashing out in a momentary fit of rage, and yet manage to keep hold of themselves nearly all the time. Almost every parent who ever lived has reached out with a reflexive *whap!* to keep a child from grabbing a hot iron or running into the street. It is the immature, unthinking or self-indulgent person—or the one so poisoned by his own upbringing—who makes a practice of physical punishment or automatically resorts to force.

This parent, who beats or torments a child in the name of retribution for a childish transgression, is not, by any stretch of the imagination, punishing a crime. The action is completely unrelated to discipline and is rooted in the individual's own perverse fascination with the act of abuse. Maybe deep in his heart he feels that his parents enjoyed doing it to him, and now he is taking it out on his own little hostages.

There is, in fact, a very clear distinction between the disciplinarian and the abuser: the individual who disciplines has in mind the welfare and best interests and safety of the child, and he knows that these aims are not served by beating the child. But the one who abuses is indulging himself.

Aggressive "punishment" does not occur out of context. It happens in a violence-prone or emotionally unhealthy family. "The family is the place where we first learn about violence," say sociologists Murray A. Straus and Richard J. Gelles. "Children learn that love and violence go together. Moreover, they learn that since by and large it's done by loving, good parents . . . hitting is morally right." A fundamental lesson of the very important work of these researchers is that "human violence—be it a slap or a shove, a knifing or a shootout—occurs more frequently within the family circle than anywhere else in our society."

We have found that there are very close links between domestic violence and child abuse. See a battered woman, hear the thuds and outcries of adult abuse: if there are children in that home, those children are in danger. Police responding to reports of domestic squabbles would do well to take them more seriously. Where a spouse is threatened, so is a child. Even if physical battering does not extend to the children, a family atmosphere is created in which violence is the norm. That atmosphere is in itself enough to taint the development of the child, who becomes deeply involved psychologically. But there is danger in more than the atmosphere: this child is also at great risk of being abused, physically, emotionally, or sexually. Either the battering father or the battered mother may strike out at one or more of the children.

According to the combined figures of several recent studies, children are present in at least 50 percent of the homes visited by the police in connection with domestic violence calls. The majority of battered women never press charges, which increases the possibility that the abuse will escalate and include the child. Because the most severely abused women are usually the least likely to seek help, many children in violent homes *never* come to the attention of agencies that might provide protective services—a grim thought, since a nationwide study has found that over 50 percent of the children of known battering couples had been physically or sexually abused.

This is, of course, extreme. But an acceptance of less violent patterns of maltreatment is imbedded in the family code today. "There is a high level of sanctioned violence within the American family that makes it difficult to define and prevent child abuse or spouse abuse," says Murray A. Straus. "Law and social custom condone an intrafamily 'right to hit,' which far exceeds what might be permitted on the street or on the job."

So much for the safety of the family bosom. Clearly, there is much risk here for the children.

If we were to look for a likely family in which to find or expect child abuse, we would draw up a trial model of a family unit characterized by a pattern of isolation from the community and of violence within; social deviance or criminal behavior; a mother bearing her first child before the age of twenty; poor prenatal care, or none; marital conflict; and a record of previous child abuse and neglect, possibly culminating in the removal of a child by court order. We would not be surprised to find that one or both parents had been abused, neglected, or otherwise demeaned as a child, or had been raised in hatred masquerading as love. One is a substance abuser, the other an enabler. One may be mentally ill or retarded. One or both may be unemployed. There is likely to be a child in the family with medical or mental problems. If there is a grandmother in the household who might be expected to lend stability, she is likely to be a permanent adolescent herself—a teenage mother in her time, and a 28-year-old grandma.

Let me hasten to point out that this profile is a conglomeration based on known families of abuse: the highly visible ones in contact with social agencies. Obviously, in more affluent circles, the portrait of the household is bound to be different. The portrait of the abuser, however, is very much the same, no matter what the social class.

He or she tends to be a social isolate of minimal self-esteem, usually maltreated as a child, lacking a parental role model, looking to the children to provide the warmth and attention not forthcoming from his or her own parents; he does not have much in the way of coping strengths. There is a pervading sense of despair, of giving up. These sad people have no awareness that in hitting out at innocent, powerless little targets they are expressing repressed anger and hatred. They are so cut off from their feelings that they neither know nor care about the pain and misery they are inflicting. If the abuser is the male, the woman in the case is a passive collaborator who is either so addicted to or afraid of the man that she cannot intercede.

Some major studies of child deaths due to abuse and neglect have concluded that most of the homicides are committed by mothers, followed by the mothers' boyfriends and the biological fathers. This may be true, but the mothers also cover up for their men: if they do not confess to guilt themselves, they profess to have no idea what could have happened, or go out of their way to insist that the male partner could not possibly have been involved. My feeling, based on police investigations and years of personal observation, is that the "boyfriend" is most often the perpetrator. However, the dumping of newborns into the trash—an escalating phenomenon—is almost certainly the work of mothers "stuck" with babies they didn't want.

Thus, within limits, it is possible to predict the kinds of situations in which abuse is likely to occur. We can look into our schools, too, and pinpoint predictive risk factors through what we see of the lives of children and parents. We have learned that such factors as low birth weight, having a teenage mother, untreated health problems, lack of language and coping skills at school entry, and failure to develop warm and trusting relationships early on in life correlate with troubles in elementary school. In turn, we find that poor school performance and truancy as early as third or fourth grade permit us to predict delinquency, dropping out, early pregnancy, and long-term damage in general. Knowing these things, we can attack the risk factors with intensive intervention programs providing preschool education and intensive family support.

Some children adjust better than others to conflict in the family, including violence upon themselves. Many kids who have been horribly abused by hatred or neglect or physical violence rebound like spring flowers after heavy rain. Nearly always these are the ones who have felt loved by their parents no matter what the turmoil around them. Indeed, there are children who endure the most arduous conditions while growing up—poverty, the chaos of a family in which a parent is alcoholic or mentally ill, physical abuse or neglect of one kind or another—and yet go on to thrive. Not just to survive as okay people, but to thrive.

Experts on child development have not yet pinpointed why some children are more resilient than others. Current thinking is that these children, the apparently less vulnerable ones, are endowed with certain innate characteristics that shield them from the turmoil of their families and permit them to establish a relationship with a substitute parent, either a grandmother, an aunt, an older sister, a neighbor, or a teacher, who can offer emotional support. The ability to seek out a supportive person is a key element: many children in abusive or chaotic homes have equal access to a potentially nurturing adult, but they do not reach out the way resilient ones do. Physically or emotionally battered children are seldom likely to have the inner freedom to seek out the nurturing person.

Other factors, according to researchers, are frequently involved. The kids who flourish in spite of continued stressful conditions seem to come equipped with self-esteem, tolerance, and an ability to cope. Most are of at least average and often above-average intelligence, but even if they are not particularly bright, they possess and utilize some talent or skill—whether in sports or music or skate-boarding or computer graphics—that absorbs them and gives them both solace and confidence. Usually they are independent, easygoing, and quick to bounce back after ugly scenes in their lives. And they are born with the seeds of these traits.

What are these seeds? Are they genetic? Hormonal? Chemical? We don't know. Nor do we know what it is in some kids that puts them at abnormally great risk of a violent future. We can recognize parental fingerprints and environmental factors, but sometimes these are not enough to explain why an individual develops into a human monster; there is a mystery element. Is it a genetic flaw that predetermines a lifetime of uncontrollable rage, perhaps even a one-man outbreak of mass murder? Can it be a chemical imbalance, or abnormal electrical activity of the brain? We don't know, but some researchers are speculating that, just as there are children who are preprogrammed to be stress-resistant, so may there be others who are preprogrammed for violently aggressive behavior.

Over the years I have encountered many parents who are totally baffled by what they see as their child's unpredictable, inexplicable, and out-of-control temper tantrums. As a young pediatrician I was quite certain I was seeing a failure of parenting, but now I suspect that I was not always right. Something that we do not understand is going on in some of these children, something that reminds us that we do not have unlimited control over the way our children develop.

It may be of some little comfort to parents to learn that several university studies have shown some children to be difficult from birth. They are cranky, they can't take stress as well as other infants, and they are insecure. Even a small negative stress, such as a mother not smiling at certain times, makes their hearts beat faster and their nervous systems go into overdrive. Groups of such children have been tracked for several years and found to have more than the normal number of problems in preschool and elementary school. Researchers feel the problem is genetic in origin, but can nonetheless be nipped in the bud by extra doses of loving care, complete with well-timed smiles.

Other recent studies, these of youngsters aged nine to eleven, suggest that perhaps as many as 10 percent of all children are growing up unpopular with other children and with adults because they have problems with nonverbal communication that impair their everyday functioning. These kids give off messages through posture, gesture, facial expression, and tone of voice that are not what they intend to convey. They seem angry, disturbed, overeager, or aggressive when they are feeling none of these things; and through their miscues they antagonize other individuals without knowing why. They don't understand that they themselves have provoked the negative reactions of others, and they feel themselves to be unfairly rebuffed. It seems likely that the problem here is a learning disability that can be corrected by special tutoring. Meanwhile, there may be many thousands of young children who are inadvertently giving off misleading cues, and many thousands of adults who are wondering if there isn't something slightly out of kilter with their perfectly ordinary, intelligent kid . . . or have they just imagined it?

I meet many parents who find it difficult to cope and yet are doing their absolute best to be there for their children, to love them, to listen to them, to laugh or cry with them, to help them when they're in need. And some of these parents, in spite of their best efforts, have one child who is going bad. *Why?* The child has never been abused or neglected! Both the father and mother have spent as much time with him during the twelve years of his young life as with the other kids and given him equal attention. They have loved him and cared for him and touched him and held him and he is turning out to be a rotten kid. Why this one boy, and none of his brothers or sisters?

It is a rare parent who actually admits to a preference to a particular child. Almost invariably, mothers and fathers will tell me in all sincerity that they love all their children equally and treat them all alike. This just isn't so. We may love them equally and try to treat them evenhandedly, but we do not treat them all *alike*. Unless we are clones or identical twins, we are all different from all other children at birth, and it is no more possible for us—with our own genetic and environmental baggage—to feel exactly the same about each child than it is for all our children to be exact little rubber stamps of us. Inevitably, we treat each according to our own view of him or her, and we usually do it without being remotely conscious of our selective attitude.

In some families there is no attempt whatsoever to hide the fact that the firstborn son is the favorite or that the most adorable girl-child has everybody's heartstrings wrapped around her little finger. But more often the favoritism is unconscious and the display of it subliminal. There is something about the favored child, whether firstborn or prettiest or funniest or smartest, that appeals to the parent and elicits a positive response. And there is something about the less-favored child that tends to make a parent think, "He's not like me at all. He's not like anyone in this family. He's funny-looking. He never smiles. He doesn't like me." This is such a common phenomenon that we even have a label for such a child: he is an f.l.k.—funny-looking kid. A subtle interaction begins, and some of the links in the bonding process fail to connect.

Parental perceptions may also be colored by conditions in the family before and after the child's birth. What is going on in someone's life and head at the time may have a very great deal to do with whether the mother and father are apathetic or eager to have a child, responsive or unresponsive, more loving or less loving, more or less eager to take care of the child. There may be a problem with family finances that did not exist when the first child was born, or the mother has an abnormally difficult pregnancy, or the father has lost his job or taken to drugs or alcohol, or the in-laws have moved in. Any of these and other elements may create a situation in which the second child or the fourth child is perceived not as a bundle of joy arriving at a convenient time but as a little bit of a burden instead. And though the mother and father may insist that they are raising this child in exactly the same way as the others, they are not. There is a little something missing.

And as the children grow, the parents communicate better with those who have bonded early and well. In small, unintended ways—a little more attention, an extra smile or word of praise—mother or father or both show that one child is more highly thought of than another. The child who seemed slightly different to begin with is slightly more different now, and he is picking up negative cues through a thoughtless word here, an exasperated look there, and a too-hasty or mechanical hug when he needs undivided attention.

Sibling rivalry soon enters the picture. The most favored child flourishes and feels that he is *the* person in the household; the least favored child feels diminished in the correct belief that he is not the apple of his parents' eyes. The social and scholastic performance of the child who is not *the* person begins to lose its edge. Now the parents, unthinkingly, make another contribution:

"You're doing a great job in school, Henry. That is a wonderful report card. You make us proud. But as for you, Calvin! You're just as smart as anyone but you're not doing anything with your brains. Do you want to be known as a dummy?" Of course he doesn't, but the sound of "dummy" rings in his ears.

As school looms larger in the children's lives, the verbal and psychological undermining of the less favored one tends to gather momentum. "Why can't you be more like your sister? She does well in school. Look at your grades! You're stupid! You're not even trying!" Just saying these things is demeaning and hurtful to the child, who will in all likelihood respond with a burst of temper and perhaps a day of hookey. Next thing we know, the child is being whacked for being a stupid, hookey-playing dummy but his parents will still claim that they love their children equally and treat them all alike. They don't realize that the "dummy" is feeling bruised and rejected, and that when he is being ornery and difficult to deal with he is clamoring for attention.

It is all too easy for parents to slip into a pattern of subtle discrimination that makes the child feel he is not as valued or loved as he would like to be, and he becomes increasingly vulnerable to the less than wonderful world outside his home.

A recent advance in our understanding of the reasons for child maltreatment has been the development of what professionals call the "stress model," which depicts child abuse as a consequence of parental reaction to the various stresses they experience—illness, depression, a bad marriage or relationship, addiction, harassment by demanding relatives, loss of a job or home, financial problems, and even school staff calling up and saying that the child is a behavior problem in the classroom.

We know that the mere presence of such stresses does not prompt all parents to maltreat a child. Three components are usually necessary for abuse or neglect to occur: a parent who is potentially abusive because of his or her own childhood experiences; a "special" child—one who is chronically ill or hyperactive or handicapped or an f.l.k.; and a sudden crisis. We also know that the common denominator for aggressive parental behavior is a lack of self-control, so that when the crisis occurs the parent strikes out at the nearest target without a thought of holding back.

Maltreating parents, particularly in a family with a multitude of major, long-term problems, are usually unable to deal with any crisis situation. In fact, they often fail to distinguish between a minor mishap and a catastrophe. Even the breakdown of a common household appliance or the spilling of milk by a child may seem overwhelming. If these everyday stresses are compounded by the parent's reaction to a special child, the potential for child abuse increases dramatically. Furthermore, multiproblem families almost always have children who evidence behavior problems in school or at home, creating a volleying effect of abusive behavior between parent and child.

Yet a family enduring several different forms of stress is by no means doomed to be an abusive one. Parents faced with a housing problem, a sick child, and a run of bad luck may still have the coping skills to deal with a minor or even major crisis without loss of self-control; and they may have the ability to make effective use of the social services available to them. People who know how to wend their way through a maze of institutional bureaucracies to get their health care and their food stamps are patient, resourceful people who don't solve their problems by violence.

Nonetheless, they may hit out. Even parents who would not dream of damaging their children in any way may not understand the fine art of parenting. They only know the rough and ready ways handed down to them by their own parents, and they practice them unthinkingly. And so do all their relatives and friends and neighbors, so why shouldn't they? These are parents we can reach; with them, we can break the cycle.

Rather than receding, violence is becoming more deeply entrenched in our society. If we cannot trace the practice of violence against children back to its historical roots, we know very well where it has nestled and been nurtured: in the bosom of the family. The civilization of the times plays its role, too. "Civilization" is the environment of the family of man, and a quick look around will show us a present-day environment that is poison for families and a new breed of family that is hell on the environment.

7 | The New Family Ecology

They were an extended family in themselves—husband, wife, and nine children ranging in age from sixteen years down to four months—yet a remarkably self-contained one. Indeed, the family unit was so self-contained that Herman McMillan would not allow his children to go to school, preferring to teach them himself with homemade flash cards and readings from books on history and literature. The men who worked with him on the construction site where he labored spoke of his diligence and energy on the job, and how he talked about his wife and kids: "I love my wife very much. I need this job desperately. I got a lot of kids to support. The kids are the most important thing. My wife and kids are everything." And he would go home, leaving the other men to their after-work beer.

"You never know what goes on behind a man's door," a neighbor said, after the police had come and gone.

The McMillan apartment in the Bronx was a house of horrors, a trash-strewn nightmare of filth crammed into what a police official called "a darkened closet, with little access to the outside world."

The police arrived after the building's superintendent called a special child abuse hotline, opening up a Pandora's box. McMillan and his wife, who would later claim to have been enslaved and battered, were arrested and accused of raping, sodomizing, beating, torturing and otherwise abusing their nine surviving children.

Three other children had disappeared after being born at home. The nine children, traumatized into little whimpering animals, ended up in foster homes.

"He seemed like the perfect family man," a coworker observed. The irony of this appalling case is that, on a superficial level, it involves an intact family in the traditional format—a husband, a wife, and a large brood of children. Yet the McMillan family does not represent the "old" family by any means. It is an ugly caricature: intact but incestuous, locked into itself, violent and depraved, largely isolated from the normal world. Obviously, the McMillans are not normal, but they remind us that it does not pay to generalize about the intact and thus presumably healthy family.

No matter the conformation of the family, the social environment we have created for ourselves in the last two or three decades does not encourage wholesome, stable family life; rather, it tends to poison it. Grotesquely dysfunctional families such as the McMillans are just one symptom—a particularly unpleasant one—of what is happening in the American family today. A bigger tragedy is the enormous number of families that are simply disintegrating, either by choice or by chance. Togetherness is becoming an outdated concept. The traditional family as an institution and a structure is falling apart, seriously jeopardizing the security and welfare of our children and *their* children as well. The extended family of several generations and many relatives, wherever and whenever it actually existed in this country, has practically disappeared, and even the small nuclear family of Mommy and Daddy and two or three kids is on the decline.

No question about it. The traditional two-parent, single breadwinner family, with grandparents ready to come to the rescue at a moment's notice, no longer represents the typical family unit. The unmarried parents, the one-parent family, the working mother, the alternative-lifestyle family, the family reconfigured by divorce, the foster and adoptive family, all of them subject to the mounting stresses of the late-twentieth-century lifestyle, constitute the new ecology of the contemporary family. All the ruptures and frictions that come with a fast-paced and complex society conspire to wear people down. Even people consciously determined to be "good parents" find it extremely difficult to cope with life as it is and their own personal problems, never mind giving the children all the loving care and attention they need. And they don't know where to turn; the people who used to bail out the conventional family are scattered far and wide.

The family in whatever form molds and shapes the adults of tomorrow, and can do harm as well as good. Even the best of families can be dangerous places at times: not always cherishing, laced with pain and imperfection, miniature battlegrounds for their members. And the family that looks like one of the best and prides itself on its place in the community, yet inflicts secret abuse and neglect and other harm upon the children, is a family that threatens us all. Such families do not have the excuse of poverty and ignorance for their actions; they epitomize the American dream but are instead helping to destroy it from within.

See the face of such a family: it looks just like our own—or maybe the family next door.

Take the Piersons of Magnolia Drive in Selden, Long Island. They were regarded by their neighbors as a cheerful, fun-loving group, always ready to break open some beers and invite folks over for a party. James Pierson was a steady family man, a good provider, generous and loving with his wife and three children. His wife, Cathleen, suffered from a kidney ailment but was a lovely lady nonetheless. Cheryl, in her mid-teens and known as a good, sweet girl, took excellent care of the house when her mother was ill. Her older brother, Jimmy, was a bit of a handful but a fine young fellow, and little JoAnn was as cute as she could be.

All in all, a nice, ordinary American family—but revealed as less than nice and more than ordinary when James Pierson was found shot to death in his driveway one icy February morning. Cheryl had paid a classmate to kill him. By that time Cathleen was dead and did not have to hear what she already knew—that her husband had been taking their daughter to bed.

At her trial, Cheryl testified that her father had had sexual intercourse with her two to three times a day. James Pierson had physically and verbally abused both Jimmy and Cheryl. He had physically attacked his wife when she had confronted him about his sexual activities with his daughter. Cheryl feared that seven-year-old JoAnn would be his next target. And so she had taken out a contract on her loving father.

When I talk about saving the family to save the child, I am not talking about keeping the members of a nonfunctioning family together just for the sake of togetherness—that certainly would not have helped the McMillans or Piersons. Rather, I am talking about healing the families that can be healed; but more than that, I am talking about saving the family as an institution. The family has always been the best system we can imagine for raising children and ensuring that their basic psychological needs are met. The genuinely intact family unit, whatever its shape or size, provides security and a sense of belonging. Caring parents instill values, nourish religious beliefs, guide their kids in matters of morality and sexuality, encourage high aspirations, provide an environment wherein the child is able to become a productive and responsible human being—all this, and even more! Truly, the work of a family is a monumental task.

The question that arises is whether the family in its present state can function effectively and provide for the essential, nonmaterial needs of children. And I think the answer is no. I complain that our child protective system is failing our children, but the inescapable fact of the matter is that the most important part of the system—the heart and core of the system—is the family. And the family itself is failing. It seems to have lost its way.

I know there must be millions of parents out there who still cling to traditional values, still try to imbue these values in their children, still try to build a foundation for the future. But I think that many—whether they live in squalor or in splendor—want what they want when they want it, and never mind the kids or a better tomorrow. They are engulfed by the stampede to grab as much of the world's goods as soon as possible and let the chips fall where they may. Some of the chips are flying fragments of family, mainly our children, but that doesn't seem to matter. Material possessions count for more.

I don't know where these parents are going. Neither do they.

I talk to parents who lament that the demands of their dual professions leave them little time to be with their children—when in fact they could manage very nicely on one paycheck for a while and spend some time on the very important job of parenting. I talk to others whose time and energy are consumed with the unfulfilling jobs that bring home the paychecks upon which the family genuinely depends for survival. I talk to wives who would be unfit mothers if they could not get out of the house on at least a part-time basis to pursue a career. I talk to single mothers who don't want to work outside of the home but are driven to by economic necessity. I see families in which there is no sense of family, no grounding in a culture of continuity, no concept of personal accountability or of anything but instant self-gratification. They are bewildered people, both parents and youngsters, virtual strangers to each other who seem to have no joint purpose or plan or sense of belonging. The fullness of life is passing them by.

What do these parents actually want for their children? I should have thought that they would be alarmed by the national infant mortality rate and the lack of a national health care program for all children, but I don't hear much of an outcry. I should think they would be outraged by a public education system that turns out more and more unskilled illiterates every year, yet I see them sitting back and permitting this system to continue its downhill slide. And why have they not been galvanized into action by the abysmal quality of the street life to which we expose our urban kids—drug runners and addicts, homeless people lying in rags, casual murders, and mindless acts of vandalism? Instead of protesting, they bring the street world into the home in the form of substance abuse, domestic strife, and video entertainments of the most violent and pornographic kind. Or is it the other way around, and does all this start in the home and spill out into the street? Probably the latter. After all, most of our attitudes are born in the home.

When we are honest with ourselves, we acknowledge this. We know that kids learn by example, that they absorb family attitudes and imitate parental behavior. And what do they learn in many homes today? Self-indulgence. Abusive language. Violence. Bigotry. Use of dangerous substances. Distorted attitudes toward women, sex, race, religion, discipline, honesty, the work ethic, and the family itself. All this starts very early on.

In the thirteenth century, or so it is said, the Holy Roman Emperor Frederick II persuaded himself that his native tongue was the natural and universal language. He theorized that all children would speak it spontaneously even if they were never to hear it spoken by others. To test this premise, he ordered that a group of babies be removed from their mothers immediately after birth and placed with nurses who would take scrupulous care of their physical needs but remain completely silent.

And so it was done. The children never heard a word and never spoke. To the last one, they became ill and died.

This may be an apocryphal tale, but it does point up the importance of affectionate cooing and cuddling between caregiver and child. The babies were deprived of what babies need most: a warm, secure, bonding relationship, the give and take of love.

But if they had lived, what then?

Permit me a digression.

In generations past, starting a family was a significant step, giving marriage partners considerable pause. Could they handle the financial responsibility? Were they mature enough to be parents? Were they ready to dedicate large chunks of their lives to the welfare of the children they hoped to have? Were they willing to sacrifice some of their personal pleasures? These were important considerations in a time when parenthood was regarded as a cornerstone in the personally rewarding life. Now, for many people, it's just one of the things they want to try in their pursuit of fulfillment . . . or the careless consequence of a casual act.

But parenting is not a task to be haphazardly undertaken or performed. The stakes are too high for fooling around. A necessary requirement for the normal growth and development of the infant and young child is a close and mutually satisfying relationship with an affectionate adult.

Freud noted that a child's development is based largely on the repetition of activities that have been experienced passively during infancy and early childhood. This primary phase in the developmental process is called the imprinting stage: the time when a parent's smiling face, support, comfort, and love envelop the newborn infant. The mother experiences the joys of nursing her child. Such a parent-child relationship produces a consistent, need-satisfying experience for the child that makes it possible for him or her to respond lovingly to his own children.

This is not an old-fashioned, outdated concept; it is as true today as it ever was in Freud's Vienna. The child who is deprived of this kind of nurturing may be literally stunted by the lack—measurable psychologically, physically, and mentally. Maternal deprivation syndrome may be observed in a baby whose mother pays no attention to it because she is immature or afraid or alone or in a postpartum depression, or if her mothering instinct is deadened by drugs or alcohol. She may feed the baby and change its diaper when necessary, but for the rest she leaves it in the crib, untouched and unloved. If this pattern is continued, the child fails to develop normally.

A hospital physician can spot the deprivation syndrome very soon in a child who is brought in because of "failure to thrive." We can tell the age of a child by x-ray of the wrists. In a child who is not given emotional and physical stimulation, we will observe that the bone age is notably retarded: a ten-month-old child, for example, will present a bone age of five months. But if that child is subsequently held and cuddled and talked to in a gentle tongue, the bone age comes back to normal within five or six months.

That is the really encouraging news: not all serious damage is irreversible. This is true too of crack babies; even those who are very seriously damaged show dramatic improvement, mentally as well as emotionally and physically, when they are held, touched, and loved over a period of time. The actual reversal of retardation seems somehow magical, yet it is possible.

Evidence continues to mount that a close parental presence in the first six to twelve months of life is a vital factor in the child's development. Scientific studies going back almost half a century have demonstrated that infants deprived of physical contact, though fed and otherwise cared for, exhibit aspects of psychological and physical stunting. Now, new research shows that it is not merely the parents' loving presence or expressions of affection that affect the mental and physical growth of the child, but the actual experience of being touched and even massaged.

The new findings suggest that touch releases certain brain chemicals and inhibits the formation of others, resulting in important consequences for psychological development. Holding, touching, stroking, and carrying an infant all serve to soothe, stimulate, and communicate at an age when the tactile sense is the most mature sensory system. Babies who are stroked and massaged gain weight quickly. They are healthy and alert. Those who are touch-starved may become psychologically and physically stunted, irritable, hard to raise—in other words, candidates for abuse.

But babyhood isn't the only time parents need this basic form of communication with children. When parental words and reason make little impact, touch still counts: hands-on expressions of affection, even a little roughhousing, are tonics for children right up to adolescence—or whenever such demonstrations of affection start to embarrass them. Bonding goes on, and with it, attachment.

Some developmental psychologists, among them Jerome Kagan of Harvard University, are critical of the attachment theory of infant-maternal bonding and of assumptions that the events of infancy, especially the mother's demonstration of love, can seriously influence the mental health and behavior of the growing child. According to Kagan, the commotion about attachment is mainly a sign of contemporary mores. He plays down the long-term impact of parenting, believing that genes contribute to much of what we become.

But my clinical observations, my day-to-day dealings with children and families, lead me to believe—and strongly—that life experiences and mothering have the major influence on the future well-being and behavior of the child. I've seen touch-starved babies come back to life when loved, and I've seen others shrivel in mind and body when deprived of loving. Certainly, one must always consider the importance of genes and inherited predispositions in the makeup of the future adult, but there is overwhelming evidence that the result is not all genetic. Environmental life influences are critical.

I don't believe that most parents fully realize their potential for harm and for good. But they are phenomenally important people in the lives of their children. Parents, and mothers in particular, are responsible for the creation of the child's personality—and that is *power*. If the mother is irritable the baby's going to get irritable, and the baby's going to cry; if the mother is serene and holds the baby with love and gives it the sense that it's protected, that baby does not cry. There is an inevitable reciprocity here: a depressed or despondent mother, an irritable or immature mother, conveys her feelings to an uncomprehending child; the child becomes irritable and irritating, and develops colic and hollers all night; the mother reacts by yelling, "I've had enough of this! I can't stand you, I'm going to get rid of you!" The developing conflict often leads to serious abuse and sometimes to the killing of the infant by suffocation or shaking, or to long-term emotional disturbance.

Parental power is awesome. And because it is, parenting is an awesome responsibility.

There comes a point, of course, when the child has presumably reached the age of reason, and what he does from then on is his own responsibility. But in very large part he remains what his parents have predisposed him to be, whether he is a dropout, a runaway, a drug addict, a prostitute, or a prince of a fellow. The lost kids on our streets are kids who have been abandoned at home, who have developed hostility, who have become emotionally damaged, and who have declared open war on society and their parents. For these youngsters the lines of communication between parent and child have become nonexistent, replaced by harsh words, severe punishment, and an atmosphere of domestic violence that becomes the only life they know. Unless they are exceptional, they cannot rise above their upbringing to become stable, civilized adults; civilization is not taught through hostility and violence.

Where did these kids learn to do what they do so well and apparently enjoy? The mob of teenage boys who went on a rampage in New York's Central Park, ending their spree with the rape and near-murder of a young woman and joking about it afterward? The gang of schoolgirls who ran amok on upper Broadway and stuck pins into some forty-five unsuspecting and defenseless women who had done nothing whatsoever to provoke the attacks? ("We did it for fun, and it was fun. We was laughing.") The boys of middle-class, conservative Howard Beach, who attacked a group of blacks just because they were black? The three Harlem boys who raped a twelve-year-old girl, burned her breast, stuck her with an ice pick, threatened to throw her off the roof of a building, and giggled about it afterward? The packs of teenage hoodlums, totaling thousands, who for the last couple of Halloweens have swarmed through the streets of New York's five boroughs, assaulting people at random and trashing and looting stores in the name of fun?

Can parents be blamed for these things? Yes. Blame society, blame poverty, blame the affluent, blame the spirit of payback, blame uncontrolled high spirits, blame the mob instinct, blame the environment, spread the blame around all you like—and the fact remains that the parents of these juvenile criminals did not set standards, did not convey to their children the difference between right and wrong, did not provide examples of common human decency within the family that could deter the children from this kind of behavior. It is, once again, a question of attitude. And attitude is learned in the family. The kind of attitude that permits the worst crimes and tops them off with laughter afterward is an attitude that is born in the family and must be changed within the family.

It might help to unplug what journalist Marie Winn calls the plug-in drug—television. Each generation is always supposedly worse than the last, but, thanks in large part to television and film, today's children are definitely not like yesterday's. They are exposed virtually from birth to the ugliest aspects of the adult world, factual and fictional, presented on screens of various sizes with little thought of the adverse impact on impressionable viewers. Our kids' childhood has been snatched away from them. We have permitted the creation of an ugly environment that started out by entrancing them and wound up enslaving them—just like any drug.

Responsible parents don't sit with their own noses glued to the tube but rather try their best to shield children from the subculture of graphic violence, sexual brutality, and mutilation-murder that passes for entertainment these days. Setting standards in the home that make it very clear that sadomasochism and sexploitation are disgusting and contemptible may be only a small first step toward that end, but it is an essential one. Certainly, limiting the availability of ugly trash, especially for young children, is both possible and necessary. Just as little kids imitate their parents, so may they imitate what they see on their home screen.

One illustration comes to mind: a five-year-old Boston boy stabbed a two-year-old girl with a butcher knife right after watching a teen-slasher film on TV. He did not understand that she might die as a result, and fortunately, she didn't. But that video should not have been on the home screen in the first place.

Obviously, many of the people who produce the gruesome trash our children have come to identify with are parents themselves. What are their kids like, I wonder? And how dare these people manipulate *our* children just to make a buck? Do they justify and excuse themselves, like the rapists and incestuous fathers who say, "Well, she wanted it"?

I regard this as a very serious problem, and one that is exacerbated by many of our daily papers and weekly magazines. Headlines and "in-depth" interviews tell us all there is to know, and more, about the flamboyant lifestyles of rock stars, sports figures, and various performers on screen and TV. If we believe half of what we read, it is difficult to escape the conclusion that some of America's favorite, most highly publicized individuals endorse a way of life that celebrates promiscuity, arrogance, substance abuse, public temper tantrums, and displays of violence. And these people are role models and examples for our youth. Furthermore, those who celebrate them know this.

With a careless disregard for the consequences, the media compound existing problems of family breakdown by reveling in the non-family lifestyle. Effectively, they help to undermine all efforts to restore a sense of family as a viable means of social survival and to impart some moral values to our young people.

Looking at current statistics, it is obvious that something is very wrong in the home. The rate of juvenile delinquency in the United States is rising faster than the growth rate of the juvenile population. Suicide is the third-highest cause of death among teenagers, surpassed only by automobile accidents and homicides. Over one million adolescents—one out of every ten adolescent females—become pregnant each year. And this is not an inner-city phenomenon: teenage pregnancy among white adolescents has risen over 140 percent in the last two decades.

More than a million children each year find themselves in single-parent families as a result of the massive number of teenage pregnancies and the epidemic of separations and divorces. It is estimated that 50 percent of the children born in the 1980s will live in a single-parent home for a large part of their childhood. Somehow, these parents are going to have to make a living—and then who will nurture the children? Forty-nine percent of married women with children less than a year old work outside the home, more often than not because a double income is a necessity; also of necessity, they leave the child with a stand-in parent for a large part of the day.

Not only have grandparents exited the family circle; aunts and uncles have disappeared as well. Now even fathers or mothers—and sometimes both—are disappearing, leaving the child with weak, ineffective, or totally nonexistent kinship networks and without parents in the home. More than half a million children are residing away from their families in facilities ranging from individual foster-family and group homes to large institutions. Some of these, as we see in the Foundling's Skilled Nursing Facility, have special needs as a result of their physical and emotional handicaps; many others have no disability but have been removed from parents too stressed by housing and unemployment problems to be able to care for their children or from parents who abuse or neglect their children as a result of these stresses.

American children today are physically healthier than in generations past but impaired in their developmental, psychosocial, and educational maturation. Problems of adolescent sexuality, substance abuse, self-esteem, judgment, self-control, and behavior in general are rampant. Adults preoccupied with self-gratification don't spend enough time with their children to guide them through the thickets of growing up, and children will always find something to fill the vacuum. Peer influence has increased dramatically while parental influence has declined. The following was noted in a recent report by the National Research Council:

At every age and grade level, children show a greater dependence on their peers than they did a decade ago.

A parallel study indicates that susceptibility to a group influence is higher among children from homes in which one or both parents are frequently absent. Peer-oriented youngsters describe their parents as less affectionate and less firm in discipline. Peer-oriented children have a rather negative view of their friends and of themselves. They are pessimistic about the future, measure lower in responsibility and leadership, and are more likely to engage in antisocial behavior.

Concerned parents know all about outside temptations and peer pressure, yet they quite rightly feel that family standards should prevail. They may wonder, then, why their kid is so undisciplined and irresponsible, why he's running with a bad crowd and paying no attention to well-meant parental admonitions. "Why doesn't he listen?" they want to know. "We set rules. He knows what's expected of him. We started explaining right and wrong from the very minute he could understand."

And when was that? Children start to understand long before they are able to take in parental explanations. Explaining isn't everything. Almost always, children go wrong because of a lack of *parenting*, and parenting means attention of a particular kind. Not just the first few months but the first four years of a child's life are the years of imprinting, when parenting is most important. Imprinting is the input of the mother and the father: it is the parental blueprint or design of love and warmth, of understanding and strength, of beliefs and values, of hopes and expectations, of rebukes and rewards, of teaching by example.

It is very difficult and sometimes useless to start disciplining a child when he has already been molded in an undisciplined environment, although it can be done; on the other hand, in the early years it is relatively easy for the parents to instill in the child virtually everything they want—for evil as well as for good. If a kid is a little monster, that is pretty much what he has been programmed to be—not deliberately, but carelessly. Successful child raising requires care. It takes discipline—firm and fair, loving and consistent.

What it does not take is force. Millions of words have been written on how to discipline children. Books, magazine articles, newspaper features, cautionary pieces in the tabloids—advice is everywhere. I won't add to it, except to underline the current maxim: *Use the rod, and spoil the child.* Which means, Want a rotten kid? Hit him. No longer can anyone claim not to know that applying the rod is worse than futile. Nobody can *not* know that any form of violence in the home is poison for everyone in it.

Angry confrontations and chronic arguing between parents create a hostility-laden, emotionally violent climate that is frightening and psychologically harmful to the children. Parents tend to say, "Oh, they'll get over it. It's not directed at them. They know we love them anyway." Do they? Or do they think they are to blame?

It is true that children need to be exposed to a full range of emotions, positive and negative, in order to grow into emotional maturity. This does not mean, however, that they benefit by exposure to a long-term feud. They turn off emotionally and become withdrawn, or have trouble learning in school, or have outbursts of temper, or become fearful at any sign of anger. And when a marriage is breaking down, whether in a semicivilized manner or in open contempt and hatred, the fallout can be extremely damaging to the children. A tormented, mixed-up kid gets caught in the cross fire of his parents' messy divorce, and his welfare ceases to be a primary issue in the marriage. It may be altogether ignored.

Men and women alike, when entangled with their own problems, experience a diminished sensitivity to their children's needs and a diminished capacity to parent. Nice people turn ugly and venomous, developing blind spots and becoming hateful aliens in the eyes of their children. Then comes the custody battle: in extreme cases, the children are virtually sacrificed in the process—even when one or both parents feels he or she is genuinely acting in the best interests of the child.

A recent case leaps to mind. Going beyond the question of custody, it nevertheless illustrates how a child can become a pawn— perhaps, ultimately, a trophy—in a war between parents. The case involves Dr. Elizabeth Morgan, her ex-husband, Dr. Eric Foretich, and their daughter, Hilary. Dr. Morgan spent twenty-five months in the District of Columbia jail for defying a court order to reveal the whereabouts of Hilary or surrender the child for court-ordered, unsupervised visits with the father, contending that Foretich had sexually abused their child. Foretich denied the charge and made angry counteraccusations. The release of the mother did not resolve the case: Hilary was still hidden and accusations were still flying.

The saga as it unfolded revealed a poignant tale of a little girl on the run with her maternal grandparents and an ego match between Morgan and Foretich, floodlit by a media blitz of phenomenal proportions. No outsider can know where the truth lies or assess the actions of the parents, although I think that any outsider is justified in concluding that the court system in this case compounded rather than helped to solve the problem. What matters in a case of this sort is the best interest of the child. Was her best interest served? Were both parents sincerely concerned for the child's welfare? Or one? Or neither? I hope that the outcome for Hilary is a happy one for her, but meanwhile she has been subjected to an extremely bewildering, traumatic experience. The little girl in the middle has been nearly pulled apart by the parental tug of war.

The case of Hilary is extreme but not unique. Child custody is disputed in about 75,000 divorces every year, and none of these disputes is without some damaging by-products. Considering the inadequacy of our judicial system in dealing with questions of custody and visitation rights, I should think that the loving parent might want to make very certain of what he or she is letting the kids in for when the battle begins.

I often hear people say things like, "Our children are better off now that we're divorced than they would have been if we'd stayed together, because there was so much conflict and so much anger and yelling and screaming that the kids suffered for it." They may be completely sincere in this belief, and on occasion they may be right, but very often they overlook what is happening in the heart of a child when the core of his life—his family—goes to pieces. He suffers during the separation process and he suffers when it's over. He no longer feels part of a family because he *is* no longer part of a family; in his own eyes, a chunk of his life has been taken from him, and he feels abandoned. He is likely to feel even more divided when he acquires another mother or father, and additionally stressed when he has to adjust to stepsisters and stepbrothers whom he barely knows and doesn't even want to like.

A new bonding process is required here and it is an extremely difficult one, often made the more so by the failure of the parents to get their own lives back on track. The new families cobbled together after broken marriages tend to be anything but sanctuaries for children. They may instead be breeding grounds for all kinds of child maltreatment. Folklore tells us a lot about wicked stepmothers, and there is much truth in those dark tales; new writings would do well to examine the role of the stepfather and stepbrother in the rise of sexual abuse. Street kids know. That's why many of them leave home.

The step-home has a lot to do with filling streets with runaways and rejects, some of them more neglected than abused.

In 1985 Sean Russell, fair-haired, blue-eyed, and unwanted, took a bus trip from Florida to New York's Port Authority bus station and became a part of the street scene. His parents were divorced; both had remarried. After the breakup, Sean lived for a while with his father, an unsuccessful actor, two-bit drummer, and parent without soul. "He was a throwaway kid," a New York friend recalls. "His father had ninety-nine women and ninety-nine friends, and if they didn't like Sean they threw him out."

Carelessly shuttled back and forth between his father and his mother, the boy took to petty crime and heavy drug use before hopping the bus to New York. Four years later he was dead—a drifter who had wandered from job to job, from flophouse to charity shelter, from one drug party and one drug deal and one hustling trick to another. He came to a quintessentially bad end, slashed to death by a knife-wielding transsexual who then slit his own throat from ear to ear.

This is a true story. I did not make it up as a cautionary tale. And I hasten to add that many very fine and stable children have been produced by decent parents struggling to parent in broken families.

I remember when Francis Cardinal Spellman used to tell his young priests: "It's not enough to be kind. Be *super*kind." When I talk to parenting groups I like to borrow that wisdom and say: "It's not enough to be a parent. You've got to be a *super*parent." The new ecology of the family has brought with it unprecedented problems, and it takes much more time and effort for today's overworked and overstressed parent to do an adequate job, much less a super job.

Many parents are just as vulnerable as their kids. They are still kids themselves, in actual years as well as in emotional immaturity, and we in the helping professions sometimes forget that parental competence and confidence don't automatically arrive with the baby. We tend to forget, too, how often the young parents need to be helped over having been victims themselves. And if we lose sight of their needs as individuals, we cannot help the child.

I remember one young mother who pulled me up short and made me consider where she had come from and how she felt. Diane was about nineteen and her little girl was three. The two of them were participating in the temporary shelter program at the Foundling, in which abusive mothers and their children stayed with us for several months or a year while the mother learned some of the basics of parenting. Our mistake with her was that we kept focusing on the child's needs and overlooking her concerns.

Diane had originally come in after having seriously abused her child. After several weeks of doing very well with us, she and the little one were allowed to go home for a weekend—and when they came back the child had a bruise over one eye. I became involved when the social worker told me about the bruise and indicated that perhaps the mother had been implicated.

I took mother and child into my office, sat the child down on my lap, and started questioning Diane in what I thought was my most tactful manner. She said the child had fallen down. I must have looked skeptical, because she started crying. The child got off my lap and, in a classic case of role reversal, put her arm around the mother and said, "Mommy, Mommy, don't cry, Mommy. Everything will be all right." And that is when Diane really broke down.

Between sobs she said, "I'm sick and tired of all you damn people worrying about the kid. I didn't do it, I didn't hurt her! She fell down! A few years ago I was the one who was abused and you were all concerned about me, but now I don't matter to you at all. Don't you *know* I can't take care of the kid unless you first take care of me? If I don't have my head straight, how can I possibly take care of her?"

She was right. We had stopped taking care of her. Barely sixteen when she'd had the child, she was still a child-mother herself and she still needed our concern. She had reminded me that we must always reach out to the parent in order to help the child. Troubled mothers need mothering, too; they need tender loving care, or they won't be able to give it.

I doubt that Diane will ever be a superparent, but she is working at being a more competent and loving one in spite of the bareness of her life. Every day I see mothers and fathers with virtually all the advantages in the world who seem to be much less caring about their children and much more critical of them.

I am aware of the problems facing parents today, but the fact is that a lot of parents have brought many of their troubles upon themselves. Within the last generation or two we have lost sight of family obligations and the purposes of togetherness. It has become too easy for the man to shrug off his commitments and just walk out on the family. It has become too common for the woman to assume that she and her kids are better off on their own. Children need *two* parents; they need a mother and a father who share the responsibilities and joys of parenthood. They need the safe harbor of a wholesome family life. I know that fate often decrees that the family be damaged, but far more often it is the individual who makes the decision—and for basically selfish reasons.

There is a great deal that can be done to make the family a nicer, less dangerous place to be, but as in all things the first steps must be taken by the individual.

The most basic steps of all: Do as you would be done by, watch your tongue, and *listen*.

Have you ever said to yourself, "I hated my father for doing this, and here I am doing exactly the same thing"? Do you, like your mother, scream at your kids and throw things at them? Did *you* enjoy it? Do you ever find yourself saying things that were said to you and you swore you would never say? . . . "Crybaby

. . . stupid . . . I can't stand the sight of you . . ." And, of course, your kids are quietly resolving, "I'm never going to do that when I grow up"; whereas, in all likelihood, they are going to do exactly that, complete with the look of contempt and the threatening body language. Somewhere along the line this has got to stop, and it might as well stop with you. You yourself will be happier for it.

Something else is almost as basic: as a marvelous food writer has observed, "much depends on dinner." Absolutely. Food is elemental, food is basic, and nurturing through food is of the essence of the family. The family that eats together is the family that is together—for a while, anyway. It is specious to insist that the schedules of all the family members are so different that they can't all get together for several meals a week. If parents care about the family, they can get back to the traditional practice of having breakfast and dinner for the whole family instead of providing a soup kitchen where kids can come and go as they please. The family dining table is, or should be, a center of family togetherness; and the family meal schedule can, or should be, a framework for the consistent, predictable, and disciplined life that all children crave even while they seem to rebel against it.

Much also depends on schools and the parents' attitude toward their children's education. An astonishing number of parents seem unaware that they are actually responsible for their children's education, and that it is their obligation to become actively engaged in the development of a curriculum suitable for their kids; if they can't be bothered they have no right to complain. And if they don't already belong to a lively PTA they should push for a parent-teacher partnership and get involved with it. Such a partnership is one of the most valuable supports for beleaguered parents, and a bulwark against child abuse.

In a kinder time, neighbors were friends who cared about each other and each other's kids. They would notice when a mother was depressed or overstressed, or a child was pale and withdrawn, and they would offer to help by running errands or taking over a few hours of baby-sitting or whatever else was needed to lighten a load. Now they say, "I mind my own business. I don't care. I know mothers who abuse their children, but it's nothing to do with me. I can't help. I got enough with my own kids."

Some day—and this is the dream that I have—neighbors will be neighbors again. Meanwhile, what is an overstressed mother to do?

Call Parents Anonymous, for one thing. This is a nationwide organization whose members are or have been abusers or have an inner dread that something is going to trigger them into an abusive act. Of all the countless "anonymous" groups in the nation, this is among the finest. These parents, no matter what their financial and social circumstances, are comfortable together and genuinely care for each other. Nobody blames; everybody helps.

For people who shy from group meetings and feel more comfortable with private consultation, there is private counseling. It should be pointed out that there is no longer any stigma attached to discussing problems of parental overstress with a family or marriage counselor. This is fine, and admirable, for those who can afford it and for whom it works. Yet, more and more, people are finding strength in togetherness. If it cannot be found within the biological family, it must be sought wherever it exists.

There is a growing recognition in the United States that families have been seriously weakened during the past couple of decades and need a support system. In response, parent support programs geared to helping two generations at once have been popping up all over the country. Most of them have little or no connection with government agencies, and participation in them is no more demeaning than participation in a neighborhood playground group. Formal and informal, local and statewide, located in housing projects, storefronts, church basements, and schools, these groups are becoming a network of new social units—today's extended families. In a movement that cuts across racial and socioeconomic lines, parents and teachers and other people who care are joining forces in programs like these:

• Missouri's Parents as Teachers, a support and counseling program that caters to all income levels and reaches well over fifty thousand families. Any parent with a child under three can sign up for monthly group meetings to share child-rearing experiences with other parents, and in-home counseling visits to discuss parents' problems and the child's development. It offers a no-pressure, drop-in-and-chat approach.

• The Family Focus Center in Evanston, Illinois, a nonprofit parent support program run by the Chicago-based Family Resource Coalition. It offers professionally run parent workshops, a mothers' support group, and child care as a respite for the mother. "These institutions are acting as extended families," says one energetic participant, who has helped to form a reading club and raise money for the center. "A parent has to have a helping network." Middle-class parents use the center as a place to socialize and exchange ideas and are actively recruiting low-income minority parents.

• Avance of San Antonio, a program geared to low-income Mexican-American women with children under four and dedicated to teaching mothers how to teach their children. A nine-month program of weekly parenting classes runs the gamut of what mothers need to know, from how children learn and how to make toys for them to the essentials of nutrition. Meanwhile, the little ones are being cared for in several bright playrooms. Field trips to the library and local shopping mall are also arranged.

• The Beethoven Project in Chicago, inspired by Chicago businessman-philanthropist Irving B. Harris and financed by a combination of station, federal, and private funds. The program is open to every baby born in six of the twenty-eight high-rise buildings in the nation's largest public housing complex, the Robert Taylor homes. Pregnant women, young mothers, and preschoolers receive intensive support and a full range of services including free prenatal care, counseling, home visits, and access to a drop-in center where classes, day care, and health care are available. The aim is to educate the young mothers for their own future and equip them to help their babies to be fully prepared for kindergarten at the Beethoven Elementary School when they turn five.

• Homebuilders, a crisis intervention agency started in Tacoma, Washington, in 1974 and expanding into other areas. The Homebuilders on-site program, aimed at keeping families intact and functioning, is founded on the premise that a child is best served by remaining in his own home and in his own community even when the family is in deep trouble. Unlike other helping agencies, whose workers are commonly burdened by caseloads of twenty to forty families, Homebuilder team members concentrate on no more than two to three families at a time. On call twenty-four hours a day seven days a week, staffers spend many hours daily with the clients in their own homes in an intensive and highly personalized effort to help the family members pull together the threads of their own lives and make effective use of community services.

• Maryland's statewide Friends of the Family, which runs about a dozen drop-in centers offering a range of services such as classes on child care, literacy tutoring, teenage group meetings aimed at pregnancy prevention, breakfast and potluck dinners, and playrooms where parents can leave their children under someone else's care while they go to a class or take a nap. The focus of these centers is to cut into the isolation that parents often experience and encourage them to be with other people. "We are trying to do all the things that a grandmother or aunt used to do," one of the providers says.

A significant point about these programs and a thousand others is that they all make some provision for child care. They offer respite that is often desperately needed. When we get down to the bottom line, child care of one kind or another is *the* most essential need for the overstressed and often overworked parent. An occasional morning of peace, or even an hour or two with adult friends, can be a lifesaver for the mother—and just as much of a break for the child.

The respite has such miraculous effects that we cannot help but see how valuable a nationwide system of day care—and in some cases, night care—would be. More than just a backup for an exasperated parent, the well-regulated child care center is a human support system demanded by the new ecology of the family. It is today's essential bailout. Where we don't have indulgent grandparents and aunts, we have to provide our own.

Yet even more can be done. Let industry provide day care for the working mother. Let parent-school groups provide it in before- and after-school centers, rather than let the latchkey kids hang around an empty home. Let the neighbors, the community, and the government at various levels each do their part to get these extended family support systems into action. Let an ecology-conscious government, if that is what it is, consider the massive cost of cleaning up toxic spills and compare it with the pitiable monies spent on cleaning up the family environment—and then spend the money where it can do the most good. Let us put our children first.

Whatever it takes, let us do it. The new extended family may be an odd-looking assemblage, but it is a vital adjunct to the new ecology.

8 / Lisa's Legacy: School Alert

"Concerning a teacher's influence," the late author-teacher Haim Ginott wrote, "I have come to the frightening conclusion that I am the decisive element in the classroom. It's my personal approach that creates the climate. It's my daily mood that makes the weather. As a teacher, I possess a tremendous power to make a child's life miserable or joyous. I can be a tool of torture or an inspiration. I can humiliate or humor, hurt or heal. In all situations, it is my response that decides whether a crisis will be escalated or de-escalated, and a child humanized or dehumanized."

No question about it: A teacher is almost as influential as a parent, and sometimes more so.

The death of six-year-old Lisa Steinberg in November 1987 prompted a proliferation of inquiries, none more pertinent and compelling than that conducted by the New York City Board of Education. According to the Board's report, the signs of abuse displayed by the little girl should have been noticed by personnel at Lisa's school, P.S. 41 in Greenwich Village.

In fact, they were.

"Lisa's disheveled appearance (hair, fingernails, and clothing) was observed by at least eight people," the report said. These individuals included teachers and school aides who were accustomed to seeing her as a normally well-groomed child and who might have been expected to voice concern. "Bruises were noted on Lisa's face, forearms, and back by at least five people," the report continued. But school officials apparently accepted the explanation that she had been struck by her baby brother. "Her excessive absences and latenesses," tallied afterward, should themselves have been an indication that something was amiss in the Steinberg household.

These three elements—the look of neglect, the bruises, the poor attendance record—were sufficient reason for a report of suspected child abuse to be made. Indeed, Board of Education regulations *require* that all such cases be reported. Yet in spite of regulations and suspicions, appropriate authorities were *not* alerted, and Lisa died. A few parents of students at P.S. 41 have told me that teachers did report their observations "to the guidance people there," but there is no knowing how far their comments traveled along the chain of reporting.

Could Lisa Steinberg's death have been prevented if an abuse report had been appropriately lodged by school personnel? The Board's report concludes that this is an unanswerable question: "However, if the question is whether school personnel are properly trained in the recognition of child abuse, what to do when child abuse is suspected, and what their legal obligations and responsibilities are, the answer has to be a definite no."

Not only that. School personnel in this case, as in many others, lacked clues that might have helped them put two and two together. The teachers who noticed Lisa's condition had no way of knowing that Hedda Nussbaum, Joel Steinberg's companion, had previously been treated at Bellevue Hospital for a beating, or that social workers had ever visited the Steinberg home, or that the police had responded to a complaint of domestic abuse at the apartment a few weeks before Lisa's death, or that baby brother Mitchell was far too small to beat up on his sister. School authorities were never in possession of these bits of information. Perhaps they would not have realized the significance even if they had been. But perhaps they would have.

Since then, child abuse recognition training has been made mandatory throughout the New York City school system. Every guidance counselor, teacher, and administrator has been briefed on how to detect and respond to cases of abuse and neglect. The Board of Education has distributed hundreds of thousands of copies of an information-packed desk reference called *Child Abuse Alert*. School personnel have been reminded that they are required by law to report suspected cases of abuse to a state hotline number. Everybody in the system knows—more or less—how to identify the various types of abuse and abusees, how to recognize abusive parents, and how and to whom to report; everybody in the system has been informed of their rights, responsibilities, and legal safeguards in regard to reporting. The program is a model of its kind.

Yet, even today, many school systems in New York State and throughout the nation have only the sketchiest plans for dealing with child abuse. Dismaying numbers of educators are still reluctant to get involved in what they consider the family's private affairs. And teachers at all levels have conflicting opinions about the function of schools.

A teacher speaks: "I see 150 kids a day. It's difficult to do all the things that need to be done in six hours and twenty minutes and be aware of everything that's going on. I think people ask too much of the teachers in the schools. They want us to feed Johnny, they want us to integrate Johnny, they want us to bus Johnny, they want us to civilize Johnny, they want us to discipline Johnny, they want us to counsel Johnny—they want us to do seven or eight things, and teaching Johnny to read seems to be the ninth. But education should be our primary focus."

"The classes are large and many children are disruptive," says another. "Discipline is a major problem. There's a desperate lack of time to pay enough attention to individual kids. If you have a class full of difficult, troubled, backward children whom you know you must get to pass a certain reading test or math test, the pressures on you are very, very hard. At the same time you have to understand what the school means to many of these kids. They come from chaotic homes, some of them from families where there's a lot of drug use. Some I think were damaged before birth. There are kids who catch up on their sleep in class and there are kids who would have nothing to eat if we didn't give them breakfast and lunch. Here they have some sense of structure and they know that nobody's going to hurt them. School is a haven for them."

Schools are not always the havens they should be. I believe that the common impression of big-city schools as hotbeds of juvenile criminal activity—gangs preying on students and teachers, drug dealers blazing away at each other with Uzis—is a highly colorized version of reality. But exaggeration does not change the fact that urban crime has a disastrous impact on our everyday lives. We are not even particularly surprised when we read that a day care center in Brooklyn teaches preschool tots how to take cover if gunfire erupts. In some inner-city high schools there is an atmosphere of street brutality that is an abuse in itself and teaches students that violence is okay for those who can get away with it.

Not perhaps generally known is that *deliberate* violence against children is permitted and even encouraged in the majority of classrooms throughout the nation. Teachers and principals spank, whack, beat, switch, or paddle children two to three million times a year. Most of the victims are students in elementary school. According to Federal Department of Education statistics, about thirty thousand children a year are injured severely enough to require short-term medical treatment, and more than one hundred thousand a year are whacked into long-term emotional and learning problems.

It is illegal in all states to subject hardened criminals to corporal punishment, but in most states it is perfectly legal for school personnel to discipline children by beating them—short of using "deadly force," as they say in Texas, or provided that another adult is present as witness. Twelve states have laws against this form of child abuse and some school systems forbid it. But the Supreme Court, as recently as March 1989, has upheld the archaic principle that the schoolmaster or schoolmarm has the right to wallop the child.

And for what sort of crimes? For so trivial an error as underlining instead of encircling answers on a quiz. For snickering in a kindergarten class. For not completing homework. For hitting another child! The irony is indeed rich.

Experienced caregivers know that inflicting physical blows is a pathetically ineffective method of instilling book learning, good manners, or obedience. Teachers are kidding themselves when they claim that corporal punishment is discipline. It is vengeance, retribution, sadism, or simple loss of control. If children learn anything from being hit by school staffers, it is that it's okay for the powerful to hurt the less powerful, and that school is not a very nice place.

I received a letter the other day from a father in a southern state. He writes: "My son is ten years old and he is afraid to go back to school this fall. He tells me that his teacher uses a paddle about three feet long, three inches wide, and one inch thick, covered with black tape. This must be stopped. . . . My son just came in and said, 'Dad, don't say anything about my teacher, or he'll get mad and whip me.' The boy is scared to death."

This is legalized, institutional abuse. Most other industrialized nations have long since done away with sanctioned hitting in schools. It is to our shame that we have not.

There is another form of abuse in schools that is not legal but is nonetheless too common for comfort. It occurs when screening and hiring procedures are shoddy and unsavory individuals manage to get too close to the children. For example:

- A teacher handcuffs students in his office and then beats them.

- A convicted child pornographer is hired to teach.

- A man with a record of eight arrests on charges including public indecency and a sexual assault on two seven-year-old girls is licensed as a teacher and sexually molests two girls in junior high.

- A female teacher believed to be an addict is charged with possession of drugs.

- A male teacher previously found guilty of endangering the welfare of a child resumes his teaching career and is arrested and charged with third-degree rape.

- A nineteen-year veteran of public schools is charged with sexual abuse and endangering the welfare of a minor.

- A high school principal is found guilty of purchasing crack.

- A teacher is discovered snorting cocaine in the school parking lot.

- A female teacher hits two students on the head with a high-heeled shoe, cutting them seriously.

- A coach molests a brain-damaged special education student.

And so on. All this, in what should be a home away from home.

And yet the school is, and rightly so, a place and institution that most people trust. Too bad that the rotten apples keep on bobbing up.

According to the National Committee for Prevention of Child Abuse, more than two-thirds of the children who are abused or neglected annually in the United States are between five and seventeen years old, which means that they are of school age although not all of them attend school. The three- to four-year-olds are another vulnerable group, and a good number of these are in preschools. Clearly, well over half of the children reported in cases of abuse, as well as others who are not reported, do go to school and spend a good part of their waking hours under the supervision of presumably responsible and caring adults.

I do not expect these adults to do the job of parents, but nonetheless they are *in loco parentis* for significant chunks of the child's lifetime. Other than the parent or substitute no one else in the child's life has so much contact with and is in a position to know so much about the child. Between them, the teachers and the principal and the guidance counselors are familiar with his attendance record, his usual behavior, his normal appearance, his interaction with his peers, his ability to function at grade level, and how much his parents are involved with the school. They can recognize a physical or personality change when they see one; they understand the significance of disruptive or belligerent behavior in the classroom, even if they cannot divine the precise cause.

Teaching professionals are thus in a unique position to do more than pound knowledge into youthful heads. Indeed, there is more to the educational directive than that. A major part of the educator's mission is to teach the skills appropriate to functioning in society while at the same time civilizing the child and developing his or her potentialities. Surely it is logical to take the next step and concede that abuse and neglect set up blocks that inhibit a student's learning ability. The child who is healthy, happy, and secure at home has the makings of a good student; the child made wary and distressed by maltreatment becomes a learning problem.

This, obviously, is the business of teaching professionals. And taking note of a child's pain is the business of all child-oriented human beings.

Like it or not, educators and their staff colleagues represent the first line of defense against child abuse and neglect. One and all, they are literally and figuratively on the spot. In every state in the United States, its territories, and the District of Columbia, all individuals associated with the education of children—principals, administrators, teachers, school social workers, counselors, nurses, and day care operators—are required by law to report suspected child abuse.

Yet for a variety of reasons, school personnel have been reluctant to report suspected cases of abuse or neglect. For anyone, the decision to report is laden with conflicting emotions, and even mandated reporters share a widespread fear of getting involved in a situation that may prove, one way or another, to be beyond them.

What often happens is that a kind of disguised shifting of responsibility gets under way. In many areas, class teachers don't know whether it is their duty to report or the duty of the principal, guidance counselor, school nurse, social worker, or someone—anyone—else, and they have a tendency to wait for one of those other people to do it. But it isn't someone else's duty; it is everyone's.

Some teachers believe that an abuse report will adversely affect teacher-student rapport; others fear retribution from irate parents. But rapport actually tends to be enhanced by a teacher's display of concern, and in any event is less important in the long run than a child's overall well-being.

The possibility of retribution is something else.

In spite of all the information supplied to school personnel, many members of the educational system believe that, if a member of a school staff makes a report that turns out to be unfounded or unprovable, the child's parents will sue that person—or the school or maybe the whole system—for slander or defamation of character or whatever. This misapprehension leads me to believe that teachers have not been doing their homework.

It is true that anyone knowingly or willfully making a false report is liable for damages. However, reporting laws in most states make it very clear that individuals who report *in good faith* are immune from liability. They do not need to know for a fact that abuse has taken place; they only need to have reasonable cause to believe or suspect that a child is being maltreated. This is the kind of judgment call that teachers make every day.

It is virtually impossible for individuals in a school situation to provide proof of abuse in the home—and they don't have to. Obtaining such proof is the job of trained investigators, and once the case gets into their hands the original reporter has little to do with it. A wrongful report may subject an individual to criminal sanctions only if it is held to be malicious.

The other side of the reporting coin is that, by law, *failure* to report a suspected case is a crime punishable by sentences ranging from a few days in jail and a ten-dollar fine to a year in prison and a five-thousand-dollar fine—supposedly implemented only when the individual has knowingly or willfully failed to report. Here is another judgment call, this one on the part of the court: hard as it is to determine by superficial observation whether a child has been neglected or abused, or if the reporter has reported out of spite, it is just as hard to determine the willfullness of nonreporting.

The nation's laws, as they stand now, have teachers in something of a bind. When three elementary schoolteachers in Atlanta were arrested for failure to report suspicions of child abuse, other teachers felt both confused and fearful—especially since the accused teachers denied having suspected anything at all and investigation failed to substantiate allegations of child abuse. It is not surprising that a blunder such as this should prompt teachers to think twice before reporting.

More often than not, however, the reluctance of school personnel to report suspected cases is due not to fear of personal repercussions but to a combination of two other factors: fear of parental reprisal against the child, and a lack of faith in the child protective system. "What's the point in reporting?" teachers ask. "Nobody does anything. Nothing happens to make things better."

But if policies and procedures were firmly established and communicated throughout the community of parents, teachers, and social services, and there were a direct and viable channel between the school and the child protective system, complete with built-in safeguards for the child *and* his parents, something would happen to make things better. Yes, in all major cities that system is overloaded, but nonetheless, if pressure is brought to bear on it by educators who make reports and then follow up on their reports, it cannot fail to respond, even if it has to demand more resources from local government. But the process must start somewhere.

Last Halloween I chanced to be walking through the streets of my neighborhood when hundreds of small children in costumes that were mostly creatively homemade erupted through the doors of the local grade school and lined up on the sidewalk for their annual parade. Chirping and chattering, they romped from block to block, shepherded by teachers wearing makeshift disguises and slightly embarrassed looks. There was a sudden rain shower and a chill in the air, and the kids pushed their Batman masks back over their heads for rainhats and wrapped their witches' cloaks around them to keep out the wet gusts. They giggled and laughed and pranced through the streets as though it was all great fun. Four or five children had no costumes but did have funny hats and smudges on their faces. For some reason it struck me that their teachers, not their parents, had offered them these little tokens of belonging. One small boy, quite neatly but cheaply dressed, had no suggestion of a costume. He passed me by without a dab of paint or a smile on his face, without a mask or silly hat on his head, a solemn six-year-old who had no connection with the festivities around him. I wondered how he, of all children, had been overlooked.

And I thought of Lisa, the one child in her class without a Halloween costume on one of the last days of her life. I worry about that little boy. Did his parents belong to a religious sect that prohibited such activities? Or was it that his parents had not thought to dress him up and his homeroom teacher had run out of funny hats before she got around to him? Or had she simply not noticed that he was the only one of all her kids who had nothing festive about him? The costume was not her responsibility. But I hope she will notice should the child outgrow his clothes or start coming to school with bruises on his body.

A little boy such as this may be responsive to a compassionate teacher. Fearful of volunteering anything about his home situation, he may be gently encouraged to confide in someone who cares.

Absenteeism is another signal that, curiously enough, often goes unheeded. Lisa's flagging attendance record is one case in point, but there are others that are even more blatant. Two of the nine McMillan children, for instance, apparently attended school for some time and then dropped out. Did the school authorities not follow up on this truancy? Or try to determine whether there might be other school-age siblings to be enrolled? If there was any such effort, it clearly came to nothing.

The case of Nicholas Lebron Alvarez came very close to being fatal for him. He is the half-brother of five-year-old Jessica Cortez, who was beaten to death by her mother's live-in lover. More than twenty hours after the little girl's battered body was taken away, nine-year-old Nicholas was found cowering in a closet, malnourished and suffering from multiple fractures caused by repeated beatings. School officials said that there had been truancy problems with young Nicholas, namely, he had been absent from P.S. 147 for about eighty days—almost half the school year—for each of three years in a row. I cannot imagine why attendance officers did not descend upon his home to learn the reason for this phenomenal record of absenteeism and incidentally notice conditions in that squalid place that warranted attention by the child protective agency. In fact, a halfhearted inquiry was attempted by an investigator for the Bureau of Attendance, who simply dropped the case when he found it difficult to establish contact with mother or child. He was not obliged by law to go any further, but he could have and he should have.

Obviously there was a major slipup here on the part of truancy investigators, but I fault school personnel, too. Again, there is no law decreeing that persistent absences are grounds for a child abuse report, nor is there any provision for the school system to take a neglect petition to court. But even the most basic inquiries were apparently not made. Normal procedure in the case of absenteeism is for the principal or teacher to call, visit, or get a message through to the parents to find out if there is a problem at home that is affecting the child, and suggest a consultation. If there is a persistent lack of response, it is time to call in the attendance or truant officers and *keep track* of their investigations. But it seems this did not happen in the case of the McMillan children or Nicholas Lebron. They were shrugged off as if they did not exist.

As stressful and time-consuming as an educator's job may be, it cannot be so engulfing that a few phone calls become a major additional burden—phone calls that may save a child from the burden of his pain and perhaps even save a family.

Recognition training, if it is to be of any value, has to deal with both parent and child. Sensitizing the teacher to the significance of scabs and unwashed hair is only the beginning; what is even more important is for the teacher to understand *why* some parents abuse their children, what personality forces interact to bring about a parent's violent or neglectful or insulting act against a child, and what stress factors can impel a parent into abusive behavior.

It is essential for school personnel to realize that most child abusers are not aware that their behavior is abusive. These parents are
usually astounded and none too happy to find out that it is, yet
they are nearly always willing to cooperate in a school program
designed to help them with their child's behavior problems and
other parenting difficulties. Behavioral parent training has helped
a good many families. And when parents *are* aware that they are
hurting their children, they may be defensive and angry when first
approached, but almost always want help desperately.

On the other hand, parents who are engulfed in a mass of unresolved psychosocial problems and who lack coping skills on any
level do not respond well to approaches from the school. Yet these
people also need understanding and compassion, for they are
among the most desolate of human beings and their children among
the most gravely endangered. What is indicated here is a direct
telephone call by teacher or principal to a community child abuse
prevention program or parent helpline requesting an appointment
for the stressed parent—and a follow-up call several days later to
make sure that the parent has shown up and is being helped. Such
calls are neither accusation nor betrayal; the first is like calling an
ambulance, and the second is a concerned inquiry as to the patient's
progress.

On a day-to-day basis, the sensitized teacher is in a strategic
position to observe and evaluate each student's appearance and
demeanor. Yes, I know that a classroom load of thirty-five ricochet-
ing youngsters is enough to occupy the full attention of any diligent
teacher—but normal, trained attention should reveal even subtle
abnormalities.

There are bodily signs of abuse and neglect, there are behavioral
signs, and there are silent signals that children give off. It is possible to recognize them all. No serious observer will mistake the
obvious clues—the bruises, the welts, the contusions, the burn
marks, the split lips—for the less serious, less frequent battle scars
of the romper room. By the same token, the aggressive, disruptive
behavior of children in need is not difficult to distinguish from
normal high spirits. A child whose attitude and acts are destructive
may be imitating the violent behavior of his parents or making a
pitiful bid for attention; in either case, he is yelling for help.

Habitual truancy and chronic lateness with flimsy excuses are
typical of a child who is having problems at home or in school or

both. In fact, a child who is abused at home is often subjected to further, unwitting abuse in school: he hasn't done his homework or he gets to class late; he is chided for it and perhaps disciplined, and he feels singled out for negative attention in front of his class.

The child who comes to school much too early and hangs around after activities are over is usually not an overeager student but a kid who doesn't want to go home, either because there is no one there to supervise or care for him or because there *is* someone there—someone he fears. Kids like this are crying out for help and protection. Others come to school inadequately clad for the weather, or conspicuously growing out of hand-me-down clothes, or with their hair tangled and unclean. Sometimes a child will have such bad body odor that his classmates refuse to sit anywhere near him, although they will make faces and giggle and point. Or a child may be consistently hungry and show physical symptoms of undernourishment. He may come to school so tired that he sleeps in class, suggesting that he has been up all night because of family habits or disruptions, such as night-long substance abuse or domestic violence.

All these signals are signs of neglect, signs that a parent is unable or unwilling to care for the child, signs that any teacher or other staff member should be able to recognize.

Sometimes it takes a little detective work to interpret signals correctly, and sometimes that extra little bit of effort might prevent a death. Or so one can say in hindsight. But hindsight gives us some pointers for the future.

I think of a case in Santa Clara County, California, one in which the child in question had been involved with the social services system prior to his death. The core of the case is this: here was an overtly mistreated child who died as a direct result of being mistreated. He had been beaten, deprived of food, and then force-fed as a punishment for some minor misdeed until he vomited and then choked on his vomit.

The child had previously been removed from the parental home in another county because of neglect and was later returned by social services in accordance with regulations current at that time and place. Because of the move from one county to another, there was no procedure or mechanism to monitor the case and keep track of the child's situation at home. It was later determined that parental drug use was a major factor in the deterioration of the family and contributed to the child's death. A review of this case resulted in a number of observations, one of which is this: the school had known that the child had at times stolen food. In retrospect, it is clear that this behavior was related to the parent's use of food deprivation as a method of discipline. School (and law enforcement) personnel would be wise to consider the possibility that food larceny may be a sign of neglect and hunger, rather than a simple conduct problem.

Why does Johnny steal food? Yes, in retrospect, one might suppose him to be hungry. Yet "food larceny" is more than merely a "simple conduct problem," and hindsight might have suggested a problem at home that was affecting his school behavior. It is unfortunate that school personnel had had no way of knowing that the child was from a high-risk family. Had they known, they might have been more alert.

Far more often than they realize, teachers come into contact with children who show symptoms of physical or emotional neglect, or physical or sexual abuse, and overlook them because they are not geared to recognize the cues *in the population* in which they present themselves—"nice" children from "nice" families. Educators know intellectually that abusive home situations may exist on any economic or social level in the community, but, like spouses who deny their loved one's drug use, they don't really want to know about it and they don't let themselves become aware.

The Cochrans, for example, lived in a trim-lawned, four-bedroom colonial home in a New Jersey town. Stuart Cochran was a successful contractor who could set his own hours; his wife, Mary, worked part-time as a restaurant bookkeeper, starting early so that she could be home in the afternoon to spend time with her children. There were four of them, three girls and a boy, and they all went to the same school.

No one at the school thought to question the number of times that Molly, the youngest daughter, came in late or not at all, on each occasion turning up eventually with a note from her father. No one wondered how Charles had managed to break his finger and get a burn mark on his arm at the same time; or how Peggy got the ugly bruises around her neck, or asked why Jean had become so withdrawn and depressed that she never smiled any more.

Later, Mary Cochran would say she had known that her husband was physically abusing all the children; he hit her, too. But until the kids got together and said, in effect, "Mom, we've got to get out of this, with or without you," she had no idea that her husband was regularly sleeping with Molly, and, as the mood moved him, Molly's older sister Jean. Or so she said.

And although the troubled siblings exhibited many clues, the teachers noticed nothing wrong. They did not expect to find child abuse in the "nice" families of their "nice" town.

Another factor obscuring recognition on the educational front is what I call the headline syndrome. When most people think of child abuse they think of the hideous cases that make the front pages of the tabloids and the lead stories of the evening news—the broken legs and arms, the subdural hematomas, the scaldings and the brutal deaths. But these cases represent only about 3 percent of all those that are reported, and very few teachers will ever see a child on the verge of such a state. Teachers are infinitely more likely to be confronted with signs of minor physical injury, neglect, sexual abuse, and emotional maltreatment, and those who have done their homework will know how to read them. And early detection and referral to protective services may very well prevent some of those headlines.

Timely observation of parental attitudes may be as pertinent and revealing as any scrutiny of the child. Teachers who take the trouble to consult with parents about a child's behavior are in a position to make assessments. Are the parents concerned about the child, or do they lack interest in his progress or his school activities? Are they aggressive or defensive? Apathetic or unresponsive? Reluctant or eager to participate in school programs or functions? Normal or bizarre in manner? One meeting with a parent can often make a lot of little indicators click into place.

If there is reason to suspect, the report must be made immediately; abuse situations seldom get better on their own.

Any school system or district or individual school can sweep away the difficulties of reporting by mobilizing its own policies, resources, and personnel within the guidelines of the state or local department of education. Directives from upstairs mean nothing unless they are implemented by knowledgeable, caring human beings who are not afraid of some degree of involvement in a child's well-being.

I would suggest that each school create a team to receive and assess suspected cases of abuse brought in by any staff member or associate—*any*, from bus drivers and cafeteria servers and paraprofessionals to student teachers and nurses and athletic directors, from guidance counselors to full-time teaching staff. The report should be in writing and must specify the reporter's reasons for suspicion. Proof should not be expected of the reporter, who is obviously not a professional investigator; nor should unsupported accusations and vague doubts be acceptable. The following elements *are* acceptable as convincing evidence of abuse or neglect:

• Eyewitness observations of a parent's neglectful or abusive behavior

• A child's description of being abused or neglected

• The parents' own admission and description of abusive or neglectful behavior

• Accounts of child abuse or neglect by spouses or family members

• Children allowed to be in physically dangerous situations or left alone for extended periods of time

• Demonstrated parental inability to care for the child due to mental illness, retardation, or drug or alcohol abuse

Having spelled this out, I must repeat that "proof" is hard for a teacher or any other noninvestigator to come by, and that there are many other indicators—as discussed earlier—that must be viewed with concern by any individual who cares about the welfare of a child. These are all grist for the school child abuse team.

After in-school assessment determines that there may be need for child protection, either a designated team member or the principal reports the conditions to the Central Registry or local child protective agency.

From that point on, it is the duty of the agency to investigate the case and develop the facts. If this agency knows its stuff and is not totally swamped, it will provide the services needed to help both parent and child and rehabilitate the family. The reporting individual does not *have* to do anything more, and neither does the school. But if the child is to be truly served, the school team will develop an ongoing liaison with the protective agency. It must insist on obtaining feedback demonstrating that the response to any of its reports is constructive, effective, and maintained as long as necessary. And the original reporter, if a teacher, should have the opportunity to continue contact with an agency social worker to exchange observations about the child's home situation and progress in school.

Perhaps, in this way, one of the cracks in the child protective system can be stopped up, and at least some children saved.

For all that, prevention is the real heart of the matter, and knowledge is the basis of child abuse prevention.

Bearing in mind that the primary function of the educator *is* to educate, we have to ask ourselves if our school curriculum is addressing itself to a very major subject: family life. Other societies make this a priority. In Sweden, for example, both boys and girls are given classes in sex education, child care, home maintenance, and the dynamics of family life.

Unfortunately, American educators are wary of giving even carefully edited courses in sex education, largely because both parents and teachers feel that sexual matters are private and should be dealt with in the home. The truth, of course, is that a good many parents, even those who are well-informed and caring, don't do a very good job of explaining the facts of life to their children. What the school can do is provide the objectivity of a classroom setting and a matter-of-fact course that supplements, and in many cases corrects, what the kids have learned elsewhere.

But it must do more than that. I advocate a curriculum of much greater scope: a human sexuality curriculum that includes and emphasizes an understanding of the family unit, preparation for parenthood, and the long-term responsibilities of child-rearing. Teens and preteens must be made aware that sexual activity is filled with emotional, physical, and social consequences, that raising a baby is very, very difficult and confining for an unprepared, immature child-mother; that it takes a father as well as a mother to rear a child; and that ill-treating that child, or any other, is a crime, even though they themselves might have been reared with a belt buckle. Such basic lessons in life can be started in elementary school or even earlier. Preschool toddlers know very well what their homes are like and what makes them hurt.

My ideal curriculum would include these topics, at age-appropriate levels:

- Self-esteem and coping skills

- Human biology

- Responsibilities and rewards of family life

- The how-to of proper parenting

- Teenage pregnancy

- The dead-end of drug and alcohol abuse

- The whats and whys of child abuse

- The unacceptability of all forms of violence

Some educators think all this is beyond them. I think not.

Several years ago, five Kentucky teachers designed a model course for high school students in one of these subjects, called "The Prevention of Family Violence." The project, headed by Eva May Lloyd, a home economics teacher at Ballard High School in Louisville, was begun at the request of Martha Layne Collins, governor of Kentucky at the time and herself a former teacher of home economics.

Mrs. Lloyd initiated the four-week course in conjunction with her home economics class, 40 percent of whose members were boys. According to her, home economics these days is a lot more than "stitching and stewing." The emphasis today, she says, is on gaining life skills, and on social problems like unemployment, teenage pregnancy, and family violence.

The violence-prevention curriculum covers physical, emotional, and sexual child abuse; missing and exploited children; date rape; and abusive treatment of the elderly. Now taught statewide, the course is a graduation requirement for Kentucky high school students, and several other states have adapted it for use in their public schools. Its teachers report positive results. Students who are in abusive situations at home have been moved to seek help from teachers and other sources, and the feeling is that the course has great potential for reducing all types of abuse in the future.

A different tack is taken at the Henry Eggers Middle School of

Hammond, Indiana. As part of its regular educational curriculum, Eggers has a program called the "3 C's"—Coping, Caring, and Communicating. Its purpose is to help students through the difficult transition years of adolescence by addressing problem issues such as sibling rivalry, teenage pregnancy, teen suicide, and drug and alcohol abuse. In line with this purpose, and aware that continuity is not always to be found in the home, Eggers has gone beyond the concept of the standard class year and created small learning communities in each of which students are taught for three years by an unchanging team of teachers. The teachers thus become familiar, trusted adults in the child's life—virtually an extension of the family.

This kind of approach, positive though it may be, is insufficient in schools that have to deal with an entire range of ages and problems. These schools need massive doses of outside help to mobilize the personal resources of teachers, parents, and children. Such help is often at hand in the form of a variety of nonprofit programs that can function in any community. One such is EPIC—Effective Parenting Information for Children—an organization based in the State University College at Buffalo, New York, but willing to travel anywhere.

EPIC, funded by state agencies, county youth boards, and private foundations, is a sort of package program that can be brought into any school or school district whose educators and community leaders want to support it. Parent participation is fundamental. EPIC's philosophy is rooted in the proposition that destructive juvenile behavior and adult maltreatment of children are both primarily due to lack of effective—or any—parenting education. Thus, one component of its program prepares children of all ages to be responsible adults with positive parenting skills. Another gives workshops in parenting for parents of children in two different age groups. Parents of young children come to grips with such topics as fostering self-esteem, single parenting, communicating with teachers, and coping with daily conflicts and family crises; parents of adolescents tackle such issues as teenage values, adolescent suicide, identity and independence, emerging sexuality, and teen pregnancy.

Another project with a somewhat cumbersome name—Parents and School Partnerships for the Prevention of Child Abuse and Neglect—is the product of a collaboration between Bronx Community School District Ten and the Family Life Development Center of Cornell University in New York City. Much like EPIC in concept, the District Ten program unites parents, schools, and community agencies in an antiabuse campaign with a dual thrust—to involve parents in prevention efforts through free workshops that make parenting easier and more fun, and to help at-risk and abused youngsters grow into healthy, caring adults with positive parenting skills.

There are several things about the District Ten model that, in my view, go beyond the purely educational everybody's-here-to-learn approach to grasp the nitty-gritty: the parent hotline for families seeking immediate help and information on problems related to parenting; the Safe Place in schools, where parents can go for respite from crisis; school-based support groups that provide a warm and supportive environment in which parents can ventilate their problems and explore options for dealing with them; special parent-teacher meetings in which the participants let down their hair as far as it will go and tell each other how they endured physical, mental, and sexual abuse as children, and how, at last, they are learning how to stop abusing their own kids.

I have heard these parents and teachers comparing notes and I have seen their tears. They tell each other what they cannot bring themselves to tell their children—that they were abused by their own parents. They say, "I know I hurt my kid. I hate myself." They say, "Who hurts the child? Who is it who ever hurts the child? The *parent* hurts the child." They say, "My kid does bad things in school because I do bad things to him at home. But I can't talk even now about the things that were done to me." And eventually they do talk about them, saying, "What we never want to do is the bad things done to us." "I look at my kid's face and I say to myself, Did I do that, Did *I* do that? God help me if I ever, ever do that again."

The group therapy approach isn't right for everybody, moving though it may be. But it is my feeling that a parenting program of this type, whether devised by a parent-teacher cooperative effort or by an organization such as EPIC, should be in place in every single school in the nation.

But that situation will be a long time in coming. Meanwhile, the main sufferers are the kids of the underclass. Over 45 percent of American children between the ages of three and five are enrolled in preschool programs. Children in this age group are among the most vulnerable to physical attack and neglect. A teaching staff that comes into day-to-day contact with them serves as an important detection system. Early intervention and reporting may be a lifeline for some kids, but it doesn't exist for children who do not attend preschools.

There is, however, a possible solution.

Educators know that when children of poor families start school they lag behind their more fortunate classmates and seldom, if ever, catch up. About a decade ago the Missouri school system launched an early-intervention project called PAT, or Parents as Teachers, in an attempt to forestall that problem. Specially trained teachers started going into homes every six weeks to recommend games and toys that would stimulate learning and, in effect, brief parents about what to expect at each stage of their preschooler's development. The program proved to be so effective in preparing children for school that Missouri's education department set up a national PAT center in St. Louis to help other school systems develop similar home-training programs.

The program is admirable in itself. But why not use it also to help spot abuse in the home? Surely all the responsibilities of teachers in schools carry over to those who work off-premises.

When the school as an institution starts bursting the bonds of conventional education, it becomes a very potent force. One dynamic person can make a change—one principal who says, "We have a problem, we are going to do something about it, and this is what we're going to do." But that one person doesn't have to do it all alone. There are immense and virtually untapped community resources available, not the least of which are parents—all of whom have strengths as well as weaknesses. An energetic parent-teacher partnership is a powerful combination.

But, teachers say, the parents don't even want to come to school! My answer is, yes, they do, if there is something there for them. They come when there are programs giving them information and support. They come when they have a share in deciding what's best for their kids. They come when they feel that their presence matters, when they realize that the people at their kids' school care for *them*.

Teacher power plus parent power adds up to a tremendous force—a force that can prevent child abuse.

9 | A Medical Prescription: Treating Child Abuse

A six-month-old child was brought in, crying his heart out. There were black-and-blue marks on his body and our initial examination indicated hemorrhages of the brain. The parents' attitude was a curious if familiar mixture: truculence, fear, denial, shame. They said they had hit him a little bit, but not hard, because his nonstop crying had driven them nuts. What we had here, it seemed likely, was a classic case of child abuse.

We did a spinal tap and found the baby had meningitis. He had been crying because he had an infection and a fever and was feeling miserably ill. We started him on antibiotics right away, but it was too late. When he died, as he soon did, it was not because of the abuse but because of medical neglect. Instead of bringing him into the hospital while there was still a chance, the parents had let him become fatally ill. Why, we wondered. Was it because they felt guilty about hitting him? Or had they really not known that he was terribly sick? For whatever reason, they had been unable or unwilling to take care of their baby. I believe they simply didn't know how to care for a sick child.

Cases like this are one reason why many child advocates today focus on the prevention of child abuse and neglect rather than waiting for abuse to occur and treating the victim after it has begun. And this, of course, is where physicians and hospitals come in, because we in the medical professions are usually the first people to see the mothers and the fathers and their newborns. And in fact it is only fitting that physicians should always be in the front line of the battle, because physicians were the first to devise a means of fighting back against the enemy.

A quarter of a century ago, Dr. C. Henry Kempe, who coined the term "battered child syndrome," conceived the first defense of children as a hospital-based child protection team, a working model of which he developed at the University of Colorado School of Medicine in the late 1960s and continued at the Denver Center for the Prevention of Child Abuse and Neglect in the early '70s. Revolutionary for its time, Kempe's pioneering program employed both hospital personnel and lay people from the community.

The professional part of Kempe's team consisted of four pediatricians, four part-time psychiatrists, two social workers, a representative of the welfare department, a public health nurse, and a special coordinator. These were the hospital-based diagnosticians and treatment planners. Backing them up were the lay therapists, or parent aides, mature individuals who had experienced affectionate parenting in their own childhood and grown up to be successful parents themselves. These people were the home visitors, men and women both, who gave their clients virtually minute-to-minute mothering over a period of eight to nine months. They provided emotional support and hands-on help, a listening ear, and a night-and-day personal telephone hotline service for moments of extraordinary stress or crisis.

There were three other important elements of the Denver program. One was its close link with Families Anonymous, the support group of admittedly abusive parents who met once or twice a week to help each other wrestle with their demons. A second was the crisis nursery, a place of safety open at any and all times to a child in need of a haven during a time of family crisis. The third was the day care center where overwhelmed mothers could bring their children for mutual respite and share their feelings with others whose concerns were reassuringly similar.

Kempe's program was a landmark operation, notable particularly for its multidisciplinary approach—the combination of pediatricians, social workers, psychiatrists, paraprofessional surrogate parents, and the other lay people—*and* for its outreach into the family homes. I believe that time will prove the success of both the team approach and the home visiting program, which Kempe saw as the forerunner of a nationwide corps of "health visitors" who would go into every home for some time after the birth of a new baby to make sure that the whole family is thriving.

The treatment by team made a great deal of sense to me, though it was obvious that it could only work if members of the various disciplines were to be persuaded that it would. In New York at that time, the Mayor's Task Force was attempting to interest mental health practitioners in working with abused children and abusive parents with the purpose of getting their input and developing mental health programs for abusers. To my astonishment, we encountered enormous resistance: psychiatrists and psychologists outdid each other in their scurry to get away from the very idea of becoming involved with abusive parents. We had thought they might feel it worthwhile to study the psychodynamics of child abuse and become a part of the solution, but their phenomenal unwillingness to have anything to do with a child abuse program suggested that they were ill-equipped to come to grips with the problem. Perhaps they were too judgmental and disgusted with the very idea of child abuse to have anything to do with it. Perhaps they lacked the conceptual tools or the technology to work with abusive parents and feared treatment failures. Or perhaps they simply didn't care.

But now maybe mental health professionals would see the value of their involvement. Certainly, to me, the Denver program was an inspiration. Mental health professionals could be effectively involved, as could sympathetic but practical nonprofessionals. Kempe had successfully demonstrated the power of the team effort. He showed us all something that we have learned again and again since then: child abuse is not just one person's turf. It is not a syndrome that falls readily into any single category or discipline. Only a group of people working together and sharing information from different perspectives can approach it effectively and lend each individual's particular expertise to a totality of successful diagnosis and treatment.

Maybe some day, I thought, Kempe's model—reluctant mental health professionals included—could be replicated in every major medical facility throughout the nation. Or maybe somebody would come up with something even better.

*   *   *

In a recent year a study of child fatalities showed that 75 percent of the children who died from abuse or neglect had been born in fairly highly regarded and sophisticated hospitals. This leads us to ask: Was there nothing about the mother's attitude during her hospital stay that led to concern for the baby? What observations were made, what records were kept, what follow-up arrangements were pursued? Putting aside for the moment those cases that should have been reported to the Central Registry but were not, let us look at a few instances in which a hospital has let a child slip through its fingers, either through poor record-keeping or the discharge of newborn babies into dangerous home situations. This is hospital neglect:

• A hospital admits a three-month-old baby with fever and diarrhea. He is treated routinely and discharged to his mother a week later, a move the hospital staff might not have made if the baby's birth record *from the same hospital* had been available to them. That record showed that the mother was a homeless, mentally retarded seventeen-year-old with emotional problems; she could not possibly have cared for a child and should not have been permitted to leave the hospital with him in the first place. Not surprisingly, the next event in the child's brief history was its death.

• A premature baby is discharged in care of a teenage mother who already has two other children living in a neglectful home situation. The mother has had a recent psychiatric hospitalization but has been receiving no follow-up care. After the new baby dies it is learned that, in the dead of winter, the apartment has no heat or light and has thus been a hazard in itself. Should the hospital be faulted? Yes. A hospital, of all institutions, should make a profile of the mother and her family a standard part of the case history, and should be extremely careful about releasing newborns. This is an obligation that has nothing to do with a legal or moral mandate: It is based simply on good medical judgment.

• A hospital had treated three out of five children in one family for serious physical abuse inflicted by the stepfather while he was out on bail awaiting trial for the murder of a fourth. This information was part of the case records, revealing that what was being dealt with here was a severely dysfunctional family. The mother then delivers her sixth child at home. Both mother and child are brought to the hospital, admitted, and sent home for "routine" follow-up. But there is nothing routine about this case or this family's needs; the situation cries out for a referral to home health services.

• A severely starved newborn baby rapidly gains weight in the hospital on several occasions and fails to thrive when it is sent home. The hospital is trying to arrange psychiatric care for the mother and has requested home care visits, which is all fine and good. However, the referral mailed by hospital authorities to the visiting nurse for her information notes only that the "baby is an excellent feeder. . . . Mother needs to be taught how to burp." This is incredible. If a baby feeds well and thrives in the hospital yet almost dies every time it goes home, there is obviously something more serious at issue than the mother's inability to burp the baby.

• The hospital readmits a recently released three-week-old baby who has been seriously misfed by the mother. The baby is treated and sent home as a matter of course, although the hospital knows that the mother's male companion has recently murdered another child in the family. The referral to the nursing service on discharge advises merely that the mother is "an emotionally dependent woman [who] needs supervision in amounts of feeding and burping."

• Here is yet another tragic case that must be partly ascribed to hospital neglect. It involves the death of an infant from what the medical examiner described as low birth weight, or failure to thrive. The child and his twin had been born prematurely, somewhere other than the hospital. The mother had received no prenatal care and was seen for the first time when she and the twins came in following delivery. Yet the hospital apparently did not consider these babies to be at risk. No report was made to the State Central Registry, nor did the hospital arrange for social service intervention, nor was any post-discharge social or medical treatment plan formulated for the children. Mother and babies simply went home. Two and a half months later the police, responding to a call, found the twins alone in the mother's residence, at which time they were returned to the hospital for examination. Again they were discharged without a report to the SCR, although it seems highly likely that they showed signs of failure to thrive. When the one twin died two weeks after this second hospital visit—that is, at three months old—it weighed just seven pounds. One wonders: Was there no record of the first visit? Of the premature birth outside the hospital? No sense of the need for referral? No recognition of the child protective issues involved?

Medical examiners and coroners make mistakes, too, and although a misdiagnosis during a postmortem is obviously no longer critical in the salvation of that child, it does cast a cold light on medical misjudgments overall and makes one wonder how some medical professionals go about weighing evidence in front of them. For instance: a fifteen-month-old girl dies at a baby-sitter's home. The M.E.'s cause of death: Sudden Infant Death Syndrome (SIDS). After a jury inquest the cause of death was changed to "undetermined." The body had shown twenty-two human bite marks in different stages of healing—not in themselves a cause of death, but enough to make the trained observer suspect that this was something other than a SIDS death at the advanced age of fifteen months.

In another case, an eleven-month-old girl child was found to have died of SIDS although the body showed three bite marks. Two years before, a sibling had died at the same age and also, supposedly, of SIDS. This might have been the final judgment had not the mother confessed to suffocating both infants.

When a three-week-old baby girl was found dead in her crib, the coroner gave the cause of death as skull fracture due to accident. The little body had presented with not only the skull fracture but a healing spiral fracture of the tibia, fractures to each ankle, and bruises on the face. The mother had an explanation for each injury, and the coroner felt that the parent could not be intentionally responsible. But she had been. She made a full confession at a jury inquest.

Wrongful accusations are sometimes made because of faulty diagnosis. A two-and-a-half-year-old girl dies of a skull fracture due to blunt force trauma and the M.E. calls it homicide. However, a follow-up investigation supports the parents' story that the child, while playing, had dislodged a television set from a rickety table and brought it crashing down upon herself. Conclusion, after a period of unnecessary torment: accidental death.

These tragic vignettes do more than merely point the finger at careless diagnosticians: they demonstrate very real diagnostic problems that in fact do not always have solutions. The suffocation of a child is hard to distinguish from SIDS, especially when we are looking at a crack baby. We examine the child and there is nothing wrong with it, except that it is dead. Is this SIDS, accidental suffocation, or child murder? We can't tell. We look at a dead newborn and a mother who is depressed: which is the cause and which is the effect? We see a child who has died or is in critical condition because of some freakish accident, like a television set falling on its head. Kids of all ages manage to get themselves into bizarre situations that often result in terrible trauma and even death. But which presenting stories do we believe? How many accidental deaths are truly accidental? How many kids who are said to fall out of cribs or windows actually do fall out of cribs or windows? How many scaldings are accidental, and how many are deliberate?

Child fatality reviews, conducted in all major cities every year, confront this kind of problem all the time. Many childhood deaths are found to have been apparently unavoidable accidents. One recent review, for example, concluded that the following deaths, among others, were the result of tragic mishaps. Three children die in separate apartment fires; one infant is fatally injured when a two-year-old sibling pushes its crib into a wall; a toddler dies after pulling over a table and being struck on the head; a child suffocates while sleeping with its mother; another freezes to death while sleeping in an apartment that is not too cold for the adults in the household but is too cold for an infant. In each case we deplore the tragedy for the family, but wonder if the deaths might not have been prevented by more alert or experienced parents exercising better judgment in the care of their children.

And for all our new sensitivity and technology, we still can't be sure. Accidental trauma is common enough in children to make us be wary of making unwarranted accusations; yet abuse also is common enough that we can't brush suspicions aside without considering the possible danger to other children in the family. All too often, hospital personnel are simply not sufficiently aware of the child protective issues that may be involved in a matter of an injured child, and unless there are administrative policies and procedures in place, there may be a lack of coordination between one department and another *and* between the hospital and the child protective service.

In a run-of-the-mill case that might be replicated any day in any hospital anywhere, a family with a number of children brought one child in for hospitalization with a broken arm. The admitting physician contested the family's explanation of the injury and actually made a report to the State Central Registry, but the hospital discharged the child to the family before there was any response from the child protective agency. Then, when the agency made contact with the family, it simply referred the parents to a contracted agency for counseling and preventive services, and closed the case. There was no follow-up contact by the hospital. Two months later the child was brought back to the hospital with suspicious bruises. This time the hospital administration called in a report. The protective agency obtained a remand of the child, who was placed in foster care, and reopened the case in terms of monitoring the rest of the children.

This was a satisfactory conclusion, but let there be no mistake: there was also some luck involved. Neither the hospital nor the child protective agency had responded satisfactorily to the first incident, which effectively contributed to the child's reinjury. The lucky part was that the new injury could have been much worse; it could have led to permanent damage or even death.

The vastness of major modern medical centers demands an interdepartmental coordination that does not always exist. Children come in with hundreds of different ailments and injuries—respiratory and abdominal problems, heart defects and malfunctioning livers, meningitis and ear infections, tumors, abrasions, dislocations, fractures, burns, gashes, lacerations, internal ruptures—and they are treated by different departments, starting with obstetrics or the emergency room and going on up to pediatrics or the burn unit or orthopedics or surgery. On other visits they might go into yet other departments: pediatrics this month, orthopedics the next, surgery some other time. But unless medical records are made available and reviewed there is little or no coordination between these units, no way one physician or nurse can say, "What goes on here? This kid was in two months ago with burns—now he has three broken ribs!" And so the child slips down into the gap between departments.

Unfortunately, a slip between one department and another is the sort of thing that can happen in any busy city hospital—unless there is a mechanism in place to prevent it. That mechanism is a multidisciplinary team of trained medical and other professionals to scrutinize all cases in which maltreatment can reasonably be suspected. The makeup of this unit has to be flexible enough that a complete team is available at all times, and in general should consist of a pediatrician or other physician, a sex-abuse expert who is usually a gynecologist, a child psychologist, a social worker, a nursing supervisor, and a member of the administration staff. Groups like this, often called SCAN teams for "suspected child abuse and neglect," investigate reports made to them from within the hospital, usually from the emergency room or pediatrics department or burn unit, and from the outside by some other medical facility or the police. When a SCAN team is put into place it becomes, in time, a smoothly functioning consulting team that meets on a regular basis to discuss ongoing cases and forms a close working relationship with local law officers and family service agencies.

I would add that the hospital physician of today is well trained to pick up on most cues. Unless he or she is maniacally overworked or totally unsensitized to the concept of abuse and neglect, the medical practitioner *more often than not* is able to recognize abnormalities associated with child maltreatment. Until the mid-1980s it was legitimate for physicians to claim that their medical training in this area was insufficient or inadequate, but today there are enough training sessions, seminars, and conferences for even the least zealous of young physicians to become familiar with the many aspects of inhumanity to children. In addition, there are many books and pamphlets and clinical studies and illustrated case histories within easy reach of every single medical professional. There is no need for ignorance anymore, nor any excuse for it. Nor is there an excuse for not reporting suspected cases on the grounds of unfamiliarity with reporting procedures and requirements. Medical practitioners are required by law to report reasonable suspicions. They know it, *and they do know how.*

Among mandated reporters, hospital physicians—particularly in the emergency room—are the most likely to see early abuse cases and the most qualified to identify the symptoms. If they are in doubt, second opinions or guidance is near at hand. Procedural information is right at their fingertips. Hotline numbers are posted in emergency rooms. Instructional materials about indications of child maltreatment have inundated virtually every hospital in the country. What more can staff doctors need?

On the other hand, mental health and drug rehabilitation professionals, on staff or otherwise, are still too often outside the loop in terms of spotting child abuse or the potential for it. The psychiatrist or psychologist treating a mother or father who is paranoid, schizophrenic, or seriously depressed, or the counselor or therapist who is working with a parent's drug problem, seldom deals with the family unit as a whole. Does the client have a spouse? Are there children in the family? How are these children? Is the parent a good parent in spite of his or her illness or addiction? Is there any possibility that the children are being abused? Does the family need a support system? These questions have not surfaced often enough and have too seldom been pursued.

There is always a possibility of abuse or neglect when a parent is sick. Mental health and drug treatment experts have to recognize the fact that they cannot work in a vacuum: the individual must be treated in the context of the family unit, and an integral part of all rehabilitative programs must be the health and safety of the children. In fact, the mental health professionals can play a major role in setting up full-service counseling services and parenting programs for clients and their families, but to the best of my knowledge they have made no such move as yet, and certainly not in a hospital setting. Neighborhood clinics might well provide the best and most comfortable environment for the delivery of a family package of treatment and counseling.

In recent years, drug rehabilitation programs such as the "Anonymous" groups have recognized family and parenting responsibilities as an integral part of their treatment and have expanded their rehabilitative services to include the provision of human support services and parent education programs. In so doing, they have achieved a close collaboration with child protective services and community child abuse prevention programs—providing a signpost for mental health professionals to follow.

Inevitably, questions of privacy and confidentiality arise in the treatment of individuals with substance abuse or mental problems. A therapist suspecting the possibility of child abuse in a client family is in an awkward situation that calls for the exercise of every measure of his or her professional acumen. The situation must be carefully and honestly assessed. Is there, in the therapist's objective judgment, persuasive reason to believe that abuse is taking place? If a report is made, how can it be done with minimum damage to the doctor-patient relationship? Neither I nor anyone else can determine the therapist's best course of action in any particular situation, but the practitioner does not, in fact, have much latitude. The law requires that, if there is good cause to suspect that abuse is taking place, a report be made to the Central Registry. Professional judgment may also indicate that the abused child and indeed the whole family need the human support network available through the child protective services. It may be hard to persuade people that anything good could possibly come of a child abuse report, but in fact it can be a very positive, helpful action.

Private physicians—family doctors, general practitioners, and pediatricians—can be in an even more uncomfortable position with respect to possibly abusive clients, so much so that they can be considered part of the problem rather than any part of its solution. The medical profession as a whole originates a very small percentage of the abuse and neglect reports made to child protective services—and most of these come in from hospitals or clinics. Doctors in private practice are extremely reluctant to report their suspicions.

Many, perhaps even most, will say they have never seen a case of child abuse. My response is that they are simply not looking. Child abuse is far more common than many of the life-threatening pediatric problems, and the mortality many times higher than most. It is just as important to make a diagnosis of child abuse as to make a diagnosis of Wilm's tumor or any other cancer. In both cases, early diagnosis and management can be life-saving. But private physicians seldom think of child abuse as a disease; in fact, they don't want to think about it at all. For the most part they are middle-class individuals dealing with middle-class clients, and they prefer to believe that child maltreatment is a problem that affects only the underclass. It is much simpler to accept the story that a child keeps falling off his bicycle than to consider the proposition that he is being deliberately battered.

If doctors in private practice do suspect abuse, they may be confused as to where their responsibilities lie: their clients are not only the children but also the parents, who appear to be people in good standing and who may be peers or even friends. And of course they pay the bills. There is an element here of not wanting to blow the whistle on somebody who seems to be basically okay. In fairness, too, the private physician very often cannot emotionally accept what he suspects may be abuse. He must be wrong, he says to himself; it must be something else. At this point he may push the matter aside altogether in order to avoid confronting his own feelings, or he may decide that he will delay making a report until he is sure of his diagnosis.

Then again he may have some other ideas. One is cover-up: "I don't think it's necessary to report. I'll just put a cast on this kid's arm and send her home." Another is the personal touch: "I'm going to work with the family and solve this problem without any outside interference." And then there is: "I don't think the system works. There's no point in reporting because nothing ever happens. There's never any feedback." Or: "My patient goes around telling everybody I reported her for child abuse when she says she didn't do anything wrong. Now I'm losing patients and I also have to go to court and I don't have time for that."

Most doctors don't have much skill for it, either. They are not trained in courtroom techniques, and they very often get tied up in knots. They admit this readily—they are, after all, doctors and not lawyers—and their ineffectuality in court scenes is a major reason for their reluctance to get involved in a case that is likely to head for trial. Even physicians who are eager to testify are unprepared to deal with court procedures, defense attorneys, and the rigors of cross-examination, and do a poor job of presenting evidence. This is a common phenomenon, so widely recognized that in recent years there have been several texts and annual seminars for physicians on the subject of *how to testify*. I hope their instruction is good; I know it is necessary.

Some doctors are reluctant to report because they fear the retribution of an outraged parent, guilty or not. Most of all they fear—they say—being sued. But who among them is not aware that they are mandated reporters, legally obligated to report suspected child maltreatment? And that if they report in good faith, they have immunity from any liability, civil or criminal, that may result from such a report? I think this alleged fear of liability is a smokescreen for the more practical concerns that they might lose business and waste precious office hours in court without accomplishing anything for the child.

One of the most important things these physicians do not grasp is that they may have a lot more to lose by *not* reporting than by reporting a good-faith suspicion. If they fail to report an initial episode of child abuse and the child is permanently harmed after a second episode, they may indeed be sued—for malpractice. A California Supreme Court ruling of 1976 established the principle that a battered child, through an attorney, may ask a jury to award damages for a physician's negligence if further injury follows failure to report observed or suspected abuse. Such action may be brought by the parent not involved in the original abusive incident.

Fear of suit aside, there are a lot of physicians who, for one reason or another, don't want anything to do with the child protective system. To them I would say: "One, if you don't like the system and you don't report, all you are doing is hurting one person—your patient, the child. You are allowing that child to be further abused or neglected or possibly killed. And two, if you suspect abuse and you don't want to make the report yourself, then send that child to the pediatric emergency room of a hospital for a workup, and let the hospital's child protective team do the investigating and reporting."

In making such a referral, the private physician must be sure that the hospital of his choice has a SCAN team or a close equivalent that can provide effective management of abuse and neglect cases and cooperate closely with the child protective agency and family support services. In the absence of a child abuse team or a concerned on-the-spot physician, there is no guarantee that the child will be given the best possible protection or that the referring physician will ever receive any feedback.

This is a weak area in a basically strong system. How does the referring physician know what he is getting his young patient into? Is he simply going to pass the buck, send the kid to an ER, and forget about him? Or is there a real human being at the end of the line when the doctor makes his calls? Every hospital, not only those with SCAN teams, should have a round-the-clock child protective liaison, either a medical social worker on the hospital staff or an on-site representative of the local child protective agency, to deal with physicians' referrals and questions and maintain a full-time link between the medical and child protective services.

"Linkage" is the key word. For all our big-city SCAN teams, there can be no effective medical attack against child abuse and neglect without a link between private physicians, hospital personnel, child protective agencies, law enforcement personnel and family support systems in the community. A fully functioning process of cooperation and coordination is essential if health care professionals are to carry out their responsibilities in saving children's lives.

There is another weak area, and certainly a touchy one, that private physicians must come to terms with. It is something that medical schools must address much more energetically than they have in the past, something that pediatricians and child psychiatrists must be prepared to approach with a much greater degree of alertness and open-mindedness than most have shown to date. I am talking about the sexual abuse of children, an issue that has leapt to the headlines in recent years and been the subject of a flood of books and articles but has not been greatly illuminated by health care professionals.

I think we are letting it become too much of a doctor's dilemma. It is not the function of an examining physician to debate the proposition that sexual abuse allegations are the product of children's fantasies, nor to be swayed by accusations made by suing spouses in custody cases. It is his or her function to examine the physical evidence, ask pertinent questions, take case notes, make a diagnosis, call for consultation if necessary, and, finally, to make a report. But—does the examining physician actually go through this procedure? Only if he or she thinks of it. Even in this day and age, many physicians cannot come to terms with the fact that adults—parents, teachers, day care operators, staff members of residential facilities, guardians of all kinds—sexually abuse teenagers, preadolescents, toddlers, and even babies. It is incomprehensible and unacceptable.

But it happens.

And certainly in the case of preschoolers and infants it is not a condition that is likely to be made known to an examining physician by the victim, nor is it usually something that leaps readily to the eye. It is easy to account for redness and rashes around the genitals by diagnosing diaper rash, or allergy to bubble bath or soap. Pediatricians do this all the time, without thinking. It doesn't occur to them that molestation might have occurred—and if they do not consider the possibility they are not going to recognize the condition and they are certainly not going to order any lab tests. I contend that they don't know what they are looking at because they don't want to know.

The chief prosecutor in the McMartin Preschool case understood this, as one of the sideshows accompanying the case made clear. In a November 1986 broadcast of *60 Minutes*, Mike Wallace asked prosecutor Lael Rubin how it was that none of the children who had allegedly been abused at the school over a long period of time had been diagnosed as molested by any examining pediatrician. Ms. Rubin's reply: "Do you really think that there were doctors—pediatricians—out there who, two, three, five years ago, were really trained to examine young children in their genital areas? Many of the doctors suggested other alternatives or other reasons for [abdominal or vaginal] pain, discomfort, urinary infections, vaginitis, all sorts of other problems. . . . What I'm saying is that not only they but parents and a lot of other people in this case were not willing to believe and accept that, in fact, children were being molested."

The fact that so many family physicians are resistant to acknowledging the possibility that their respectable adult clients might molest their children suggests to me the following: that physicians should educate themselves in the recognition of *all* child abuse signs and symptoms, especially including the child sexual abuse diagnostic indicators. That every community should have a hospital with a child abuse team. That there must be a fully trained and experienced sex abuse expert on every such team, and a child psychologist experienced in sexual abuse cases. That *all* private physicians and other persons suspecting molestation of a child refer that child for examination to the hospital team, which by its very nature must be deliberative and objective in its findings.

One such investigation is surely enough. To subject a child to repeated interrogation by batteries of experts hired by legal persons bent on proving one point or another is to abuse the child further. And the hurt child needs no more abuse.

If teamwork is one answer to identifying and healing the traumas of child abuse and reeducating abusers, it is also an important part of a major strategy in the war against child abuse—the preemptive strike. What we have accomplished by the multidisciplinary treatment approach is to demonstrate that a group of people, each of whom brings specialized knowledge to an investigation, can effect change. We can go further.

We can switch our focus to prevention. I believe this is something that medical professionals can do better than anyone, *if* they have the will and if they have community or state support.

We ask ourselves: Where do preventive efforts begin? With fighting all the evils of our society, yes, and giving our kids the educational tools to continue the fight; but when it comes down to the nitty-gritty of what we are going to do to prevent the abuse of individual children in our own neighborhoods, we must be sure that help is at hand when the babies are born and before they are born.

The hospital setting offers the single best opportunity to teach parents about baby care, give them advice on how to manage life with an infant, and refer them to follow-up community parenting services. And parenting skills are still the single best prevention against abuse and neglect.

New York State has recently instituted a program called the Pre- and Post-natal Parent Education Hospital Program, or PPPEHP, which is a statewide effort to reach every family expecting or caring for a newborn baby. My instinct is that we need a catchier handle than PPPEHP, but the concept is an excellent one. PPPEHP is a team approach to parent education and self-help that uses hospital-based health and human services professionals to teach parents about basic baby care, offer instruction on the many adjustments required to manage life as a new parent, and refer families to community-based parenting programs.

For many years it has been the goal of most child advocates to enable every young mother in this country to receive not only adequate pre- and postnatal care but a complete program of parenting education and support. *All* new parents, not only those considered at risk, lack parenting skills. Some lack role models; many lack support systems; most lack information; too many lack good medical care for themselves and their babies before and after birth. If we can reach them at this critical point of their lives, we can do a lot to reduce infant mortality as well as abuse and neglect. Maybe we can even make the American family a happier place to be. But to do this effectively, we must have some version of national health care, with particular reference to mothers and neonates.

Experience has taught us that there will be no earthshaking action by the White House or the Congress to bring about so basic yet sweeping a health care measure, but some measure of political clout must be involved if there is to be any uniformity of purpose, planning, and delivery. We had that involvement in the case of our new hospital parenting plan: the PPPEHP was initiated and launched by the New York State Citizens Task Force on Child Abuse and Neglect under the joint leadership of First Lady Matilda Cuomo and State Commissioner of Social Services Cesar Perales.

The program is designed to promote hospital participation in the delivery of parent education and support services and forge partnerships between hospitals and community-based programs for parents. I believe it should be a model for other hospital systems throughout the country.

The program has three components: prenatal, delivery, and postnatal. All parents and quasi-parents are the targets of the program, including fathers who may or may not be husbands and various closely involved individuals described in the PPPEHP literature as "other supportive caretakers."

The first phase of the program is an attempt to reach expectant parents with information about the vital importance of seeking good prenatal care early in pregnancy. To this end, the New York State Department of Health is distributing thousands of copies of a handbook called *Having a Baby: A Family Guide to Pregnancy* to hospitals and health educators as well as to prenatal and other health clinics across the state. The booklet, which is attractive and easy to read without being condescending, tells the mother everything she needs to know about choosing a health care provider and keeping herself healthy during pregnancy. Our experience in the past has been that the women who most need information and care are the last to seek it. This may be because they are uninformed and thoughtless young people, or because they are on drugs and don't want to call attention to themselves, or because they find hospitals forbidding places. To make the program succeed in its initial and most critical stage, we have to make every effort to develop innovative programs to bring in the reluctant mothers. In some circumstances this can best be done through community neighborhood clinics, which are far less alarming than hospitals.

We already have some community clinics for pediatrics and some for general care. Why not special prenatal clinics? Why not little neighborhood medical centers that include a prenatal clinic? Even then, we will have to make a special effort to encourage immature young mothers to come in and at least look at the literature—or the videos—and talk to a doctor, but this can be done by offering incentives and making the neighborhood medical center a more pleasant place. Whether this involves free coffee and lollipops or a weekly lottery with cash prizes does not really matter; what does matter is finding out which inducements are likely to work in a particular neighborhood and using them to lure shy mothers into the prenatal clinic. It is pathetic that we have to do this, but this is one of the areas in which our national non-system lets us down. Unlike many other countries, we do not have a family allowance system that offers financial incentives to encourage the use of pre-natal and postnatal services. But more of that later.

Meanwhile, within our present limits, more important than any-thing is the need to make absolutely clear to the entire community that there is no stigma attached to coming in for pre-baby care. The local media can help. Word must get around the neighborhood that every mother-to-be, whatever her personal fears and failings and social status, will be welcomed—not with pointing fingers but with open arms. This is not to say that any mother on drugs or alcohol will not receive special attention and advice, because she most certainly will, but everything that is done is carefully geared toward the needs of the mother as well as the unborn baby. Her clinic records will go with her to the affiliated hospital where she is to deliver the child.

The second phase of the PPPEHP program has to do with the critical time frame immediately surrounding the birth of the child. The mother enters the hospital and has her final prenatal examina-tion and initial meetings with her care team, consisting of a pedia-trician, primary care nurse, obstetrician or nurse-midwife, social worker or psychologist, and a nutritionist. During the predelivery time she is closely but discreetly scrutinized for any problems she might have—drugs, alcohol, depression, anxiety, a sense of being alone or abandoned, doubts about her readiness for motherhood, ambivalence about the baby, and all the multiple worries that might afflict a young mother-to-be.

During the delivery and immediate postdelivery period the team continues to observe her for telltale clues about her feelings toward the baby. Does she act bored, depressed, upset? Is she interested, is she happy, does she ask whether it's a boy or a girl, does she want to see and hold the baby? Is the baby's father at the hospital, and is he loving and attentive? Do parents and other older persons visit?

Some of these and other observations may seem beyond the scope of hospital personnel and possibly even intrusive. But if there are no off-key notes, the observations go no further; and if indications are that the mother needs more than ordinary services, these will become part of her follow-up plan.

The third part of the program is the postnatal phase. A member of the hospital team gives each mother an illustrated handbook called *Welcome to Parenthood: A Family Guide,* and reviews it with her to make sure she realizes it is not just another social services throwaway but a genuinely practical manual of information for moms and dads, dealing not only with the care and feeding of children but also with more troublesome topics such as postpartum depression and sibling rivalry. The booklet is designed with pockets on the inside covers to make it possible for each mother to compile listings of all support services and parent helplines available in her community.

Now the mother goes home, back into the community. When she leaves she takes with her a sort of prescription she can present to whatever clinic or other support system she may need—perhaps a more comprehensive parenting program, a crisis nursery, a day care center, or a drug rehabilitation program for some member of her family.

At this point we start treading on theoretical grounds. We do not yet have all systems in place to round out this program. We hope to develop a program of home visitors, such as New York City and Boston had almost one hundred years ago when public health nurses routinely visited new mothers and newborns. Costs being what they are, I suppose we will never have enough public health nurses to go around, but we can and we will train home health visitors.

The idea is that the home visitor goes into the young mother's home on a regular basis and asks how she is doing, casting an alert eye around the household to judge the situation for herself. Is the mother okay? Is she depressed? Has she enough money? Does she have any problems with housing? Is everything all right with the baby? Is the husband still working at his nice job? Is there anything at all she needs help with? Often what is needed is no more than a listening ear and a little homely advice. The visitor is a surrogate mother, available at all times by telephone and ready to offer emotional support in times of crisis or just plain loneliness. If there is any indication of medical, social, or psychological needs, the home visitor helps the mother gain access to a whole range of community services.

It is to be hoped that in the near future every community in the United States will have its own home visitor program and its own drop-in family medical center, one that serves all health functions from routine checkups to drug rehabilitation, and maintains a close liaison with the local child protective agency. Already I see a gradual—too gradual, but real—change in health delivery services from the monolithic hospitals of the past to neighborhood clinics that offer one-stop shopping for everyone. And I believe it is inevitable that Americans will sooner or later catch up with the comprehensive health care systems offered by other countries.

Perhaps when that day comes we will save the babies before they are brought into the emergency room with a deadly combination of illness and abuse.

10 / We Entrust to You This Child

December 1988. Father, we entrust to you this child whom you loved so well in life. Violence has caused her death. We are not all guilty, but we are all responsible. Children do not belong just to their parents. They belong to all society. To their neighborhoods. To their schools. And to the church. It is our responsibility.

—A parish priest

In our society, a major share of the responsibility for children at risk rests with our child protective agencies. When the family fails, we entrust our children to them.

The child whose death prompted the preceding prayer was Jessica Cortez. She had been found near death on the floor of a Brooklyn apartment after a neighbor, hearing screams, had summoned the housing police. The little girl was a pulp, a small raw body with a broken arm, cigarette burns, an open gash on her lip, bruises from top to toe, a possible skull fracture, angry welts on her buttocks, and a broken neck. All this savagery had not been the impulsive work of moments or even days; it had been systematic. The mother, Abigail Cortez, and her live-in companion, Adrian Lopez, were both charged with murder. Lopez, it appeared, had been the active abuser; Cortez the one who displayed "depraved indifference" for failing to protect her.

Same old story.

But it wasn't, quite.

The next day, Jessica's badly beaten half-brother Nicholas was found in a closet, and a day later Jessica's relatives on her natural father's side—the natural father being in jail at that time—expressed outrage not only at Abigail Cortez and Adrian Lopez but at child welfare officials, who, they said, had known for at least six years that Mrs. Cortez had abused her other children savagely and had ignored pleas by the paternal grandmother, who feared for the little girl's life, to take custody of Jessica.

Child welfare officials gave their accustomed response and denied practically everything. They had had limited contact with the Cortez-Lopez family, they claimed, and although they were perhaps not totally blameless, they felt that records would show that by and large they had acted appropriately. However, this is not what the records show. The records show that the people to whom we entrust our at-risk children, the people in the agency charged with the task of preventing abuse and keeping track of nonparenting parents, failed to fulfill their directives.

Child protection workers actually visited the Cortez home at least a dozen times during a five-year period and conducted a number of investigations. Their task was complicated by the fact that they could not always locate the woman, who sometimes called herself Abigail, sometimes Carmen, Alvarez, but nonetheless their involvement was more than sufficient to show them a disaster in the making. Indeed, for a time they made a commendable number of visits, considering their heavy caseload.

The first contact was made in March 1983, when an allegation of abuse and neglect was filed with the New York State Central Registry. The report alleged that one of Abigail Alvarez's children, Papo, was being maltreated by a parent or parent surrogate. A caseworker visiting the home four days later—and a lot can happen in four days—found the mother and a perfectly healthy, uninjured child in an "orderly" home. Two follow-up visits found no one in, but on April 13 a second neglect report was filed when Papo was admitted to hospital in an emaciated condition with bruises on his arms and legs and a broken rib.

Is this mere *neglect?* Call it what you may, a neglect petition was filed. Abigail failed to show up for repeated appointments with the caseworker and generally made herself unavailable. Papo came under city supervision and was placed in foster care, ultimately to be retrieved by relatives. It was learned that when the first caseworker had gone to the Alvarez home in March, after the initial report, the uninjured child seen in the well-ordered home was not Papo but another son, Nicholas. Papo had apparently been hidden.

With Papo out of the picture, Nicholas and his mother dropped out of sight for several months. When they reappeared, a family court judge placed the boy under agency supervision for a period of eighteen months but allowed him to remain with his mother subject to caseworker visits. I don't know if anybody noticed at the time that Abigail was extremely pregnant.

That was November 1983. In December, Abigail gave birth to Jessica. Three months later she married the father, Carlos Cortez, who was suspected by neighbors of having been the abuser of Papo. During 1984 and 1985 the agency made some eight to ten home visits to monitor the family. On all occasions the mother was found to be providing a proper home for Jessica and Nicky.

Somewhere along the line there was a rift between Abigail and Carlos, possibly having something to do with frequent visits by a man named Adrian Lopez. In August 1986 Carlos was obliged to absent himself from home because of an arrest for drug possession, which resulted in a brief stay in jail.

In September there were two separate investigations of the family. One, it appears, was initiated by Carlos Cortez, who had come home from jail to find—he said—his daughter alone in an apartment billowing with smoke because of an unattended iron. He took the child to his mother, who discovered cigarette-like burns on Jessica's back, hands, and legs. These were reported to a caseworker and allegedly seen by her. This individual put in a report that focused on neglect, not abuse. The second investigation, touched off by the same incident, was ordered by the court in connection with a custody battle over Jessica. Two caseworkers were working independently on the two separate inquiries to determine the truth of the neglect allegations; each was unaware of the other's efforts, presumably because one was checking on Abigail Alvarez and the other on Abigail Cortez.

In the event, Abigail retained custody. Caseworkers who had met with her had called her a good mother and described the home as a "warm and nurturing environment." No reference to the 1983 neglect charges were included in caseworkers' reports to the judge, never mind any suspicion of abuse.

Carlos, who would later be jailed in connection with two stabbing deaths unrelated to his family situation, faded out of the picture. Mr. Lopez, on probation after a purse-snatching, was now ensconced in the Cortez apartment. Abigail explained to caseworkers that he was a relative, there to protect the family.

Next scene: November 1987. School officials recorded persistent truancy by Nicholas and took steps to investigate. I can't find anyone who is completely clear about what happened here, but I gather that the school made a report of educational neglect to the State Central Registry and also referred the case to the Bureau of Attendance. The caseworker assigned by the latter office to investigate the complaint was told that the family had a history of neglect, but apparently failed to review the files or even locate the boy after supposedly vigorous attempts to reach the family in its "warm and nurturing environment." He then sent a mailgram to Mrs. Cortez warning of legal action if Nicky was not returned to school, but when there was no response he concluded the matter with "no resolution" notifications to school and public assistance officials.

In 1988 Nicholas was dropped from school rolls.

Was a law broken here? No, it was not. The investigator might not have been sufficiently zealous or adequately trained, but he was within his rights to base his judgment on such information as he was able—or unable—to obtain. There are no laws providing for open-ended investigation of school absenteeism.

Thus the truancy case was closed. And the walls closed in around Nicholas and Jessica, in spite of neighbors' complaints to housing and city police about the racket and filth and foul odor in the Cortez-Lopez apartment. The filth was seen by police, but, somehow, they never saw Abigail or Lopez or the children.

And so Jessica died and Nicholas survived in a closet, found almost by accident by police looking for physical evidence in Jessica's case. His mother and her lover had told police that the boy was in Puerto Rico. In fact, the boy in Puerto Rico was Papo.

When the storm broke, the city's social services boss made the usual noises about everybody being at fault. "I don't think we're blameless. I don't think the Family Court is blameless. I don't think the Board of Education is blameless," said William T. Grinker. But what blame was his agency willing to accept? Not much. After all, the agency had nothing on Alvarez-Cortez-Lopez but a neglect charge. No evidence of abuse had ever been found. "By and large, I believe we acted appropriately. We cannot predict in any given situation when tragedy will strike."

I, on the other hand, believe that in fact we have a pretty good idea what is likely to happen in a given situation when we have pulled all the pieces of the background together and taken a look at them—which is the job of the child protective agency.

For example, in September 1987 a woman named Marsha Foot

was charged with neglect after leaving her baby daughter in a Bronx crack den. Police discovered the discarded child when they raided the place on a drug warrant in connection with the arrest of a crack dealer. A Family Court judge allowed the woman to keep her daughter but ordered that the home be monitored by the child protective agency for one year and that the woman be periodically tested for drug use.

In January 1989 this woman was charged with the death of her son, Michael Anthony Baker, aged ten months. He had died in his crib after he and his two-year-old sister had been left in a closed bedroom with a heater turned on while the mother spent the night elsewhere with her boyfriend. The temperature in the room had risen to more than 110 degrees, suffocating the baby. It was then learned that, in spite of the court order, no one from the city agency had contacted the family since the previous April. Why not? Because, in a futile attempt to reduce the work load of over-burdened caseworkers, the city had transferred hundreds of cases—including the Foot case—from one busy unit to another, and the history of Ms. Foot's children ended up in one of many unattended files. And Michael ended up dead, a victim of double negligence: his mother's, and the city's.

In New York City, the Bureau of Child Welfare or Special Services for Children or whatever its name happens to be at any given time is one of the agencies of the mammoth Human Resources Administration. The HRA's function is to provide human services to the people of our city, which means that in addition to the more or less run-of-the-mill tasks of operating welfare and food stamp programs it must also wrestle with the cosmic issues of AIDS, homelessness, child abuse, and foster care. It has a massive budget of more than $5 billion a year and a work force of 32,000 employees serving about 1.5 million people. The child care caseworkers have the most thankless jobs of all. They are undertrained, underpaid, overworked, and largely unappreciated. Often they are obliged to work with massively dysfunctional families in which the parental figures are manipulative, demanding, and violent. If they can survive in the system for as long as a year and a half, that is a very long time—but often not long enough for them to see a case through to the end.

On the whole they are a sincere and dedicated group of people. But in any post-tragedy inquiry it is always discovered afresh that they have failed to investigate charges of abuse with sufficient thoroughness, to monitor troubled families adequately, to coordinate with other agencies, or to find suitable foster homes for children who must be taken away from dangerous parents.

The New York State investigation that followed the beating death of Jessica Cortez reviewed the city's handling of a sample 240 cases. The report observed that the failures in the Cortez case were not uncommon in the city's child protective system:

• In 57 percent of the cases reviewed, caseworkers had not looked up past records that might have triggered deeper concern about an immediate situation and precipitated some action.

• City caseworkers frequently did not pursue the most fundamental element of a case investigation: inspecting a child's home and meeting the parents or other individuals named in abuse allegations. In 27 percent of the cases, contact was not made with all the children and adults who were subjects of the abuse report; and in 10 percent of the cases, no worker *ever* visited the home.

• Another basic element of investigation is to make sure that all the unreported children in a household that has been reported as abusive or neglectful are accounted for and are not being maltreated. But the state report notes that in 33 percent of the cases reviewed, the worker made no attempt to do this.

• Although caseworkers investigating families reported for child abuse are expected to get in touch with relatives, school officials, neighbors, and other individuals who may have knowledge of the family, the report found that in 45 percent of the cases reviewed, this had not been done adequately.

• Caseworkers rarely saw families who were supposed to be monitored in accordance with court orders. In 70 percent of the cases, the families were not seen in what the investigators perceived as a "timely manner"; and in 85 percent of the cases a mandatory once-a-month visit with the at-risk child was not made. Even when Family Court judges ordered that troubled families were to receive counseling or other services, this did not happen in 45 percent of the cases reviewed.

• When cases were transferred from unit to unit, as in the Foot affair, a number of them had literally disappeared because their files had been lost. Many others had gone unassigned for an average of thirteen weeks. And at least one case was not assigned to a caseworker for forty-four weeks.

Is it any wonder that so many reports of abuse are airily dismissed as unfounded when they are not even investigated?

HRA's own annual fatality reviews present a sad and humbling picture of a system struggling under the burden of steadily increasing caseloads and employee burnout. Each year, a high percentage of the children who die from other than natural causes are from families whose histories of abuse or neglect were already known to HRA's child protective agency. By definition, these children were at risk. The following brief cases are a minuscule sampling of dozens that have never made the news:

A preschooler dies of internal injuries due to battered child syndrome. The stepfather is arrested and charged with homicide. The child had first come to the attention of the agency after sustaining a spiral leg fracture while in the care of his mother and stepfather, who had been found to be "caring and concerned."

Another child dies in an apartment fire after having been left by the mother with a caretaker who in turn left the child alone under unexplained circumstances. The family had first been reported three years earlier when a two-year-old had tested positive for venereal disease. It was determined that the child's father, now absent, was the likely perpetrator.

An infant apparently suffocates after rolling between a cot mattress and the wall. The mother is out, having left the child and a sibling under the care of the stepfather. The family had first been referred to the agency when a clinic doctor had reported that the stepfather and mother were, respectively, an alcoholic and heavy drug user, and that two younger children were neglected. Sporadic home visits found the children healthy, although the apartment was overcrowded and infested with vermin.

A child dies of what appears to be Sudden Infant Death Syndrome. The family had become known to the child protective agency some months before because the mother was overwhelmed and unable to deal with her other children. One child, not the deceased, was removed and placed first with a relative and then in foster care; the family was not adequately monitored thereafter.

It is true that child fatalities cannot be predicted. Families that we might consider at high risk of stepping over the line do, more often than not, manage with skilled help to weather life's storms and refrain from the ultimate act. But that line is sometimes very thin, and we must acknowledge that past behavior is the best predictor of future behavior. What has happened before in a family is likely to happen again, and to be worse the next time.

There is very little difference between abusive or neglectful families in which fatalities occur and those in which they do not occur. However, alert observers, maintaining contact with volatile families, can focus their attention on potentially explosive situations and forestall the explosions. Fatality cases in known at-risk families are horribly revealing of the worst fault in this overburdened system: nobody is keeping track.

What else happens is that cases are very often closed too soon, wrapping the perpetrators in a cocoon that provides safety for them but is potentially deadly for their children. As long as there is any suggestion of drug use or spouse abuse in the household, as long as there are any other kids on the premises even after the abused one has actually been removed, there is always danger that there will be another case of maltreatment—and the next one may be terminal, as we have seen.

Civil libertarians exercise themselves a great deal about family privacy. Should caseworkers continue monitoring after the obligatory twelve or eighteen months have passed? Does not the family have the right to assume that they can now live without anticipation of the stranger's knock on the door? Cannot their one little slip be forgiven and forgotten?

I don't think the answers to these questions are hard. A parent who has abused a child has forfeited, for a very long time, his or her right to privacy. Caseworkers *should* continue monitoring the household. They may forgive, but they should not forget. Furthermore, complaints of child abuse or neglect should not be brushed off as "unfounded" because the parents fail to cooperate and shut their doors against investigation, or expunged from the record because the allegations have not been proved. Many an unproven case has been founded in fact. Absolute proof—the smoking gun, the bloody fingerprint—is seldom easy to obtain, especially by hurried, inadequately trained caseworkers with a load of other cases and piles of paperwork to push around; nonetheless, the evidence is very often there. If a case is deemed unprovable or insufficiently substantiated in the subjective opinion of a caseworker, does that mean that it is necessarily "unfounded"? Absolutely not.

I think this issue has been well addressed by former Family Court Judge Nanette Dembitz, who in 1986 chaired the New York City Public Child Fatality Review Committee, which meets annually under the auspices of the Human Resources Administration to study and analyze all child abuse fatalities occurring in New York City. Judge Dembitz, a veteran in the child advocacy arena, brought the "unfounded" issue to the surface in a November 1987 letter to *The New York Times* in which she condemned as "a gross mistake in New York State's child-care procedure: the destruction of complaints of a child's abuse or neglect by his or her parents." As Dembitz pointed out with reference to the Lisa Steinberg case, "In 1983 and 1984 there were complaints of parental abuse or neglect, but caseworkers of New York City's Department of Social Services decided the complaints were 'unfounded.' " And because of a 1973 state law, "the entire file in an 'unfounded' case must be expunged."

The Dembitz Committee concluded, according to the letter, that an " 'unfounded' decision on some complaints simply reflected a caseworker's values or misjudgment. In a case where the fingernails of a ten-month-old boy fell off because his parents bound them tightly and harshly to prevent thumb sucking, the complaint was 'unfounded' because the worker thought the parents were penitent.

"A month later, the child was brought back to the hospital in a coma with bite marks on his stomach, broken limbs, bruises and wounds over his head and body."

And died, of battered child syndrome and malnutrition.

Dembitz sums up: "A full record of a child's injuries and a parent's attempt to explain them are important history."

I could not agree more. A few theoreticians in the field of child abuse feel comfortable with the proposition that the child protective system is being drowned in a deluge of unwarranted abuse reports: that is to say, reports that turn out to be genuinely unfounded. It is true that there are such cases. Nationwide, several thousand parents—most of them belonging to a very vocal group called

VOCAL, whose membership consists almost exclusively of persons accused of child *sexual* abuse—claim to have been wrongfully accused. At the same time, tens of thousands of actual maltreatment cases go unrecognized, unreported, and unprotected.

I really don't think that the system is buckling under the strain of too many unfounded reports and that therefore we must discourage reporting. I do think the system is hurting because the guidelines for reporting *and* reacting are not precise enough, and because it does not have the resources to deal with the present flood of reports. But surely the solution does not lie in discouraging reports for the sake of easing the load on the protective agencies. Surely it lies in improving the guidelines and screening processes of reporting, and in upgrading the agencies so that they are able to make proper determinations of the facts. Surely we can effect some small degree of coordination and follow-up so that we can maintain valuable case records and prevent the death of children whom we already know to be at risk, simply by keeping "unfounded" cases on the books as "reported but unproved."

Says James Garbarino, president of the Erikson Institute for Advanced Study in Child Development in Chicago: "Current practice requires the destruction of records pertaining to 'unsubstantiated' allegations of child abuse and neglect. That a case is unsubstantiated may have nothing to do with the level of danger the child experiences. Rather, it often indicates only that the harm the child is experiencing has not yet reached the agency's current standard for initiating intervention. . . . In a typical protective service investigation of alleged physical abuse, the worker is called upon to decide not, 'Has this child been physically assaulted?' but rather, 'Is this assault extreme enough to justify community intervention?' "

Which leaves us with the questions: What degree of assault or neglect is acceptable? How much is too much? When should the community intervene? When should a record of assault be placed on the books for future reference? When should it be expunged?

When we talk about violence against children—which includes dangerously neglectful practices—we are not talking in terms of degrees. We are talking absolutes. Neglect is neglect; violence is violence. "Unfounded" complaints should not be expunged. More often than not, they can be seen in hindsight as signposts to future abuse. This is not to say that they should be accessible to the general public; on the contrary, they should be jealously guarded as confidential documents and made available to the child protective services to be used in the event of new complaints that might otherwise be dismissed as "unfounded."

A major subsystem of the child protective agency—even, perhaps, the heart and soul of it—has become as much a part of the problem as it is part of the solution. It is called foster care, and it is employed when a parent for one reason or another is unwilling or unable to care for the child. Agency caseworkers use the system when they conclude that the child will be better off, or safer, in a setting other than the natural home.

This decision is not made by the caseworker or agency alone. Every state has a statute—in some cases dating back to colonial times—allowing a court to intervene in family affairs to protect a child from abuse, neglect, corruption, and abandonment. The authority is usually conferred on the Juvenile or Family Court.

Most of the children are quite young, ranging in age from infancy to six years, when they are removed. Adequate but not lavish subsidies and a multitude of services are available to the foster parents. Placement is supposed to be a temporary arrangement, a short-term breaking-up of the family so that it can be put back together again in stronger and healthier shape. Each natural parent is assigned a caseworker who helps devise and monitor a service plan aimed at the restoration of full parental rights and responsibilities. When, with the passage of time, the parents show themselves to have been successfully rehabilitated, the child is reunited with them and the family made whole again. If the parents are found to be intractable and unsalvageable, the child must be put up for adoption.

How well does the placement program work? The state investigation following the death of Jessica Cortez and Michael Baker had critical comments about that, too.

In many cases, the report said, the shortage of foster homes resulted in long-delayed placements. Numbers of children were being taken from their homes only to spend their days in the agency's field offices, and either bundled from one overnight placement to another or bedded down on cots in various makeshift accommodations. Unwittingly, the city had created a new subclass of citizens: a tribe of nomadic kids, shuttled by strangers from one strange place to another, hoping anxiously for permanent placements that might never come. "The potential damaging effect of these repeated temporary placements on children just removed from their homes is incalculable," the investigators observed.

In hundreds of other cases, the report continued, kids who required no clinical care but could not be permitted to go home lingered in hospitals or group homes intended for children with special needs. These were the "boarder babies," many of whom outgrew their babyhood while waiting for a foster parent.

Children placed with family members other than their parents were not necessarily better off. Relatives undertaking "kinship" care are supposed to be subject to a review within twenty-four hours, but, according to the report, this did not happen in 45 percent of the cases. Nor, in almost half the cases, were any efforts made to find out if the relatives had a history of abusing children or could indeed offer a good home. In 73 percent of the cases, the agency had neglected to check any character references for the relatives. And after placement had been established, the city often failed to make sure that the children were receiving the services to which they were entitled.

The state report also found that the city was often separating siblings while looking for placement for the children, and even when assigning them to foster homes. Almost a quarter of the children in the cases reviewed had been placed far from their brothers or sisters, compounding their loneliness and confusion.

And this is still happening. It seems that nobody is in charge.

What goes on here? Clearly, a mishmash of errors, misjudgments, and ill-considered reactions to unanticipated situations. Kids get yanked out of their homes because it seems to be the easiest thing to do—even though in many cases it is a mistake for them to be summarily removed—only to find that there is no place to put them. Or they are just as summarily yanked out of decent foster homes and returned to their biological parents when nothing has been done to correct the situation that prompted the removal in the first place. Kids are shuffled around like departmental paperwork, removed from unfit caretakers only to find themselves at the mercy of another unfit caretaker—the bureaucracy. Often they are recycled so relentlessly and so inefficiently that between placements they are left short of food, sleep, medical care, or even a wash and a change of clothes.

Typically, plans to habilitate dysfunctional parents bog down due to long waiting lists for services, poor communication among the agencies supposed to supply those services, the ease with which frightened or poorly motivated parents avoid or sabotage the plan's implementation, and the inability of the overloaded caseworkers to keep tabs on them and make sure that they *are* benefiting from the services offered.

At the same time, some foster parents are finding it difficult to cope. The bureaucracy is not supplying them with the promised help and services. Some of them have serious problems of their own and take their frustrations out on the foster children in their care. Some of the children have already been so badly abused that they exhibit extremes of behavior difficult for the best of foster parents or even highly trained professionals to handle.

Time drags by, and the child either stays in the home or gets bounced from one home to another. Not a few children have lived with as many as eight or ten different families, for periods ranging from two or three weeks to a couple of years. Some stay in one home for as long as five or six years, becoming an integral part of the family. Incredibly, given these circumstances, foster parents are directed not to become too emotionally attached to the child, because he or she is going to be taken away from them sooner or later anyway. And if they decide they want to adopt—well, of course, the natural mother has priority if she shows any sign of shaping up.

Or, sometimes, even if she doesn't.

Report from Lakeland, Florida, August 1989: Bradley McGee, born in Jerseyville, Illinois, to Sheryl McGee and some disposable male, first became known to Florida authorities in the summer of 1987 when he was two and a half months old. By that time Ms. McGee had acquired another boyfriend, Thomas Coe. The Abuse Registry of the Florida Department of Health and Rehabilitative Services received a referral from the Illinois Department of Children and Family Services alleging that the mother left the child unattended and neglected, with urine and feces all over the crib.

This case was investigated, and closed as "unfounded."

On October 10, 1987, a referral was received by the Abuse Registry stating that Sheryl McGee, her male companion, and the child had been living out of the back of a truck parked at the

Lakeland Mall, and that Bradley, malnourished and neglected, had been abandoned. Immediate investigation by HRS determined that McGee had approached a friend at the Pretzel Shop and asked her to take care of Brad. The friend refused and called upon another person, who took the little boy to the hospital because of his neglected condition. That same day, HRS temporarily placed Bradley with Mrs. Mary Coe, mother of Thomas Coe, the first of a series of temporary caretakers with whom he would be lodged within the next five months.

On March 29, 1988, he was placed as a foster child in the home of James and Pamela Kirkland, HRS foster parents since 1986. Meanwhile, Sheryl McGee and Thomas Coe got married, and a baby was born to them in June. Neither Sheryl nor Thomas made any attempt to check on or visit Bradley until the fall of 1988, when the Kirklands notified HRS that they had come to love Bradley as their own and wanted to adopt him—and in return were informed by a caseworker that Sheryl wanted Bradley back. Since reunification with the family is as important a principle in Florida as it is in New York, the agency set the wheels in motion to remove Brad from the Kirkland home.

At once, and repeatedly for the next few months, the Kirklands expressed serious concern for the safety of Bradley and pointed out that no interest in his welfare had been shown by the Coes during all the time he had been in foster care. Nevertheless the agency pursued its plan to reunite the child with the Coes. From December to May, Bradley was obliged to make biweekly visits to the home of the Coes, in spite of evidence that Sheryl had a drug problem and could not seem to establish a mother-child relationship with the little boy. To all appearances, he had bonded with his foster parents and was uneasy about visiting his mother's home. On one occasion in April he came back to the Kirklands in a disheveled condition and with a number of small injuries on his body. The Kirklands understandably feared that Bradley would be at risk if he were to be returned, and reported their reasons for concern. None of this, however, cut any ice with HRS or the court. On May 23, 1989, upon the recommendation of HRS, the court returned Bradley to his mother and stepfather for an extended home visit. Legal custody remained with HRS, which obligated that agency to see to the welfare and safety of the boy.

Mary Rae Coe, mother of Thomas, later stated that Bradley had visited her often while in physical custody of the Coes, and that she had told an HRS worker some twenty-five times that Bradley should not be made to live with them. She said that her son and daughter-in-law were extremely vicious individuals, and she knew that Bradley was being physically abused by them because they had told her of the abuse and she had personally seen bruises on him. On July 3, 1989, the Abuse Registry received a referral—probably instigated by Mrs. Coe—alleging that the mother made Bradley sleep in urine and feces and had forced feces in Bradley's mouth. This complaint was investigated by HRS and dismissed as "unfounded."

On numerous occasions throughout June and July, Mrs. Coe found Brad to be underfed, neglected, and seriously bruised. According to her account, she made her concerns known to HRS to little effect. On July 25, 1989, a judicial review hearing was held. Upon recommendation by HRS, the court ordered that Bradley should remain in the legal custody of HRS but in the physical custody of Sheryl and Thomas Coe on "extended visitation."

As it turned out, the visitation was not extended. Two days later, Bradley McGee was taken to hospital with head injuries allegedly caused by Thomas Coe in the course of repeatedly plunging the child's head into a toilet as punishment for defecating in his pants. Brad died the next day, July 28, 1989, not quite two years and one month old, a little boy torn from those who loved him and returned to the hell of his birth home. Thomas and Sheryl Coe were arrested and charged with murder. Later, the case was investigated internally and four of the caseworkers were called to account.

The HRS report concludes as follows:

Three factors were prominent during this investigation:

• HRS did not listen to nor act on information from the foster parents.

• After extensive examination of records and personal interviews, it appears that the safety of the child was not the primary concern. Reunification with the family seemed to be the guiding principle.

• The Abuse Registry was not utilized by HRS professionals nor members of the community.

The bottom line is that the tools, rules and procedures were in place to save Bradley's life and they were not used.

I think the problem shared by most if not all of the nation's child protective agencies is that they are expected to do the whole job in what should be a community-wide child welfare system. Even if your city or mine had the finest child protective agency in the country we would still have problems. No agency, least of all one that must be sensitive to the urgent needs of children, can function effectively without the input and support of other agencies. In a way, a child protective service is like an expanded 911 line: it takes emergency calls and acts upon them swiftly, going beyond the initial response to secure further services for the client. But it needs the help of the entire community in order to operate successfully.

Our experience in New York is that the people who might be expected to call don't call. The agencies in closest contact with children and their families—schools, hospitals, mental-hygiene clinics, drug-abuse clinics, and the police—are not reporting cases of child abuse and neglect and are not sharing life-saving information. In turn, caseworkers who are trying to provide emergency and follow-up services and work out reunification plans and make home visits and open three new cases at a time often neglect a most vital matter: placing their most significant findings before a Family Court judge who is attempting to decide the fate of a child.

Yet there is nothing to be gained by saying that nothing has changed. The "boarder baby crisis," during which several hundred children languished in hospital beds or overnight in city offices because of a shortage of foster homes, has apparently abated—at least for the time being. Almost two thousand new treatment slots have been created for substance-abusing parents whose children are waiting for them in foster care. Aggressive hiring and the creation of a caseworker training academy has reduced field-worker caseloads to an almost manageable level while improving worker skills and morale—although I fear that case levels will soon be skyrocketing again as the latest in cheap designer drugs reaches the streets.

At the same time, increasing numbers of nonprofit agencies are training and licensing home-care deliverers to provide foster care and day care services for developmentally disabled kids. Nearly all such efforts are admirable. But the strength of their independence is also one of their weaknesses: like our major public agencies, they operate as self-propelled entities within a helping network without linking strands—like parts of a web with no webbing between.

What we could use in New York—and in all major cities—is a department to deal with the lives and welfare of children, not merely a division within an all-purpose agency but one with its own very specific directives, its own policies, its own budget, its own administrator and its own clout. We need a fully staffed agency that can pay full-time attention to saving our families and children. What we have now is not enough of a visible presence, although it does not have the glamour or the public support of a fire department or a police department, it is just as vital a part of the city.

And yet it cannot stand alone. The only way we can deal with child maltreatment effectively is to employ a coordinated approach and establish a sophisticated network of existing agencies to exchange information about families and children who are at risk. We have the information, distributed in little pockets throughout agencies such as the police, schools, hospitals, clinics and so on, and we have the technology. To me, it's mind-boggling that we haven't already put into place *the* indispensable information tool: a computerized registration-plus-tracking system that can serve (a) as a main storage center and clearinghouse for all records of children at risk, no matter which agency makes the report, and (b) as a computerized tracking system that maintains an ongoing log of all children and families in care of the city and its hired agencies, complete with changing addresses; monitors the services that all clients are getting; keeps track of their status and progress, or lack of it; and maintains an updated file on available foster homes and the reliability of foster parents. "Unfounded" reports will not be expunged but listed as "unproved" until they are proved one way or another.

New York City has been dickering for years over which computer system will do the best job at the best price. As far as I can see, the only obstacle to installing such an efficient piece of life-saving equipment, apart from the initial cost, is the American Civil Liberties Union, which—and I am sure they will correct me if I'm wrong—seems to be more interested in issues of privacy and personal self-expression than in matters of life and death. There is no doubt in my mind that we must have, and will have, a data bank to replace the outmoded record-keeping practices we have dragged with us into the 1990s, even if we have to do some drastic thinking about the red herring of "confidentiality" and the legitimate issue of ensuring only authorized access to the files.

I think it is clear that the city does not offer sufficient support services to families in need. I don't believe this is necessarily because the services are not available somewhere, scattered throughout the city; I believe it is because they *are* scattered, and people who have trouble getting their act together in the first place need multiservice community centers in their own neighborhoods rather than discrete agencies spread all over the city.

On one level a local center might offer prenatal education and care, early childhood services to youngsters, basic and largely preventive medical services, homemaking and financial assistance, counseling and psychological support, day care and a home visiting service, and a place for overstrained parents to crash and find respite. On another, it might be the focal point for caseworker investigations and supervision. It can be, in effect, the neighborhood multidisciplinary team right there on the spot, with each member contributing his or her specific information and skills to the joint effort. Ultimately, each community center is to be responsible to the central agency, but only in the interests of total coordination and accountability. On a day-to-day, week-to-week, month-to-month basis, the neighborhood handles its own business.

The obvious advantage is that the family service system becomes personal. Relationships are formed and developed. Neighbors get to know each other. They speak up if a family needs help. Caregivers and clients remember each others' names and faces and circumstances. Teachers at local schools keep in touch, either offering information or advice or making themselves available for consultation. As in a small, tightly knit town, seriously harmful behavior can be noted, identified, and distinguished from the occasional irritable slap. Unwarranted and unnecessary reports—the genuinely "unfounded" ones—may be filtered out from the start. Distraught mothers can be reached even before their children are endangered. Children at risk can be helped quickly, before the risk becomes great. If foster homes are needed, they can be found without a city-wide search. All this can be done through the neighborhood center, the heart of the modern village.

Let us look, for a moment, at Sunset Park, a neighborhood in Brooklyn whose fortunes and ethnic populations have waxed and waned for many generations. Housed in a small brick building in a largely Hispanic section is an organization called the Center for Family Life. Run by Sister Mary Paul, this is not a city venture, but the city could take lessons. It is a model operation that works wonderfully well.

The center provides a full range of community service programs, including group meetings for parents, after-school activities for kids, and counseling of all kinds from employment to psychotherapeutic. In addition, it does something that may be a first for a neighborhood center: it has painstakingly built up a collection of reliable local families to provide foster homes for neighborhood children who must be removed from their own homes for a time. What ordinarily happens to children placed in foster care is that they are sent to the far reaches of other communities, cut off from their parents and their brothers and sisters and their accustomed playgrounds and all that is familiar to them; but the Sunset Park kids stay in their own neighborhood and can not only maintain close contact with their friends and families but can usually keep going to the same school. From the Center's point of view, another advantage is that the foster home can be very closely supervised even while the natural family is receiving rehabilitative services.

In the usual course of events, children in foster care face four options for their future, none of them their own choice. First and most desirable is a return to the family home after an absence of no more than twenty-four months, preferably less, during which time the family has been suitably rehabilitated. Second is a life in the foster care system, a nomadic pilgrimage of disturbed souls from one unwelcoming home to another until youngsters graduate by running away for one last time or reaching the age of independence, even more damaged than when the journey began. Third is consignment to a group home or larger institution in which, unless it is an extraordinary place staffed by extraordinary people, the children are likely to die of emotional malnutrition. Fourth is adoption, the most desirable alternative to reunification with the birth family.

Bearing in mind all the care that must be taken to safeguard all parties involved, particularly the children, it should nonetheless be a relatively simple matter to manage the adoption of a child who lacks a functioning parent. The waiting lists for adoptive children are endless. Whatever may be said about the unadoptability of badly damaged kids, especially those born to a legacy of crack and AIDS, the fact of the matter is that surprising numbers of eager would-be parents are available for children of any age, race, religion, color, and practically any disability. I could multiply the following example by the hundreds.

Jeffrey and Adrian Marshall wanted to adopt a baby. They made no conditions or ifs or buts. One day they received a call from the adoption agency telling them that there was a boy available, four months old; that was all they were told at the time. They were then introduced to a little four-pound boy who had weighed two pounds at birth. "He looked like a little knot," Mrs. Marshall recalls.

On meeting the child the Marshalls were informed that the birth mother had used crack right up until delivery, and the baby had spent his first three months in intensive care. He was diagnosed as having severe cerebral palsy, and doctors thought he might never walk or talk. He didn't smile, he cried incessantly, and he couldn't stand being touched. Would the Marshalls really want this devastated child?

They would; they did. "We decided we could be his parents better than anyone else," said Jeffrey Marshall.

As of this writing, Jeffrey Junior is eighteen months old. His adoptive parents think he is the best thing that ever happened to them. He gets therapy and he is enveloped in love. He is considered developmentally delayed, which means he is slow to learn, but he does walk and he does talk and he plays with other kids and he can say "A,B,C" and "Mommy" and "Daddy." He is the light of his parents' lives.

Yes, there are people who yearn to adopt, even though they know their lives as parents will not be easy. And yet the adoption mill grinds very slowly and erratically.

Babies and children in foster care are prime candidates for adoption. If, after a period of time—usually eighteen months—the birth mother demonstrates that she is either unwilling or unable to care for her child, the caseworkers tracking that child's welfare are supposed to start working for a termination of parental rights, an essential first step in adoption proceedings. Incredible though it may seem, it is extremely difficult to terminate parental rights even in the case of a child whose mother is in prison for murder and actually wants to give the baby up for adoption. The child protective agency wastes precious time—many months, during which the child is getting more and more disturbed and less and less adoptable—in a lackadaisical search for elusive family members who may or may not want to take care of the child, and then throws away more months before filing termination papers. As time passes, people wanting to adopt start looking elsewhere, and the kids they had wanted wind up being wanted by no one.

That is one major difficulty. Another is race.

Almost anyone whose character references check out can become an adoptive parent, except those who are reckoned to be too old or of the wrong color. Shrieks of denial will be raised by people in the adoption business in regard to the question of race, but they will also be shrieks of hypocrisy. I don't think it will come as a surprise to anyone to be told that the vast majority of babies in the adoption pool are black or Hispanic. It may, however, come as a surprise that huge numbers of white Americans are yearning to adopt them but are unable to do so because transracial adoption is actively discouraged by most adoption agencies as well as federal and state governments. The rationale is the preservation of racial identity. The fact of life is that black children raised in caring white families as well as white children raised in caring black families are immeasurably better off than children who are raised in a subculture of poverty, drugs, and hopelessness or left in limbo by a neglectful bureaucracy. To claim otherwise is old-fashioned racism of the most simplistic kind.

And so the kids wait, not knowing the rules and not knowing what is delaying their lives while papers are shuffled and people argue about them or forget about them; and throughout the months and years their ranks are growing and their chances of becoming somebody's child are getting dimmer and dimmer. The sad truth is that in spite of the fact that foster children are first in line for adoption, very few are ever adopted.

About 500,000 youngsters go through the nation's foster care system annually. In the course of 1990 we will probably have seen some 55,000 children in foster care in New York City alone, twice as many as in 1989. We are rapidly moving into a new state of crisis: more babies are being born into poverty, into AIDS, into crack, into abuse. More and more babies are going to need homes. But we really don't know how or where to find homes for them.

One possible solution is a radical change in our entire child protective system, with an emphasis on neighborhood-based multiservice programs for neighborhood people and neighborhood foster parents. Another is to speed up the turgid adoption process. Caseworkers can help to do this, adoption agencies can help, judges can help, and legislation can help.

Meanwhile, the children are waiting.

All children find waiting rough, especially when they have no idea what the future may hold, when they begin to realize that nobody wants them—neither their parents, nor other mothers, nor official-looking strangers. The waiting ones are the kids the system fails, just as surely as it fails the ones who die.

"Some children break," said a social worker at a large foster care facility on Staten Island, New York. "I'll never forget one kid. At the end of three months of the system, he had to be put in Bellevue. He wanted to kill himself. No hope. For two months he didn't have a change of clothes, he had nothing. And this kid was a good kid. Fourteen years old, a beautiful kid. He came in okay, and he just got destroyed."

Sandra Thomas is an eight-year-old who was brought to the Crisis Nursery by her paternal grandmother, her legal guardian since the mother had dumped the child on her and gone off to Florida. Some months before that, the little girl had come to the attention of the child protective agency when a Brooklyn hospital had filed an abuse report based on the child's vaginal bleeding and her statement that her mother's boyfriend had had sexual intercourse with her while the mother watched.

The case faded away when the mother skipped and the father went to jail for having sexually abused and murdered a young woman—nobody is suggesting we were dealing with a salvageable family here—but revived when the grandmother gave up on Sandra. A friend told her that she could drop the child off at the Crisis Nursery, which she did, explaining that she could not deal with the child's behavior. The child would not listen to her and was always getting into trouble in and out of school. Sandra had previously been referred to a therapist at Kings County Hospital and was to report there shortly, but in the meantime the grandmother wanted to be rid of her. She wanted the kid placed in a foster home, and that was that.

So. Good-bye, grandmother, hello, Sandra—even though the Crisis Nursery normally admits children no older than six and operates only as a short-term respite center, for a maximum of three days. We were not the right place for her: we couldn't send her off to school, and there were no kids her own age in the Nursery for her to play with. What we could do was provide a facsimile of a homelike atmosphere and a concentrated dosage of attention and care. Sandra was not easily solaced: understandably, she was reacting physically and emotionally to the whole spectrum of abuse and neglect and rejections that she had suffered. Nobody loved her, nobody wanted her, and she knew it. In context, the behavior to which her grandmother had been objecting was not abnormal.

Sue Sawicki, assistant director of the Crisis Nursery, got on the telephone to the city protective agency, known at this time as the Child Welfare Administration (CWA), to plead for the speedy placement of the child. CWA said it was a PINS case—Persons In Need of Supervision—and that they had no authority. PINS said it was a case for CWA. CWA said it was not. PINS said it was. And so on. And so on. Finally CWA was pinned to the mat and grudgingly assigned the case to a Brooklyn unit for evaluation and placement.

While these and other discussions were under way the child had to be taken on four separate occasions to Brooklyn's Kings County Hospital for a multitude of psychological and psychiatric evaluations, which added up to a new burden of traumatic experience for a child already damaged by repeated abusive insult.

The days passed. Sandy remained in the Nursery, feeling more and more depressed and unwanted. She knew that the staff cared for her and loved her and she was becoming quite attached to the workers, but she desperately wanted a home—or at least a place that was more right for her than this crisis center for little kids. She had already had her crisis; now she wanted some life.

Volunteers took her to the park, to the movies, to a music and dance performance; they couldn't take her home. Sue called CWA: *What was holding things up?* The Crisis Nursery was no place for an eight-year-old to be held indefinitely. This was pure bureaucratic abuse and neglect. When was placement going to be arranged? Well, placement could not be made until all the psychiatric and psychological evaluations had been completed at Kings County Hospital, and that would take several more weeks.

Several more weeks! This was intolerable. Our Sandy did not deserve the additional trauma caused by the lack of responsible action on the part of the agencies involved. But at every turn, with every telephone contact, we became more deeply entangled in a bureaucratic mess. Nothing was moving. I spoke to the child and assured her that we loved her, that we would find a place for her with other children, that she would soon be able to go back to school. She seemed unconvinced. More than once she said to me that she wanted to die, that she had been told her father was dead (he wasn't), but that she wouldn't be seeing him after death because he was good and therefore "up there" whereas she would go "down there" because she was bad. Nonetheless, she thought she would be better off dead.

We attempted to straighten this out with her but not before the shrinks at Kings County Hospital had started exploring the child's "suicidal ideation," which struck us as a perfectly normal reaction to everything she had gone through. While this was going on I received a phone call from one of the administrators of the child protective agency with whom I had been conferring regarding Sandy's placement. He had heard of the child's supposed death wish, and had a suggestion for me: "Why don't you," he said, "use your influence to get the child placed in a psychiatric unit?"

This was too much. I was being asked to put this poor child in with crazies to vegetate for the rest of her life because she was causing so much trouble for the agencies! Was it not enough what her family and the bureaucracy had already done to her? This was like putting the last nail into her coffin. I wouldn't hear of it.

This time I didn't call a press conference; I called an emergency meeting of Crisis Nursery staff, our New York Foundling director of mental health services, and the assistant director of Blaine Hall, the Foundling's live-in therapeutic center for acting-out preadolescents. I wanted a complete roundup of expert opinion on the state of this child and what we could do to salvage her. The consensus: she was not crazy, she did need psychological help to carry her over her horrendous past experiences, and she needed to be loved and cared for. Eventually she should be placed in a loving foster home, but meanwhile our very own Blaine Hall was the perfect place for her to grow into her real self while maintaining contact with the people at the Crisis Nursery to whom she had become attached. Great idea! Unfortunately, every bed in the Blaine Hall program was filled, and there would not be an opening for at least a month. We had run into another dead end.

But, in fact, we hadn't. Next day, I got a call from one of the associate administrators of the Blaine Hall program. He said that he had found space and was setting up an extra bed for Sandy, and that she would be cared for with other kids and given her lessons as long as she needed before going to a foster home. And so it happened. I saw her, with a happy face, coming home from the park the other day; she threw her arms around me and simply said, "Thanks."

Of course this is not the complete story. I have omitted about fifty-five phone calls and as many frustrations in our attempt to save Sandy from the bureaucracy. And she is only one little girl. Multiply her by thousands. Think of those thousands, all of them waiting for a home that may never materialize. Think of the system to which we have entrusted these children.

Is this a caring, trustworthy system?

By any definition, it is not.

11 / The Courts: Poor Joshua

Joshua DeShaney, nine years old, is paralyzed and severely retarded, the victim of brutal beatings by his father. Because of this maltreatment he will have to be institutionalized for the rest of his life, at a cost of well over fifty thousand dollars a year. It is not known, as of this writing, who will pick up the tab. But what does that matter? He will never be mended.

Joshua is also the victim of Wisconsin's Winnebago County Department of Social Services, which failed to remove him from his divorced father's custody despite regular reports of abuse over a period of nearly two years and a series of hospitalizations for serious injuries.

Then, what was left of Joshua was again made a victim by the U.S. Supreme Court in a six-to-three ruling that absolved Winnebago County of constitutional responsibility for Joshua's fate.

Melody DeShaney, the boy's mother, had given Joshua, then barely a year old, into the care of her husband Randy after their divorce, feeling that she herself was too alone, too young, and too poor to give the child the kind of life she wanted to give him. But Randy DeShaney, whisking the boy from Wyoming to Wisconsin without leaving a forwarding address, beat Joshua into near-oblivion. DeShaney's second wife knew this and subsequently told the police; doctors at the hospital to which Joshua had been taken a number of times reported their suspicions; and at one time the Winnebago Department of Social Services actually took the child away from his father, but then returned him. Still, the department kept tabs on Joshua and, through the social worker on the case, documented the little boy's days by the marks on his body: a bump on the forehead, a scraped cornea, a mark on the chin that looked like a cigarette burn, a cut on the face, a bloody nose, a swollen ear, bruises on both shoulders, bruises all over the body. Let there be no mistake—*the department knew all this.*

Joshua was unconscious when he was next taken to hospital in March 1984 and rushed into the operating room for emergency brain surgery. Doctors then found evidence that his head had been repeatedly bashed and damaged over a period of time. Apparently no one in the Winnebago Department of Social Services was in the least surprised, but they had made no effort to contact the mother until that final hospitalization when he was not expected to make it through the night. He did make it; now he is little more than a vegetable. As for Randy DeShaney, he was convicted on child abuse charges, sentenced to two to four years, and has since been released.

Melody DeShaney's action against Winnebago County's inaction ultimately reached the Supreme Court. The county's welfare officials had known that the boy was in danger, she charged, yet did nothing to protect him. They had violated their constitutional duty by failing to intervene.

The Supreme Court rejected this plea.

"A state's failure to protect an individual against private violence simply does not constitute a violation," said Chief Justice William H. Rehnquist. "While the state may have been aware of the dangers that Joshua faced in the free world, it played no part in their creation, nor did it do anything to render him more vulnerable to them." The ruling prompted an impassioned dissent by Justice Harry Blackmun. "Poor Joshua!" he wrote. "Victim of repeated attacks by an irresponsible, bullying, cowardly and intemperate father, and abandoned by respondents who placed him in a dangerous predicament and who knew or learned what was going on, and yet did essentially nothing except, as the Court revealingly observes, 'dutifully recorded these incidents in [their] files.' It is a sad commentary upon American life and constitutional principles . . .

that this child, Joshua DeShaney, now is assigned to live out the remainder of his life profoundly retarded."

In sum, those whose duty it is to make their best efforts to protect our children cannot be faulted if they do not do their job. They had placed him in that predicament. They knew he was in danger. They did nothing. Yet they bore no responsibility for what became of him. Poor Joshua, indeed.

For Joshua, the court of last resort was no help to him or to his mother. His case should have been settled many months earlier before a less lofty tribunal. It should have been resolved in a court designed to protect children—a juvenile court, a family court, the kind of place where little Roxanne Felumero's fate was decided back in 1968.

She, it will be remembered, was the little girl taken from adoring foster parents and returned, by order of the family court, to the arms of the mother and stepfather who killed her. The analysis following that case demonstrated that every mistake that could possibly have been made was made, by everyone involved in her protection—except the foster parents. They knew the child was being abused when she visited her home. They wanted her, they feared for her, and they begged to be heard, but the caseworkers did not present their pleas to the court. The court, in its turn, was twice in the dark because one judge presided over the first phase of the proceedings and a second judge heard the rest.

And so the little girl died. After that, everything was supposed to change. The family court system in New York City was to be thoroughly overhauled, beginning with a special part allocated to abuse and neglect cases as distinct from all other family issues. The rest of the nation would see how we did it. Has anything changed, even now?

Only minor details.

Down in Florida, twenty-one years after Roxanne's death, little Bradley McGee was horribly abused after being returned to his biological mother and her companion. The truly saddening and disheartening aspect of Brad McGee's death was, as in the case of Roxanne, how little attention was paid to the pleas of the foster parents. They had loved him, they had wanted him, they had given warning that he would be seriously at risk if returned to his mother and her lover; their pleas were ignored, and Bradley died.

Stories coming out of family court proceedings cross my desk all the time, some from official files, some from newspapers. They oblige me to recognize, again and again, that children are very seldom adequately represented in any court of law.

Juvenile courts, and in some states family courts, are the traditional forums for abused and neglected children. They are generally responsible for handling juvenile deliquency cases, child protection, adoptions, and a range of domestic matters. These are the only courts in which children's cases are pleaded. While children obviously cannot plead their own cases and must therefore rely on adults to speak for them, the family courts do not have the rigidity of practice and procedure that exists in other civil courts or in the criminal courts.

Family Court proceedings—certainly in New York, and I believe elsewhere—provide the crucial point of decision in the lives of many of the city's malfunctioning families. This is a rather alarming consideration in light of the frantic pace of the proceedings and the many flaws in the system, but until such time as state and city have a fully functioning computerized registry it is Family Court that has greatest access to information on each case that reaches it. Family members, attorneys, and the staff of various agencies all add their input to the portrait of the family that emerges. And if the Family Court does not have the prestige and clout of the criminal courts, it does have the power to determine the future of the children in the family. For the most part it uses its authority wisely, assessing all facts and evaluations and ordering appropriate interventions for the families brought before it. Sometimes, like all systems, it fails; and when it does it is either because the presiding judge has not confronted the very fundamental question of the parents' competency to meet their children's needs or because something has gone completely haywire in the handling of the case—the featured players are, quite literally, crazy and irresponsible, or the child protective services have failed to fulfill their responsibilities in terms of protecting the children or bringing appropriate case material to court.

At times in these courts you feel as if you are in a kind of netherworld, a twilight zone in which everything is somehow out of kilter and each case is a jumble of the bizarre and the incomprehensible. Here is a mother, a paranoid schizophrenic. A previous court returned her first child to her from foster care for no good reason that one can see. At that time she refused supportive services or psychotherapy, and no one forced them on her; she has her rights. She lives with her brother, who is mentally ill. Recently she gave birth to a second child and murdered the first. She is not even going to prison. Surely this is not real life! But, oh yes, it is. This kind of thing happens often in a court where dockets are full and proceedings are so long-drawn-out that nobody has a handle on what has gone before. The fact is, there seldom is time to do anything thoroughly.

A courtroom in Family Court has all the serenity of a subway station at rush hour. It is a cacophony of sound, of angry voices raised in accusation and denial; a shifting mosaic of lawyers and law guardians, police officers, delinquents and caseworkers, court officers and clerks, physicians and psychologists, distraught and sometimes strung-out parents; a jumble of overlapping, interrupting cases that seldom come to happy endings. Presiding over all this is a judge who has to be firm but compassionate and very, very quick on the uptake to get through all the cases that come before him or her in the course of an average day. That day is roughly divided into six-minute periods—six minutes for each of the approximately fifty cases of wife-battering or delinquency or child abuse and neglect that each judge handles, on an average, every working day.

Some cases can be dispatched handily. Others, involving adoption or removal of a child from an abusive home, must be given more time. Mistakes are inevitably made. Caseworkers unfamiliar with the needs of the court often prepare their materials poorly or make inappropriate recommendations to the judge. Sometimes the judge is insufficiently conscious of dangers in the home and may unthinkingly expose children to great harm by dismissing removal petitions or returning children to parents or other caretakers who do not protect them. As the Dembitz Fatality Review Committee of 1985 observed: "If the authorities of last resort fail to realistically appraise the danger to the child in his home, the protective purpose of the whole system can be defeated."

An area where the court has shown itself to be less than alert is in directing and obtaining full investigations of the homes into which a child is to be placed for custody. Has the child protective service obtained a full picture of the home and family to which a child is to be returned? Is the perpetrating parent fully rehabilitated? Is the other parent a fully responsible, nonabusive parent? These matters are seldom probed in depth, never mind satisfactorily answered. The assumption that one parent is "bad" while the other is an innocent bystander has led to the incarceration of the bad one and the removal of the remaining children to a foster home while the supposedly innocent one, who may very well have been equally involved in a crime against a child, is likely to be granted unsupervised visiting with his or her other children. As noted in one annual fatality report, "[The] tendency to separate only one parent out as the dangerous or responsible party meant that unsupervised visiting rights were granted to very questionable people."

Similarly, Family Court rarely makes a full investigation of the extended family before placing the siblings of a severely abused or murdered child in the custody of grandmothers or aunts or uncles. Whether the fault lies with caseworkers who do not present clear evidence to the judge that the entire family of the abused child is involved in an intergenerational saga of violence, substance abuse, and neglect, or with the judge who must hasten on to the next case, the fact is that inappropriate in-family or kinship placements are often made without an overview of the entire family circumstance. In one case that I believe can be mirrored almost infinitely, a boy was removed from the home of his abusive mother and placed with an alcoholic grandmother who lived across the street. In fact, throughout his life he had been shuttled back and forth between the two households and had been abused and neglected in both. The court order notwithstanding, he continued to move back and forth between the two homes—which made no difference to him at all, since that was life as he had always known it. The judge could not have known this; the child protective agency most certainly should have.

There is not only a tendency to regard a kinship home as a safe home, which is not necessarily so; there is a lack of follow-up by overburdened social workers responsible for keeping track of client families.

Even when the court directs specific supportive interventions, as it often does, there are limits to how far it can go to enforce its orders. Typically, a judge might order a parent to undergo drug rehabilitation, a child to receive psychotherapy, a family to be supplied with homemaking services or home nursing care, or the home to be monitored frequently and on a long-term basis by the child protective service. But very often—in fact, *more often than not*—the judge's orders are either not carried out at all or are not put into effect for weeks or even months. Usually, lack of cooperation by the court-ordered parent is largely to blame, but this should be anticipated and met by firm countermeasures to ensure compliance. For instance:

Case One. Mother's obstinacy, and a bureaucratic hitch. A Family Court judge orders visiting nurse service to a family with five children. However, the mother refuses to take the children to a clinic for regular checkups, and the visiting nurse is unable to go into the home to attend to the children without orders from a physician specifying a treatment plan. Result: no visiting nurse. And no follow-up report to the court, either.

Case Two. A mother's lie. The court returns three of six children to a mentally retarded mother and alcoholic father on the stipulation that a homemaker be provided for as long as the children are home. The mother subsequently says that the children are able to care of themselves, and the homemaker service readily agrees to discontinue homemaking.

Case Three. Agency apathy. A court returns three of seven children to a mentally retarded and mentally ill couple with orders for homemaking services, psychotherapy, remedial education, and supervision by the child protective agency. None of these services are rendered. Gradually, the four remaining children drift back home from foster care to a family situation that is totally unchanged.

Time and time again, the judge's prescription calls for long-range and extensive family assistance to bring the parents up to a minimal level of parenting, but this intervention is simply not provided. The result is that mistreated children who have been removed from their homes spend years in foster care, loving it or hating it, and in many cases return eventually to a home with all the old problems and often new ones.

Here is a current news clip about a mother whose five children were taken away from her and placed in foster homes, one after the other, because they had been neglected and sexually abused. On the principle—mandated, in fact, by state and federal law— that everything possible should be done to reunite such children with their parents, the mother was inundated with rehabilitative services. According to the story, "She had 'parenting' classes, a 'parenting' aide, a therapist, a homemaker, and a driver." This blows my mind! I am all in favor of rehabilitation, but a parenting aide when there are no children at home? And a *driver*? Meanwhile, a group of nuns was furnishing this woman's squalid apartment and supporting her petition to the Family Court to get her children back.

All this was happening between January 1985 and November 1987, at the end of which time a judge returned four of the women's children to her, in spite of the warnings and expressed fears of foster parents. Two months later the mother, severely hung over and incapable of dealing with four rowdy, screaming children, killed her youngest child, still a baby, by bashing his head against the sink with the idea of quieting him. An autopsy showed an unhealed broken wrist and other signs of previous abuse.

So much for reunification.

This time, the mother went to prison. She has now served less than three years and her release is being sought by her current lawyer, who claims that she has been a model prisoner. Perhaps she has, but this has nothing to do with her being a model mother. An evaluation team, at first reluctant to acknowledge improvement in her mothering capacities, now feels she may possibly be capable of caring for her children. The foster parents still think not. One couple has adopted their foster child and would like to take another. The children themselves indicate some fondness for the mother, but they don't want to go back "home." What will happen? I fear that the three children still in foster care will be reunited with their mother and be endangered once again.

It is very sad when qualified foster parents who genuinely love and care for their temporary charges—although "temporary" can easily be as long as five or six years—have to relinquish them to dangerous parents. But it is equally sad when the shortage of foster homes, particularly for hard-to-place children, is so acute that standards for placement become dangerously lowered. I see nothing wrong in placing a child with a single person; in fact, I think it can be wonderful for both. But a single woman with a full-time job and no parenting experience is not my idea of a likely candidate for foster motherhood, especially if the child is the fragile survivor of a crack-addicted, syphilitic mother.

The thirty-nine-year-old secretary who took in little Regina as a preliminary to adopting her was thoroughly screened by the agency that placed the child, and prepared by months of training to look after her. A woman of solitary habits and apparently no close friends, she had told coworkers that in her middle years she was looking back at a life of little accomplishment and ahead to years of loneliness, and had decided to adopt a child to give some meaning to her life. I am not unsympathetic to her lack of fulfillment, but I don't regard it as suitable motivation for taking a child into her home. She would have been far better off to have done volunteer work and gotten herself a cat. I am not being facetious when I say this.

But the woman took in a child. Only a few months later, the little girl—then one year old—was dead. She had had a crying spell and wouldn't stop, and the woman could not stand it. By her own account, she had a few unaccustomed drinks and shook and struck the baby and threw her on the floor a couple of times, and that was the end of two lives.

Only one thing emerges with any clarity from this tragic tale: foster parents for the most deprived and most fragile of abandoned children must be selected with special care and approved by an authority other than the foster-care provider—specifically, an informed court.

Here is another kind of case, representative of several and perhaps many. A woman I shall call Eva Nelson is among a group of mothers accusing the Brooklyn Family Court of victimizing them and denying them due process. Eva Nelson's husband was awarded custody of their six-year-old daughter three years ago, in spite of allegations by the little girl and her grandmother that he sexually abused the child. While these charges were, presumably, being investigated—though it is not clear whether a full investigation was made—the child was placed in a series of foster homes and then returned to the father. Meanwhile, the mother, according to her account, had to submit herself to a battery of psychological tests while her husband was spared these procedures.

In the course of a visitation with her daughter, Mrs. Nelson found her to be lethargic and extremely undernourished. She took her to Kings County Hospital, where the girl was diagnosed as suffering from malnutrition. In a Family Court proceeding that followed this incident, the hospital resident testified that the child was "by far the worst case I have ever seen of emaciation and loss of fat tissue." Nevertheless, the judge not only returned the child to her father but removed all visitation rights by the mother. It had been traumatic for the child, the judge reportedly said, to have been taken to the hospital. Said the mother, "I am afraid my daughter is going to be another Lisa Steinberg, and no one is doing anything to stop it."

Attorney Steven Mandel agrees that women like Eva Nelson are being unfairly treated. With reference to the group of which Eva Nelson was a part, he observes, "All these women are being diagnosed as being paranoid and delusional. The truth is, you're not paranoid when people are coming after you and your children." Mandel believes that women's charges of sexual abuse are being ignored by the court. "It's being treated like rape was twenty years ago. Judges don't want to believe that men who are well-educated, intelligent, and successful could do these things. They just look at these charges as a way for a woman to get back at her husband."

For some reason this puts me in mind of Elizabeth Morgan, Hilary, and Judge Herbert B. Dixon, Jr., of the District of Columbia Superior Court.

When a special part of the Family Court was set aside to handle child abuse and neglect cases, it was thought that this would enhance the expertise and sensitivity of the judges, attorneys, social workers, and physicians dealing with these very particular cases, and permit them to focus on matters of maltreatment to the exclusion of, say, delinquency or adoption cases. But this well-intentioned move has not substantially improved the workings of the Family Court. We are still faced with antiquated and cumbersome administrative procedures, poor record-keeping, poor scheduling, and endlessly frustrating postponements. I look around at some of the courts today, in a relatively new building that is aging before its time, and I see bedlam—dreadful working conditions, no space, no dignity, nothing to respect; a scary shortage of trained social workers, of judges, of probation officers, and of all manner of rehabilitative social and psychiatric services; and an increase in the courts' caseload due in large part to the devastating impact of drug abuse. Our kids' courts are swamped to a truly dismaying degree. In 1989, 28,000 neglected and abused children were brought to the attention of the family courts—an astounding 760 percent increase over 1983's 3,300 children, and a mighty leap from the 19,000 children who went through our family court system in 1988.

It would seem that we are looking at an escalating crisis in which the very systems designed to intervene are inadequate to meet our needs. This is not because the original design was wrong; it is because the problem has outstripped us and we have to scurry to catch up with the times. This is a dangerous situation: the times demand fully functional juvenile and family courts to help bring some modicum of safety and stability to the lives of children. The children's court, by whatever name, is the court of *only* resort for embattled children. Whatever comes afterward is too late; it is nothing. It is in kids' court that the crucial decisions determining a child's future are made: his life, his death, his happiness, or his everlasting pain.

If I were to suggest what improvements might be made in the juvenile justice system, I could only point out the obvious—which means that there is not a single person in the child advocacy system who does not already know what is needed:

• More judges, and certainly more experienced than some who apparently feel that the Family Court is the kindergarten of the court system and who cannot wait to move up to a "real" court; and longer terms of service in the abuse part so that a judge who hears the first phase of a case will hear it through all its developing stages.

• A greater respect, within the judicial system, for the family and juvenile courts throughout the United States. New York State's Chief Judge, Sol Wachtler, has noted that Family Court, created to handle domestic and child welfare issues, is considered the stepchild of the state's judicial system. Resources and support are minimal. "This is something that is intolerable," Wachtler declares, "because there is no more important court in the system than the Family Court." He strongly favors merging Family Court with the state's Supreme Court, which has greater resources—and of course sounds more important. Cases are currently heard in a cheap, unkempt physical environment that breeds disrespect; family courts are accorded low funds, low priority, low prestige, and inadequate resources to handle the volume of work. All this suggests a need for reorganization, basically to be brought about by more attention to the importance and specific needs of these courts and by adequate funding for increased personnel and operating expenses. Also needed is a higher caliber of attorney to represent child welfare agencies; a training course in courtroom procedures for caseworkers; increased and *better* law guardian representation for the children who appear before these courts.

There are those of us who are always saying that we need *more* and then there are those others who tend to scoff and say, well, of course, more may be better, but where is it going to come from and who is going to make it happen?

The answer is that individual initiative can get a lot done.

When David W. Soukup was presiding judge of King County Superior Court in Seattle, Washington, he became concerned about the court's frequent inability to determine just what placement or judgment really was best for the child in the long run. In his concern he began looking for ways to ensure that the child's best interests could be effectively and consistently presented to the court. There was really only one answer: an effective spokesperson for the child, someone who could genuinely be that child's advocate and be prepared to represent the child at all court proceedings.

Traditionally, the child's advocate in the court is the *guardian at litem*, a lawyer appointed by the court to represent a minor during litigation. Very few court-appointed attorneys, Soukup realized, had the time or training required to conduct the type of thorough investigation that would elicit all the pertinent information the court needed to make a proper decision. Nor were many fully fledged attorneys eager to devote their professional lives to defending children. The answer, the judge decided, was to recruit and train ordinary citizens as volunteers, people who were willing and able to make a long-term commitment to each child for whom they would serve as a *guardian at litem*.

Judge Soukup's concept became a reality in January 1977, when the CASA—Court Appointed Special Advocate—program was born. In its first year the program provided 110 trained *guardians at litem* for 498 children in 376 cases. Soon, news of this innovative way of representing children began to reach other child advocates who were concerned that the best interests of the child were often frustrated by the very system designed to protect them. CASA programs sprang up in Rhode Island, California, Arizona, Arkansas, Florida, and Connecticut, and continue to take root in other states. As a pediatrician, I urge my colleagues throughout the nation to bombard their local family and juvenile court judges with requests to establish a CASA or CASA-type *guardian at litem* program. Legislators in every state should propose and pass laws mandating the appointment of such programs until there is one in every community in the United States.

The function of a CASA volunteer is to conduct an independent investigation for the court in a child dependency matter, following it up with a formal report to the court that makes specific recommendations for a course of action in the best interests of the child. As an officer of the court, the *guardian at litem* is in a position to conduct a wide-ranging investigation, interviewing all individuals relevant to the matter and reviewing all relevant documents and records. And as an advocate for the child, the CASA plays an equally important role in providing continuity to both the child and those who interact with the child over a period of time—people such as social workers, law enforcement agents, foster parents, and judges.

Here is a Los Angeles County case that I believe illustrates the role of the CASA guardian at its best. It is not a matter of an abused child, or a child unjustly removed from its home, but a case of child abuse averted; it could have been a life-threatening neglect situation, but it was not. And at first look it seems like an unusual case, yet I am told that there are thousands very much like it.

Baby E was born to unmarried parents, both of whom were deaf mutes. At five months he underwent a tracheotomy for tracheal stenosis, or constriction of the windpipe, and returned home after the operation. Unfortunately his parents could not hear his sounds of respiratory distress and were therefore unable to deal with his condition. As a result he was judged a dependent child and placed in foster care for his own protection.

The parents agitated to get him back. They loved him; they were not abusers. The court, however, refused to return him because of his parents' inability to take care of his medical needs. And then at last, after almost two years of frustration, the parents' attorney requested the court to appoint a *guardian at litem* for the child—a CASA volunteer.

Within a few months the volunteer had pulled together all the resources necessary for Baby E's safe life in his own home. With the cooperation of parents, grandparents, a social worker, and a visiting nurse, the CASA guardian succeeded in doing three essential things: obtaining the necessary equipment to manage the treatment of the child, including a monitoring and alarm system; having the parents trained in the use of this equipment; and convincing a judge that Baby E—by this time an energetic little toddler—could be safely returned to his parents.

This did not close the case. The CASA guardian continued to visit Baby E at home, checking continually on his health and helping the parents obtain speech therapy for him upon completion of his medical treatment.

In many cases the crimes against children are horrendous enough to qualify for the criminal court system, but few child advocates are in favor of resorting to the criminal court except in special circumstances—for example, the prosecution of a murderer—because of the higher level of proof demanded in criminal courts under the rules of criminal law and procedure. The practice of permitting the children's courts to employ looser evidentiary standards is a two-edged sword: the less substantial and well presented the evidence, the less likely that the case will be resolved in the best interests of the child; whereas in the criminal court, the higher level of proof demanded is more than can be expected of cases involving the secretive crimes of child abuse, neglect, and sexual molestation. The prosecution must thread its way through minefields in attempting to prove that the defendant engaged in abuse with the requisite level of intent demanded as an element of the alleged crime.

And yet I can see no justification for some of the egregious miscarriages of justice in our criminal courts when child abusers are tried for the ultimate crime.

Here is a brief list of charges and sentences resulting from prosecutions for the homicide of a child:

• A father is charged with first degree manslaughter in the battering death of his child. Sentence: 4 to 12 years.

• A mother is charged with first degree manslaughter in the battering death of her child. Sentence: 4½ to 9 years.

• A stepfather is charged with first degree manslaughter in the death of his child. Sentence: 3 to 9 years.

• An uncle is charged with second degree manslaughter in the battering death of a child. Sentence: 2⅓ to 7 years.

• A mother's boyfriend is charged with criminally negligent homicide in the battering death of a child. Sentence: 0 to 3 years.

• A mother is charged with second degree manslaughter in the battering death of her firstborn. Sentence: 0 to 4 years.

• A mother is charged with murder in the burning death of her child. Sentence: commitment to state hospital.

• A mother is charged with attempted manslaughter in the battering death of her child. Sentence: 5 years probation.

• A mother is charged with the starvation death of her child. Result: acquittal.

In two separate cases of children dying in fires after being left alone, two mothers were arrested. One had the charges of endangering the welfare of a minor dismissed. The other pled guilty and received an unconditional discharge.

Contemplating these sentences, or in some cases nonsentences, it is difficult to get a grip on the attitude of the judicial system or the individual judges toward the killers and the killings. Surely leaving a child unattended and letting him burn to death is criminally negligent? Perhaps not by legal definition, but by my human definition it is. And surely, in principle, there should be equal sentences for equal crimes. But consider this inconsistency: the toughest sentence—4 to 12 years, which is little enough—was given to a father who battered his three-and-a-half-year-old daughter to death. Yet in what appears to be the very similar case of a mother's boyfriend battering a two-year-old boy to death, the sentence was only 0 to 3, and the judge remarked: "Any one of us as parents sometimes raise our hand and cause something to happen. I don't think that you are a danger to the community [in that] you really intended to cause this result." Does this judge think that battering a child to death is an understandable little slip of the hand? Is he sympathetic toward excessive corporal "punishment" of two-year-olds by parents or casual male companions? Is his judgment as poor as his grammar? What sort of people do we have on the bench?

There are inconsistencies, too, in the sentencing of three of the last four mothers on the prosecution list. A judge is entitled to use his or her own discretion, but I find it puzzling that there cannot be more standardization in the sentencing for perpetrators with mental or emotional problems. One mother with an apparent personality disorder and possible drug reaction is committed indefinitely to a state hospital; another, diagnosed as a paranoid schizophrenic, is sentenced to 0 to 4 years in prison; a third mother, mentally retarded with a personality disorder, is sentenced to 5 years probation in a special halfway house.

This is far from equal treatment. There ought to be a law.

And what can I make of the woman who was acquitted in the starvation death of her child? I don't know. Her case leaves so much open for speculation that I cannot speculate. Except . . . is she in close touch with the city's supportive services? Has she had another child or children since then? I worry about them.

In any event, society, as expressed by juries and by judges passing sentence upon child abusers, does not appear to believe that child murder is a particularly serious crime. With a few dramatic exceptions—for example, the cases of Joel Steinberg and the Cortez-Lopez pair—the sentences handed down would lead one to think that children are no more than little animals to be snuffed at an adult's will. I wonder, often, if it ever occurs to the child killers that they might actually be held responsible. I wonder, too, if stiffer sentences for all child abusers might not help to deter them—or at least keep them out of action for a very long time so that they might hurt and kill no more. I do not believe that child murderers, on balance, are salvageable human beings. But I do believe that some parents, driven by extreme stress, may come very close to killing their kids and yet be successfully rehabilitated through the orders of an insightful judge. For instance, in one case a mother pleaded guilty to attempted manslaughter in return for sentencing to a special rehabilitative halfway house—a common plea for someone looking for an easy way out, but a genuine request for access to a two-way street in this particular case. The judge was unusually conscientious and aggressive in insisting upon guarantees of the safety of another child in the family, and did not accept the plea until that child had been freed for adoption. What was achieved here was an intelligent and positive resolution of a human problem.

*   *   *

Who speaks for the child in cases in which there is neither law guardian nor activist judge? Only the prosecutor. That is not enough. By one means or another, an abused child or even a dead child must be heard. When children are able to speak for themselves, they should be accorded the right to do so within a reasonable time after the alleged abuse has occurred and without being further abused by the judicial system. This seldom happens.

More and more, lately, children are being featured in *adult* court, either as absentee puppets being given voice by supposedly expert witnesses, as in the Morgan-Foretich case, or in person as victims of abuse, as in the McMartin trial. The Morgan-Foretich case turned into a battle of the experts, in which two opposing sides virtually canceled each other out and nobody knew what Hilary would have contributed—because Hilary, the key figure in the case, was not represented by a child advocate. And the McMartin case was an extraordinary proceeding that permitted the voices of abused children to be heard—and scorned.

Whenever a child is involved in a case of whatever sort, that child should have a trained advocate in court.

The child molestation trial of Raymond Buckey and his mother, Peggy McMartin Buckey, who directed the Virginia McMartin Preschool in Manhattan Beach, California, made some kind of history. It lasted thirty-three months, not counting an eighteen-month-long preliminary hearing, making it the nation's longest criminal trial; it cost taxpayers about $15 million; it saw 124 witnesses, produced 63,000 pages of testimony, entered 917 exhibits, and resulted in a verdict that satisfied no one, not even the jurors. The Buckeys were charged with performing lewd and lascivious acts on eleven children over a period of several years, and the court heard chilling accounts of rape, sodomy, and bizarre satanic rituals.

The children's evidence had been obtained through interviews by Children's Institute International, conducted primarily by staff social worker Kee McFarlane, who made use of anatomically correct dolls in eliciting their stories. Videotapes were presented in court.

The defendants were found not guilty on fifty-two counts.

The sum of the McMartin case was that the children's testimony was not credible to most of the jurors, even though the consensus— it seems—was that someone or some people had molested some of the children. The children's statements were for the most part dismissed as fantasies scripted by overzealous therapists; the jurors apparently would have preferred to have heard the children speak for themselves without "prompting" or "coaching." I admire those jurors; they worked hard with the evidence that was presented to them. I believe they came to the only possible conclusion in the light of what they were given. But what a mindless mess this whole case was!

One really nasty piece of business stands out for me: Kee McFarlane, who had worked gently with the kids in territory that was then unknown, was attacked by the defense as some kind of brainwashing evil genius who led the children into making false and lurid charges. Compared with the time the children had spent at the McMartin Preschool, how much time did McFarlane have to pervert them? Not much. As John Cioffi, father of two of the children involved in the case, said to Ted Koppel on *Nightline*:

"Kee McFarlane saw our children for approximately ninety minutes when they were three and four years old. If she could convince them that they were raped and sodomized, and they still feel that six years later, she's a hot property."

A primary question is: Was there any fact in the children's stories, or was the whole thing fantasy? Could so many children who were allegedly abused be lying or fantasizing? Could they all have been inventing the accusations that put the McMartins on trial? Why should they?

More than one of the young accusers, now several years older, has said: "I was there. I know what happened to me."

I believe these children. I believe these children were molested; I believe that they were further abused by the long nightmare of the court proceedings, and abused again by a verdict that, in effect, held them to be liars. Children in adult courts are treated, at best, with paternal condescension and polite skepticism, or as fantasizing little freaks coached by outsiders with agendas of their own. All this is done with kid gloves, of course, because not even the deadliest of attorneys wants to be obviously beastly to a child, but the effect is the same: humiliation for the child, and often disaster and despair. Children are being made targets in situations that turn adults to jelly. And yet the overwhelming evidence from current literature leads to the conclusion that false disclosures by children are extremely rare. That is not to say that children never lie or elaborate; it is merely to point out that even in studies where investigators actively sought to elicit false reports of abuse, it was found that children as young as four years of age are highly resistant to suggestion. They know what they know, and let us not make the flighty assumption that children are less credible witnesses than adults.

In cases involving very young children, the spokespersons must do all the talking because the children cannot possibly make known their own concerns. What person can honestly say he is expressing a child's wishes and best interests? Are "wishes" and "best interests" necessarily the same? These are difficult enough questions, but in cases involving children who can, to some degree, speak for themselves, the issues become even more complex. For a child required to appear in court, the functions and attitudes of all the other people appearing are very baffling and often intimidating, and kids cannot be expected to handle court appearances without very specialized help. The present legal system does not and cannot work for them. At the very least, each child who has to appear in court *for any reason*, including a custody matter, should have the help of a court assistant, a trained volunteer to explain the court process and prepare the child for the kind of questioning he should expect.

But that is only the bare-bones beginning.

The judicial process in child sexual abuse cases is in need of a major overhaul. It is becoming clear that a child's best interests may not be served in a legal system that was designed for adults, not for children, unless reforms are made specifically addressing the issues involved in working with children before and during the court process without adulterating the child's evidence with adult input. There are real problems encountered in trying to prove beyond any reasonable doubt that a child was indeed sexually abused, especially when the abuse was allegedly perpetrated by a parent, a family member, a friend of the family, a teacher, or another equally trusted and supposedly respectable person. There seldom is any direct evidence; eyewitness testimony is rare, and often there is no physical or medical evidence that sexual abuse has occurred. Usually, the only proof is circumstantial. The case in court becomes an issue of who is telling the truth: the victim child, or the adult offender. It is an unequal match, that between adults and children.

And this has to change. Measures can and must be taken to minimize additional trauma to the child witness and help support the child through the process of testifying—not only for the sake of the child but to enhance his or her ability to tell the truth.

The American Academy of Child and Adolescent Psychiatry has drawn up recommendations for protecting children undergoing abuse investigations and appearing as witnesses; my colleagues and I have some of our own. Combined, here they are:

• Children alleged to have been sexually abused should be interviewed and examined only by specially trained investigatory personnel who possess a knowledge of child development, the family dynamics of child sexual abuse, and age-appropriate techniques for interviewing children. The court should choose, or have access to at all times, a multidisciplinary panel of nonpartisan professionals consisting of—for example—a physician, a psychologist, a social worker, a sex abuse expert, an attorney, a law enforcement officer, or possibly the child protection team at the nearest major hospital. This team works for the court and for the children, not for the defense or prosecution.

• The initial interview should be videotaped whenever possible to (a) minimize duplication of efforts and spare the child an appearance before the grand jury and (b) serve as a record of the professionalism of the interview should questions later arise as to how it was conducted. It must be recognized that how the child is questioned will affect the responses. Failure to establish rapport with the child, and the use of coercive, threatening, repetitive, tricky, or biased questions will of course be confusing and ultimately self-defeating.

• Cases involving child witnesses should be given priority on the court docket in order to preserve the freshness of the child's recollections, and also to avoid protracting any anxiety and fear that may result from any part or anticipation of the proceedings. Delaying or prolonging a case involving children can only impede impartial and appropriate judgments. A prolonged trial makes it almost impossible to obtain a conviction. Cases can be thrown out of court, or a mistrial declared for a variety of reasons, or jurors may suffer burnout or become sick, or children may become confused and their stories vague with the passage of time. Further, a child must be given the opportunity to proceed with his or her own life. Consider McMartin again: two and a half years spent for nothing!

No—let me retract that; it was not for nothing. It was years of lost time and a lot of pain and a massive letdown for the children who took the courage of their convictions to court, but they did not do what they did in vain. Those kids did something for every abused kid in this country, and they have a right to be proud. So do their parents, who listened to their children, believed in them, and hung in there with them.

• The uses and limitations of videotapes and closed-circuit TV are still being debated, the key issue being that—according to the Sixth Amendment—"the accused shall enjoy the right to be confronted with the witness against him." In fact, in some instances it may be helpful for the child to take the witness stand against the defendant. If it is deemed necessary for the child to testify before the defendant and a jury, he or she should not have to appear alone but should be accompanied by a trusted yet impartial adult. And there should be as few people in the courtroom as possible. Following testimony, the child must be allowed to talk about the experience. It should not be assumed that, just because the ordeal of testifying is over, the trauma is all behind the child. The shame and the fear go on.

• Any changes in legislation or court procedures dealing with sexually abused children should be consistent, practical, fair to all parties concerned, and adopted on a *national* level for all states and municipalities to follow. Briefly, what I mean by this is that standardized protocols should be established nationwide. If the use of videotaped testimony or closed-circuit television is to be accepted anywhere, let it be accepted everywhere; if a child's "live" testimony is to be used in court, let there be an established procedure with all possible built-in protections for the child.

• Tentatively, I would suggest establishing special child abuse prosecution units within the court system, using prosecutors who have been trained and have become experts in this area.

As a pediatrician and not a legal expert, I am no doubt naive in my belief that change in our judicial practices is possible, if our legal giants could only recognize that children are not little adults but victims of an antiquated system that makes very little provision for them. In truth, I don't see why change in something so basic and important as our legal system—the system that protects the rights of all of us—should be so difficult. The layman in me says, *Clean up your act, get down to common sense and goodwill, and practice law for the benefit of people who don't know how to bend it to their own uses.*

People like children, for instance. Children like Roxanne and Bradley. Children like Hilary. Children like poor Joshua.

12 / The Politics of Child Abuse: Promises, Promises

February 12, 1986. Our children are our nation's future, and we must do all we can to ensure that their lives are filled with the care and concern of those who love them and want them to develop to their full potential.
—President Ronald Reagan

At the time that Mr. Reagan made his declaration, the Reagan-Bush administration had already made significant cuts in essential children's programs, including education for the handicapped, summer youth employment, services for runaway and homeless youth, food stamps, child nutrition, Aid to Families with Dependent Children (AFDC), and Medicaid; and had proposed elimination of all juvenile justice, delinquency prevention, and legal services programs. Even as the President spoke, more cuts were being planned in Medicaid, AFDC, child nutrition programs, summer youth employment, child abuse prevention, child welfare services, Head Start, programs for runaway and homeless youth—virtually every program that related to the well-being of children.

The pattern of promises and cutbacks in our most essential services has not changed. President George Bush has earnestly declared that children are "all special," because "they are the very future of freedom," but under his administration we see further cutbacks in the most basic programs for the youngest, poorest, and most helpless of all Americans. Even the federal nutrition program known as WIC—for (pregnant) Women, Infants, and Children—is threatened with serious reductions because our government apparently can no longer afford it. This means that the prenatal care and regular checkups provided to women who receive the food supplements offered by the program will also be dangerously compromised.

What is more important than the health of mothers and children? Stirring declarations about how much we love them, I suppose. But that's politics in the U.S.A.

"Politics" is not actually a dirty word. There's good politics and there's bad politics, and if you are going to do anything intended to help people of any age and on any level of society, you can scarcely avoid getting mixed up in some form of politicking. I try to stick with good politics, but I must confess to making some errors in judgment.

My involvement with politics was not a result of a deliberate decision; it simply became inevitable. As a physician interested in the problem of child maltreatment, I was deeply engaged in the search for solutions, and I actively supported legislation on all levels to protect endangered children. In New York State, that legislation became effective in 1964. But the City of New York needed more than a state law to deal with the disease of child abuse and neglect in its own backyard. Child abuse seemed rampant in the mid-1960s—although nothing compared with what it is now—and I was both concerned and extremely vocal about the quality of our children's lives. I felt it was essential to get city officials committed to creating effective machinery for combating this blight, but, even though I was chairman of the Committee on Child Abuse and Neglect for the New York State Medical Society, I had no idea how or to whom to make an approach on a city level.

I was fortunate in meeting an important child advocate in the person of the late Dr. Howard J. Brown, then commissioner of health services in New York City. Dr. Brown approached Mayor John V. Lindsay, advising him of the scope and importance of the child abuse problem in New York City and suggesting that it might be appropriate for the Mayor's office to take some action.

Lindsay's immediate response—all things are relative; I am now talking about a date in April 1967—was to ask me to serve as special consultant on child abuse to him and Dr. Brown. In the following year the mayor appointed a special task force to study the effectiveness of existing child protective programs for reported cases of abused and neglected children. I was named chairman of that task force, which started work in 1969 and turned out to be the first Mayor's Task Force on Child Abuse and Neglect in the country.

I have been with it ever since, serving under four mayors: John Lindsay, Abe Beame, Ed Koch, and David Dinkins. Throughout these past many years, the members of this task force—always carefully selected for their sociological, medical, and legal expertise—have given their time and dedication to a difficult and often heartbreaking mission. As a task force, we have been effective and productive. However, we have also experienced our frustrations. At times we have been less than optimistic about the future of children. However, in the process of interacting with various mayors and their commissioners, I have learned a great deal about the workings of the bureaucracy.

I quickly discovered that the way for any citizens' advocacy group to make an impact for change was to involve people who basically had nothing to do with the problem. Those who already had jobs in the system were resistant to change; a bureaucracy is rarely willing to recognize its own deficiencies and endanger itself by making reforms from within. I found that there were many focal points that one might address in order to change public policy for children, from community organizations to foundations and from lawyers to people in the media. Publicity, as we all know, can do wonders, and I did not underrate it. Nor did I overrate it, because I soon discovered that significant change rarely results from media coverage alone; more often, it is a product of interaction among many groups and people—including the bureaucrats, who are seldom willing to change themselves.

But they are more willing to accept change than one might think. I found that, in the operations of the Mayor's Task Force, the development of a network of bureaucratic friends and media people played a significant role. There are many, many elected and career officials who often do the right thing if someone or some group of people on the outside shows them the way and makes clear a political motive for action. And after all, child protective decisions and policy statements are not made in isolation; they are arrived at in the midst of a complex and changing social and political climate.

Inevitably, by the late '60s, local interest had led to national concern. It was apparent to all of us in the field of child health and welfare that what was happening in New York was also happening, if perhaps on a less intense scale, throughout the country. Nothing can take the place of specifically directed neighborhood efforts, and I think that New York can and should take the lead providing replicable models, but a national problem has to have national programs and solutions. And, as other people in other parts of the country began to realize at the same time, a national program was something we did not have. There was no agency in government that spoke solely for the needs of children, or did anything about them; nor did President Richard Nixon exhibit the remotest trace of interest in matters relating to the welfare of families and children.

And that is why a number of concerned citizens began descending on Capitol Hill to insist that child abuse was a serious national problem that demanded federal intervention: people like myself; the late Dr. C. Henry Kempe, director of the National Center for Prevention and Treatment of Child Abuse and Neglect in Denver; Dr. Brandt Steele, professor of psychiatry at the National Center in Denver; Dr. Ray E. Helfer, a pediatric colleague of Kempe's and coeditor with him of *The Battered Child*; Mr. Douglas Besharov, then executive director of the New York State Assembly Select Committee on Child Abuse; and Jolly K., a dynamic, articulate woman who had survived a horrific childhood to become a battering parent herself and the anonymous founder of the self-help support group called Parents Anonymous.

Pleading the cause of children, we talked to every senator and congressperson we managed to buttonhole. Over the weeks and months we met with Senator Hubert Humphrey and his staff, Senator Walter Mondale and his staff, New York Representative Mario Biaggi and his staff, Colorado Representative Pat Schroeder, Senator Jennings Randolph of West Virginia; the Honorable Tip O'Neill, Speaker of the House; to anyone who would listen to us. Between us, we must have talked to hundreds of people. We went to hearings in Denver, Washington, and New York; we presented documents, case studies, slides, graphs, plans. To our near-despair, few cared to listen and fewer chose to believe that child abuse was a serious problem demanding federal intervention.

As it turned out, however, we were being listened to by people who counted. Senator Mondale attacked the problem with the zeal of a ready convert and proposed a bill to establish a federally funded national center on child abuse and neglect and to provide demonstration grants to finance projects aimed at treating or preventing child abuse. Representative Schroeder, a powerful and caring voice of support from the beginning, carried Mondale's bill in the House.

As I glance through my notes for the closing months of 1973 I am struck by the similarity between what was said at the hearings, what had been said ten years earlier, and what we are saying even now. Dr. Kempe of Denver was our chief spokesman at the 1973 hearings; although he died in 1984, we can hear him today.

Dr. C. Henry Kempe:

"In order to insure each child's basic rights, society must have access to the child from birth until school age, the most critical time of child development. This is best done, in our opinion, through implementation of the concept of universal health supervision. We suggest that a health visitor call at intervals during the first months of life upon each young family, and that she become the guardian, so to speak, who would see to it that each infant is receiving his basic health rights." [All were and are in favor of this. It hasn't happened yet.]

"A national computerized child abuse report registry should be available. The high mobility of abusive parents makes it essential that any physician be able to ascertain whether a given child is listed in a national registry. In this way, it will be possible to discover if a child has experienced repeated injuries, thus increasing the likelihood that a correct diagnosis is made." [A computerized central registry had already been proposed for New York State. It was opposed by the New York Civil Liberties Union because of the "potential abuse of such a centralized record-keeping system," according to one of its functionaries. "What frightens us," she said, "is the possibility of allegations being made and nothing being done to clear the record of the person falsely accused." There is no reason, however, why this should be regarded as an insoluble problem. New York State already has a Central Registry; it simply needs to be more sophisticated and computerized.]

"There is a pressing need for the development of a network of adequate foster homes for interim placement of children while parents receive help from lay therapists and Families Anonymous groups. A period of foster care placement should be seen as a temporary measure to help decrease pressure and to minimize crises while parents are learning how to cope with their problems." [That is still the idea; that is still not the practice.]

"It is clear that the departments of social services are not able to perform the task of preventing or treating the problems of child abuse and neglect. It is impossible to approach a multidisciplinary problem with a single-discipline service unit. We must develop a multidisciplinary service unit which can cut across many of the traditions and unworkable rules and regulations that are built into most protective service departments." [Turf barriers are still a problem; services are splintered; our child protective services do not field multidisciplinary teams.]

Kempe said it all. He talked of the need for a network of crisis nurseries and day care centers in each community, of visiting homemakers, of the warehousing of hundreds of thousands of preschool children, of family life or "parenting" education, of a comprehensive plan to bring all services together. In the years since then, we have been stuck in a revolving door. We go in with a plan, and we come out with nothing. Not much has changed in almost twenty years.

But at least in 1973 we had a national platform. The hearings demonstrated the horrors of child abuse to those who had known little of them, and documented the shocking weaknesses in federal, state, and local child protective efforts. And we were heard.

The congressional response was the nearly unanimous passage of the Federal Child Abuse Prevention and Treatment Act of 1974, properly known as Public Law 93-247 but more often called the Mondale Act because of its chief sponsor. The act established the National Center on Child Abuse and Neglect (NCCAN), within what was then called the Department of Health, Education, and Welfare, as a focal point for federal efforts to address the issue of child maltreatment. From the outset, NCCAN was intended to offer leadership in establishing child abuse as a national concern and federal priority.

NCCAN opened for business with an annual appropriation of about $19 million, most of which was allocated for demonstration grants, technical assistance, and grants to states that qualified under the eligibility regulations of Public Law 93-247. Unfortunately, the Center was not allowed to fund established treatment programs unless they were demonstrating something new. Thus, it could not and did not support good programs that had shown themselves to be effective in treatment and prevention of child abuse, nor could it make funds available to continue their existing work.

That effectively shut out those of us who had labored in the front lines for ten or more years to bring the plight of abused children to the attention of national leaders and had cheered the resultant creation of the National Center. It was a letdown of major proportions to Kempe, myself, and others to learn that there would be no federal funds available to continue—never mind expand—our successful intervention programs. We had hoped to fund and support major treatment services; we wound up with a kind of think-tank operation that did surveys and held conferences and hired public-relations firms to develop public awareness campaigns. After all our efforts we were left to scrounge for our own funding from foundations or private sources.

And in spite of all the public awareness that was being aroused, many effective prevention and treatment programs were finding it very difficult to obtain fiscal support from state and local governments, which were in the habit of giving low priority to child protective services and specifically to the prevention of child abuse. At the same time, it was almost impossible to obtain grants from private foundations, which had and still have a very limited interest in anything relating to child abuse and neglect—I suppose because there is no hope of isolating the affliction or finding an effective vaccine.

It occurred to me that there were national organizations in America that did their own fund-raising to support and treat other social and medical problems, organizations such as the American Cancer Society, the American Heart Association, the American Lung Association, and the United Cerebral Palsy Association. Why not—I thought—a national association that could undertake a major fund-raising campaign to help support child abuse prevention and treatment programs throughout the United States?

I felt then, as I do now, that no program should be completely dependent on federal, state, or local support, since government funding on any level can be cut off abruptly if fiscal crisis makes it necessary. I believe that there should be comparable involvement and support from the private sector, that people should recognize that child abuse is everybody's business and therefore participate in efforts to break the cycle of generational violence. And it has to be a comparable contribution: public and private activities can coexist and flourish only if they are coequal in their efforts.

As I saw it, the way to go was to enlist the cooperative efforts of the leading child abuse experts and child advocates in the country and bring them together in a national organization that could speak with one compelling voice. Public awareness of the problem was no longer an issue. The public was aware; it was just not contributing. We had to find a way to meet the enormity of the needs we had discovered, a way to expand treatment programs and provide funding for community facilities throughout the country. We needed clearly focused support, and we needed money for something more than Band-Aids. In short, we had to have popular support for a nationwide anti-abuse campaign, and we had to have a national organization to push it.

Spurred on by this thought, I started lining up my troops. My first big gun was New York State Assembly Minority Leader Perry B. Duryea. A close friend of mine and supporter of the project, Duryea had established the New York State Assembly Select Committee on Child Abuse in 1969; in 1973, he had sponsored the New York State Child Protective Services Act, which has been proclaimed as the most progressive child abuse legislation in the nation. Among the founders of the new association, he was our only certified politician.

My next invited volunteers were indeed hands-on experts in the field of child abuse: Dr. Vincent De Francis, renowned social worker and director of the Children's Division of the American Humane Association in Denver; Dr. C. Henry Kempe; Dr. Eli Newberger, child advocate and child abuse expert, then director of the Trauma X Project at Children's Hospital in Boston; myself. Joining us later were Sara O'Meara and Yvonne Fedderson, founders of Childhelp USA.

Much hard work, many months, and many meetings culminated in a press conference in Washington, D.C., on December 22, 1975. Perry Duryea made the announcement: "The nation's leading experts in the prevention and treatment of child abuse," he said, "have joined together to form the National Alliance for the Prevention and Treatment of Child Abuse!" Flashbulbs, cheers, applause!

It was a stirring moment for us all, and we felt that something had truly been accomplished—but, as would-be fund-raisers, we were still left with the major question of how to get the public interested in our cause. We had already decided that what we must do was focus on some famous individual and persuade him or her to support our efforts and be our national spokesperson. What we didn't know was who or how.

It took us a very long time and a lot of maneuvering to come up with any likely possibilities. I myself finally settled on Frank

Sinatra. What bigger name was there? Who could be better? The world knew him and admired him, he had influence, he had charisma, he could hold an audience in the palm of his hand; he could be enormously persuasive. He was not at that moment at the absolute peak of his popularity, but perhaps that would make him more available. Anyway, it couldn't hurt to ask.

One little drawback was that I didn't know how to get to him. I spoke to numbers of people and I asked around, especially among my few show business contacts, and eventually I was told that the only way to get to Sinatra was through his lawyer, Milton A. Rudin, who reputedly ran Sinatra's life for him—although I cannot imagine anyone but Sinatra doing that—and handled all his business affairs.

I wrote to Mr. Rudin, of Rudin & Perlstein, Beverly Hills, California, and after a while he wrote me back saying that he was coming to New York and would like to meet with me to discuss the National Alliance and Mr. Sinatra's involvement. I set up the meeting and asked Mr. Arthur Zwiebel, an old friend and the director of development at the New York Foundling Hospital, to join us and give me the benefit of his fund-raising expertise.

The meeting went very well. I found Mr. Rudin to be a very affable and concerned human being who came across as really wanting to get something done about child abuse and indicating that Mr. Sinatra's involvement was a real possibility. Subsequently we had several enjoyable dinners and meetings, all of which ended on a very friendly and positive note. I began to feel quite optimistic that we were getting closer to the fulfillment of our hopes for a successful Alliance with a prominent spokesman spearheading our efforts. I kept my fellow members fully briefed, and they, too, were filled with optimism for the future of the Alliance and the likelihood of getting financial support for innovative and cost-effective programs.

Enthusiastic correspondence passed back and forth, all of it enormously encouraging. It seemed that Mr. Sinatra planned to become totally involved with the Alliance and the problem of child abuse. I had yet to meet him personally, but there were plans in the offing: Milton Rudin wrote to me in December 1977, saying, "Please advise us as to your available time in January or February, and we will get back to you."

I could not help having the feeling that something good was

definitely going to happen with Frank Sinatra. To me and my colleagues, it certainly looked as though we were about to achieve our hopes for a star to lead our fund-raising activities.

Not long into the new year, I was vacationing in Puerto Rico when I received a call from Rudin inviting me to a birthday dinner party he was giving for his daughter at the 21 Club in New York. Sinatra would be there, and Rudin was making arrangements for me to meet the famous singer and talk about his involvement with child abuse and the National Alliance. I cut short my vacation and flew back to New York to attend the dinner and have an informal meeting with Mr. Sinatra.

Rudin had arranged for me to sit with the star; his wife, Barbara; his daughter; and comedienne Totie Fields and her husband. Accordingly, we met, we talked, we dined. After dinner the Sinatra group left for a midtown disco and I went along with them.

The stretch limo dropped us off at the disco, which turned out to be almost completely deserted. Perhaps it was too early for the younger set to be up and about. No sooner were we seated when Sinatra took himself off to another part of the club to meet with some associates. I felt a little awkward, sitting with strangers in an empty room, but the jukebox was playing one of my favorite dance numbers and I was moved to ask Barbara Sinatra if she would care to dance with me. I thought I sensed a touch of apprehension or anxiety on the part of Mr. Sinatra's daughter when Barbara accepted and we rose to leave the table, but perhaps she was just stifling a yawn.

We danced, we enjoyed ourselves, and we came back to the table.

Mr. Sinatra eventually rejoined us, and soon we left, the Sinatras returning to the Waldorf Towers and I to my apartment. The next day I delivered my book *Somewhere a Child Is Crying* to the Waldorf Towers with a short note thanking Mr. Sinatra for a pleasant evening and looking forward to the major role he was to play in fighting child abuse.

After that, nothing. *Nothing.* I had had my first and last meeting with Frank Sinatra and my first and last dance with his wife. What had happened? Had I stepped on her toes—or on his? I will never know exactly what I did wrong. All I know is that there was no further word of Frank's interest in child abuse or the Alliance. We had lost Mr. Sinatra, I felt, because of my naïvete.

Not long afterward, Mr. Sinatra's career skyrocketed once again and has remained in orbit ever since. He has become involved in many excellent social programs and fund-raising events. One of his interests is the Barbara Sinatra Children's Center, an outpatient facility for sexually abused children, which opened in 1986 on the campus of the Eisenhower Medical Center at Rancho Mirage, California. I like to think that something I said or did that evening might have played some small part in inspiring the creation of the Center and in the good works that are being accomplished there.

Maybe Barbara enjoyed our brief meeting more than Frank did.

But the National Alliance had lost Frank Sinatra, so once again I began our search for a famous individual who would consent to be our spokesperson. We had wasted precious time. During the many months I had invested in the Rudin connection, the programs at the scattered child abuse prevention centers had run critically low on the funding necessary to continue their services to the kids and their families. We would have to move quickly.

I had already used up most of my connections with show business when I got to talking with Dr. Joseph Santo, a dentist turned restaurateur who ran the elegant Sign of the Dove on Manhattan's East Side. He suggested that his good friend Tip O'Neill, frequent visitor to the restaurant and Speaker of the House of Representatives, might be interested in helping. And, indeed, as someone who had heard a great deal about the problem in 1973, he was.

However, we were still looking for our star, somebody possibly in the entertainment community. Joe Santo enlisted the help of his brother and partner Berge and his wife Henney, and they, it turned out, knew somebody who worked with Sophia Loren.

Sophia Loren. Well. Why not? A famous star, a mother, a beautiful woman, a person known and respected throughout the world. She probably wouldn't give us the time of day.

Ms. Loren proved to be approachable and receptive. We invited her to be our spokesperson and, in a letter dated September 18, 1979, she wrote:

I am pleased to accept the role of National Chairperson for the National Alliance for the Treatment and Prevention of Child Abuse. The prevention and treatment of child abuse is a worldwide problem and one that must be addressed by every Nation in the world. Any part that I can play in assisting your organization in the United States, I am pleased to do.

With all due caution, I felt that we were on our way at last. Sophia Loren was our official national chairperson, and Tip O'Neill and his wife Millie were our national vice-chairpersons.

The wheels of politics began to turn. Speaker O'Neill and Congressman Mario Biaggi sponsored a resolution in Congress requesting that the President of the United States proclaim the month of December as National Child Abuse Prevention Month. President Jimmy Carter signed the proclamation in November 1979. It was the first such national recognition of child abuse prevention in a presidential proclamation, and it was in effect a joint call upon the public by Congress and President Carter to support the National Alliance's treatment and prevention programs.

A White House ceremony launching what was to be a nationwide campaign to solicit help from the American people was held on January 28, 1980. The members of the National Alliance were there, Sophia Loren and Speaker Tip O'Neill were there, Congressman Biaggi and many other notables were there, and we all met with President Carter in the Cabinet Room of the White House. This was indeed the culmination of a lot of hard work and dedicated effort by a lot of caring people throughout a lot of years.

President Carter said: "Our nation's children are our nation's future. One of the most serious blights on the prospects for the children of our country is child abuse and the damage that results from it. I urge all communities, public agencies, private agencies and the business community to support needed social, educational and health services to strengthen families during the critical child rearing years."

This was the first major presidential declaration of commitment to children that we had heard for quite some time.

Ms. Loren declared her support for the National Alliance and said, "The National Alliance will try to awaken the world's consciousness against this sordid and persistent crime."

At long last, our campaign was off to an auspicious start.

The press coverage, however, was not all that might have been desired. Jack Anderson, in the *Washington Post*, commented on Tip O'Neill's appreciation of Sophia's beauty, and observed that she in return had found something nice to say "about the rumpled, white-maned congressman." O'Neill had said that he wasn't used to running on his looks, and then admitted that he didn't go to movies much.

And some more of the same: publicity for the pols and Sophia, but not much for the sponsors. Still, the Alliance had made the papers, and we were making great plans for a fund-raising drive throughout the country with Sophia Loren playing a major role as an attention-getting star. Preparations were already under way to stage two major fund-raising events featuring Ms. Loren, one in New York and one in Los Angeles. There was just one small hitch: expenses. We identified this problem when the bills started coming in.

The member agencies of the Alliance had each contributed five thousand dollars as seed money to cover expenses associated with the planning and production of the White House ceremony, including all expenses incurred by and on behalf of our spokesperson. But we had unfortunately made a couple of unwarranted assumptions: one, that the White House event would quickly generate the beginnings of a cash inflow; two, that a figurehead for a new fund-raising effort would realize that we were not in a position to dispense luxuries.

Silly us, naïve again. We simply had not figured in a realistic estimate of costs, which should have included Ms. Loren's two-way trip by Concorde, accompanied by her son and a friend, their hotel and dining expenses, the limousine at their disposal, and the various little petty items that always crop up on business trips.

By the time we had finished paying our bills, we had run out of money. Our investment of hopes and plans and cash had left us with ashes in our hands. We had blown everything on the White House ceremony and our star. Plans for the New York and L.A. events had to be dumped immediately; Ms. Loren would be available only if we were able to subsidize her expenses for any future appearances.

So there we were with empty coffers and no Sophia Loren to help us fill them. My colleagues and I, jaded with stars, slunk back to work on our respective projects and our separate fund-raising efforts.

Does nobody speak for the children?

In fact, *everybody* speaks for the children. Talk is cheap, and it is convenient for politicians and other public personalities to have their pictures taken with children and express their concern. The costly and difficult part is actually doing something.

In the election of 1988 one would really have thought that the hour of the children was somewhere near. Candidate Michael Dukakis referred to children as "our joy and our future" and warned us about the new challenges facing the American family. Candidate George Bush claimed to be haunted by the lives of inner-city kids and observed that the "national character can be measured by how we care for our children."

Yes, indeed. We need only to look at the national infant mortality rate, the numbers of children who live in poverty, the state of our schools, the state of our national mental health, the human cost of cocaine, crime, and crack, and the complete absence of any national initiative or plan for dealing with child abuse to form an idea of our national character.

> President George Bush: "One thing I'm going to do is raise the level of public debate about how best to help our children. I'm going to talk and talk and talk until our country is working together to reach our children."
>
> Marian Wright Edelman, president of the Children's Defense Fund: "The mounting crisis of our children and our families is a rebuke to everything America professes to be."
>
> Senator Christopher Dodd (D-Conn.), cosponsor of the Act for Better Child Care: "Never before has there been a constituency so popular but with so little political clout."
>
> Representative Patricia Schroeder (D-Colo.): "The tragedy is that the power base in Washington is not built around children's issues. You don't gain power talking about children. You gain power talking about tanks and missiles and all that crap."

Pat Schroeder knows. When her daughter was two years old, Schroeder began pushing for child care legislation. That child, as of this writing, is twenty, and the child care bill finally got through Congress in 1990.

Said Schroeder: "Child care is not a power issue. Children don't vote. They don't have political action committees. Plus, I don't think there are too many members of Congress who couldn't come to work because of lack of child care."

I am quite sure she is right. Luckily, we have a President who has promised to talk and talk and talk.

The nation's representatives in Washington have consistently paid lip service to children. In fairness, many of them mean well, and some are zealous, forceful advocates, but they experience the same frustrations as those of us who work within the child protective system: when the meeting's over, the shouting dies down and people go home until next year. Or for another decade.

The first White House Conference on Children was convened in 1909 to discuss and marshal support for government planning on behalf of children. Since that time, once every decade, the federal government has convened such a conference, reaffirming its commitment to monitor and report on children's status in society. "Monitor and report?" Good idea for 1909, but surely we should have gone beyond it by the 1990s. Keynote of that first conference: "Home life is the highest and finest product of civilization and a child should not be deprived of it except for urgent and compelling reasons."

Some highlights from some conferences since then:

1919: The conference set standards for the Children's Bureau approved by Congress in 1912. The Bureau was to focus its work narrowly on infant/maternal mortality and health and launch educational programs for mothers to reduce the incidence of deaths associated with childbirth. Today, we observe an incidence of neonatal mortality that is higher than ever.

1930, the year of Child Health and Protection: Broad in scope, this conference dealt with almost every aspect of childhood and adolescence. Keynote: "The family has its limitations. There is need for extrafamilial institutions to supplement parental responsibility." President Herbert Hoover, although not one of our more highly regarded chief executives, commented very wisely on the role of parents versus extrafamilial institutions. "Such responsibility as was assumed for children outside the home," he said, "was in the beginning largely based on what we call 'charity.' We have seen what was once charity change its nature under the broader term 'welfare,' and now those activities looked upon as welfare are coming to be viewed merely as good community housekeeping. In a word, parental responsibility is moving outward to include community responsibility. *We must force the problem back to where the child is.* This primarily means, and should mean, the home. Our function should be to keep parents, not replace them." That observation, made in 1930, could easily be addressed to the problems confronting the families of the '90s.

1950: The conference pledged to "work to conserve and improve family life" and called for further study of the underlying causes of broken homes and divorces. Children were beginning to emerge as inhabitants of the social scene rather than just junior members of the family. President Truman said: "We cannot insulate our children from the uncertainties of the world in which we live or from the impact of the problems which confront us."

1960: This conference was concerned with adolescents, or "teenagers in trouble." Keynote: "Finding ways to turn youths' isolation and discontent away from destructiveness and delinquency and toward constructive citizenship." The conference viewed changes in the family as ominous signs heralding the future breakdown of society, and focused on the antisocial behavior of youngsters from disobedience through political apathy to crime. A large number of recommendations called for parent education beginning in high school to help young people understand the responsibilities of marriage and the privilege of parenthood. But in the past thirty years, we have not taken action to prevent family breakdown. Essentially, nothing has changed for the better.

1970: Ironically, in the year of Kent State, the White House Conference endorsed a Children's Bill of Rights, thereby transforming children's developmental, health, and educational *needs* into their "rights"—such as the right to be wanted, loved, educated, and generally cared for. The proclamation was of course heartwarming, but it gave no indication of what it means as a practical matter to fulfill these rights.

Today, children are still powerless, inconsiderable little nothings blown about by the winds of political and social expedience. They are unable to articulate their own interests or organize themselves into a constituency. Lacking the power to vote, they have neither voice nor influence within the political system. And I don't suggest they should have. It is a given that responsible adults, preferably voting adults, must speak for them and act for them.

Regrettably, positive programs have rarely grown out of conferences. There is always a great distance between rhetoric and reality, between recommendation and implementation, and this distance is especially noticeable in children's affairs. The attitude is that children can wait; they will always be with us; there is no urgency to look to their needs. They are oblivious to the discussion about them, and ultimately the discussion is oblivious to them:

children get lost in the welter of words and will only be rediscovered when the politicians need them.

And that is cynical, dangerous politics.

There is something new in the wind as the new decade finds it pace. It has something to do, I think, with our sense of ourselves as Americans. We have gotten pretty tired of hearing about our poor record among the civilized and not-so-civilized nations of the world; we're ashamed of our shocking infant mortality rate and the growing numbers of children in poverty and the increase in crimes against kids. This is not what America is supposed to be about. Our conscience is beginning to hurt. Or perhaps what's hurting is our pride. No matter; whether we are moved by pride or shame or competitive spirit, let us get moving.

Since the mid-1980s, Harris polls and other surveys have shown that a majority of the public is willing to spend more money on children's programs, including medical care for poor children, prenatal care for poor women, and job training for teens. Very little that is concrete has yet come out of this newly enlightened attitude, and very little *will* come until the public insists that our elected officials produce some action instead of just talk. The fact of the matter is that those of us who have spent our lives working with troubled families and developing programs to help them know very well how to tackle the multi-problem of child abuse. There's no mystery about it. And if there is magic, the magic is in the method. All that is needed now—and that is a monumental *all!*—is a formula consisting of two things: committed national leadership, and specifically allocated funds. The children have been shortchanged for long enough.

Our federal government, by its wholesale neglect of children, has been one of their chief abusers. *What are any of our foreign and domestic and internal policies worth if they do not look toward the reality of our future, which is the children? What are our priorities?* We talk of our environment in terms of rain forests and pollutants and endangered species; we seem not to understand that children must be at the heart of our environmental concerns. We have given our children an environment that is an abuse in itself. Nor will we ever grasp this concept until it is national policy to make the welfare of our children a national issue, implemented by a department devoted solely and explicitly to that purpose and backed by the monies to coordinate and maintain effective programs on a nation-wide basis.

Meanwhile, states and countries and towns try hard to deal with child protection on a local level even though it is not a local problem. They bumble along as best they can in a fragmented, disjointed way, totally lacking national guidelines and ignored in the national budget. In permitting this, Washington is abrogating responsibility for millions of nonvoting citizens, leaving them ill-provided for and ill-equipped to learn and prosper.

Assuming that the federal government does take hold of the reins and sponsor a national child abuse treatment and prevention program, what should it do to begin with? My answer: Make an assessment of all existing programs and demonstration models. Eliminate those that are not worth the carrying charges. Pump funds into programs that have shown themselves to be effective and replicable: prenatal and postnatal programs, parenting training for adults and youngsters, support groups, multidisciplinary child abuse teams at hospitals, neighborhood centers offering a full range of community human support services for all families—any child advocate can come up with many more in a matter of seconds.

Let it not be thought that funding a chain of such programs will take away from the war against poverty, or the war against drugs, or the war against crime. We may never know in what heart of darkness lies the deep-down seed that grew into our abuse of children, but we do know that poverty and crime and the drug scourge feed into child abuse, and child abuse feeds into them.

We have in our hands, right now, a great many weapons—peaceful ones, of course—for attacking child abuse and defeating it. But we won't be able to use those weapons unless and until the people we have voted into office can get their priorities in order.

Whether through advocacy efforts, political activism, or direct action, our children—our future—must be at the top of our list.

13 / An Agenda: The Future Is Now

For those of us who have spent the past two decades and more in the front lines of the battle against child abuse, it is clear that the responsibility for managing abused and neglected children is no longer the exclusive province of one person, one profession, or one child protective service. It is everybody's business. We know now what we theorized many years ago: that a team of professionals representing a variety of disciplines is best equipped to manage the problem of child abuse and neglect.

The simple, indispensable keys to success are communication, cooperation, and coordination. Experts representing the different disciplines, from medicine and child care to education and the law, are the core of the team. These people must learn to talk and listen to each other. The larger team is the rest of us: all citizens, young and old, who despise our national enthusiasm for violence and our casual acceptance that parents "own" their children and may therefore treat them as cavalierly as they please. We all have a stake in what happens to our nation's children. It is time that we, as individuals and as members of a community, started acting as though we cared.

America's children are our joint and personal responsibility.

This is a time of intense media interest in the question of child abuse and neglect. I find it most encouraging that some prominent politicians, too, have turned the spotlight on issues affecting children. We should seize the moment and go with it. Child advocates on all levels of government and within the community must assume leadership in the development and implementation of community child abuse treatment and prevention programs that have been found to work.

I think a common misconception has been that the failure of our child protective efforts—and in very large part, they have failed—is due to a lack of ideas and strategies, of facilities and personnel, of preventive and rehabilitative services, of models and blueprints, and the funding to provide these elements. In part, this is true. We do need more of everything, especially trained personnel and money. But it is also true that we have taken initiatives and devised strategies that *do* work. We have some excellent facilities and services, and we have countless numbers of innovative programs that have proved themselves to be outstandingly effective.

As promising as these programs are, they can only be replicated or expanded if properly funded. Yet we know them to be workable; and we know, too, that if all of them were to be fully utilized and coordinated, we would be well on the way to achieving the goal of giving our children a second chance at a life worth living.

Two things have undercut and sometimes even totally sabotaged our efforts. One is the absence of national policy and leadership; and the other, growing out of the former, is the uncoordinated, fragmented, and often wastefully overlapping system under which we devise and deliver medical and social services to families under stress and children at risk. We have created competing bureaucracies that have squandered financial resources, drowned us all in paperwork, lost vital information about endangered children, and shunted responsibility from one agency to another until no agency or individual is accountable for any part of the process of child saving. The buck, it seems, doesn't stop anywhere.

Still, we have a great deal going for us. We have the know-how, and we have a lot of the resources. Every aspect of the maltreatment problem and every risk factor associated with it has been successfully attacked through intervention techniques we know how to deliver. Critics make much of the fact that some of these are only "demonstration" or model programs, which seems to make them think that they are not applicable elsewhere. True, community-based models may not translate exactly. A program tailored for

Newark, New Jersey, will probably not work too well *without modification* for Lubbock, Texas. But common sense and flexibility are key elements in implementing effective programs. In the course of the past fifteen to twenty years we have seen enough test or pilot projects to convince us that there are plenty of treatment and preventive programs that work and plenty that are replicable throughout the United States. And having observed them, we don't simply admire them; we study them until we know exactly why and how they work. Evaluative research has substantiated claims of program success: What we have proved on a small scale—and that is how trial runs for major programs nearly always begin—we can expand to the greater community.

To quote Lisbeth B. Schorr, lecturer in social medicine and health policy at Harvard Medical School and author of the book *Within Our Reach: Breaking the Cycle of Disadvantage*:

I have come to believe that successful programs are important even when they operate in circumstances that are unusual. First, because it is essential to understand that there *are* programs that work. Model programs—no matter how special their circumstances—show that, even in an imperfect world, something can be done to address social problems previously considered to be intractable.

In addition, knowing that we can succeed on a small scale, means we can begin systematically to address the question of how human services systems must be modified to extend successful programs to many more children and families at risk. Finding ways to incorporate into large bureaucracies the comprehensive, intensive, and personalized approaches so crucial to successful programs is surely the next frontier in the development of human services.

By the same token, we don't need any more research of the protection complex's individual components to know what works. We have tested these components. We know that prenatal and postnatal care, education for parenting, preschool programs, crisis nurseries, child abuse teams, homemaker services, self-help groups, home visitors, lay therapists, surrogate parents, day care, and a shopping list of other programs have all proved themselves. I believe the only demonstration program we still need—and I think it should be initiated as soon as possible in a number of communities—is a restructured version of the ramshackle combination of agencies and purchased services that make up our nation's present human support systems. I would like to see a program in which a complete package of essential human services is pulled together at the neighborhood level, with all previously disparate programs linked together in one center to provide a coherent combination of services.

This should be initiated, I believe, in one or more high-risk communities, where drugs and poverty and all the forms of family dysfunctioning are part of the daily scene, and also in middle-class communities accustomed to finding services from podiatry to dentistry in one all-purpose shopping mall. With the assistance of foundations and other private institutions, government at all levels—right on down to the community boards—must seek out the political and social impediments to providing coordinated services and ride roughshod over these impediments. Programs for families and children must not be stymied by pettinesses such as the not-in-my-backyard syndrome, or the knee-jerk where's-the-money-coming-from response of bureaucrats who waste millions every day. It is important for all engaged in such an enterprise to make clear to the community at large that everyone in the vicinity will benefit from the delivery of services to families and children in need—or else, some day, the cost in terms of crime and agony will hit each one of us much harder than it does now.

But that is cynical. Surely we will do what must be done out of our good hearts and our common sense. A large-scale demonstration can be started in any city or community or suburb today. It would be the neighborhood concept I have introduced in earlier chapters, developed by the city's bureau of children's services in cooperation with the targeted high-risk community. It should include a total array of family services, a one-stop shopping mall of help for those who need medical care or drug counseling, welfare payments or food stamps, a homemaker, a parenting class, subsidized day care or temporary respite, job training and housing help—in short, assistance with all family problems. At the same time, such a center could coordinate its support services to troubled families with investigative and protective service caseworkers working closely with local school personnel and law enforcement officers, so that all personnel engaged in child protection can keep tabs on at-risk children—and *prevent* their abuse.

New space being a factor—hard to find and difficult to finance—I would suggest that the first family service center or centers be based in existing child welfare community centers.

When this neighborhood family-oriented plan demonstrates its value, as it surely will, it must become an integrated part of a network linking all such centers with the central city agency, the state agency, and ultimately the federal agency that will have to be put in place to support and integrate the entire national effort. That federal agency, in effect, could serve as the children's defense department. But that part of it comes later. The first move must come from the community of child care professionals, child advocates, and private citizens who understand and recognize that the entire fabric of American life is threatened unless we spare tomorrow's children from the torment endured by today's.

Herewith, incorporating small schemes and large, is a basic blueprint for the future:

Home and family. I urge community leaders throughout the nation, whether they be figures in the church or local politics or mothers who are fed up with the way things are today, to conduct campaigns in their own backyards to promote a rediscovery of moral values and of a sense of family, whatever the family unit may be, and spread the word through neighborhood support programs and church-affiliated groups. I appeal herewith to parents everywhere to look to themselves and to their own families and their own children. Remember *love.* Love is not enough, but without love there is nothing. The first element in abuse and preventing abuse is personal responsibility. I urge parents to try to grasp the nature and extent of child abuse, and see how it ties in with the ugliest aspects of our society. Violence and hatred begin in the home. They should be vanquished right there.

I implore parents to give their children moral guidance at home, and monitor their television watching and other activities. Establish rules and stick to them. Start early. I implore them, too, to listen to their children and observe their body language. Do the little ones cry when they are taken to the child care center? Are they developing sleep disturbances? Does something appear to be frightening them? Are older children becoming nervous, depressed, withdrawn? We should look to the settings where they spend their days, sometimes their nights. Something may be seriously wrong at school, at the day care center, at camp—or at home.

Further, we must recognize that we do have the moral responsibility to step in when we have reason to believe that someone else's child is being maltreated. Relatives, friends, and neighbors of abused kids are much at fault when they suspect abuse but take no action. Tragedies develop while the time slips by and the crying does not stop. The child does not know how to escape, but nearly always someone knows or someone hears and wonders. The children who have died of abuse did not die somewhere out in the wilderness. They died next door. They were surrounded by people. The neighbors who make repeated calls to the city to complain about poor garbage collection should be the same ones who make a call about suspected child abuse. The same people who resent a child's endless crying are the people who should volunteer their help.

School. Schools can teach even if parents can't, and even if teachers are weary and discouraged. I call on them to teach what they used to teach. Common civility. Respect and self-respect. Respect for the rights of others. Respect for human life and the quality of life. Respect for country and a sense of citizenship. Civic pride. Personal standards of ethics. What is right and what is wrong. Moral responsibility.

Some parents can teach this themselves, others can't because they never learned it themselves. Whether we like it or not, we must play catch-up and fill-in, or the kids that we're trying to educate will grow up as amoral, ignorant, and violent as their parents. Younger generations used to learn these common human decencies at school. True, these lessons reinforced, rather than made up for, what was taught at home—but it is even more necessary to teach them in the schools today because many of the parents themselves were not taught these things.

Educators today complain that they are asked to do much more than they have done in the past. The truth is that many of them do less. They used to teach right and wrong along with the ABCs and multiplication tables without worrying that they might be overstepping their bounds; they considered it part of the job. Now many schools don't teach reading, 'riting, and 'rithmetic—*or* moral standards.

I would ask all educators, as part of a genuine collaboration between the school and the community, to extend their educational program to both the very young and the older students. We know—we do not merely guess, we know—that courses in family life pay off for adults as well as children. We know, too, that preschool programs are genuinely effective in giving kids a head start on their educational life. Longitudinal studies of individuals who participated in high-quality preschool programs at the three- to four-year-old level demonstrate lower than average figures of dropouts, students needing remedial education, delinquency, teenage pregnancies, and unemployment. Studies also tell us that school-based health clinics can play a major role in reducing the rate of teenage childbearing, as they have in Maryland and Minnesota. It is very clear that what is done in school has critical impact on the student's future well-being.

The clergy. Over the years the church has mobilized its membership on a variety of social and political issues. Priests, rabbis, and ministers preach about the sanctity of life, the horrors of poverty and starvation in distant lands, love for one another, respect for the family, and honoring thy father and mother. Yet very little is said about respecting and honoring the child, or about domestic violence, a major cause of family breakdown. To some extent, the church has responded to the plight of the elderly, the child care crisis, and the abuse of drugs and alcohol by adolescents, but it has given minimum attention to the devastating effects of child abuse on family stability and social integrity. Voices from the pulpit have called widespread attention to the "rescue the children" cry of the right-to-life movement, and have indeed actively and vociferously sponsored it, but they have had little to say about the children born into a life of abuse. Why, I wonder, are our church people unwilling to speak to their congregations about the beating of children, the neglect of children, and the harsh punishment inflicted upon them in the name of discipline? Why have they sponsored so few programs for the prevention and treatment of child abuse?

There is much that the church—any and every church—can do. Provide human support services within the church to those in the congregation who are in need of such services. Utilize underused space in church and school facilities for outreach activities; sponsor and organize programs for latchkey kids, preschoolers, respite nurseries, parenting helplines, child care, self-help groups, and educational courses in substance abuse, child abuse, and the prevention of untimely pregnancy. Enlist community support for such activities and encourage a spirit of volunteerism in the congregation through public awareness announcements at religious services. Arrange church "socials" and other functions to raise funds to support church or community child abuse prevention and treatment programs.

Above all, the church must join in the movement to restore a genuine sense of family, which requires dealing directly with the well-being of children and the problems of their parents.

The community and the neighborhood. Publicly funded child rescue facilities, as distinct from charitably funded or church-sponsored programs, must become available in neighborhoods throughout the city—as short-term housing in agency-operated boarding homes for runaways, children of the homeless, and children who are not wanted because they are disabled or their parents are in prison or on drugs.

Through community-based efforts, the supply of licensed family day care centers must be increased, as should the availability of respite stops for mothers and mini-crisis nurseries for children. Working mothers, and those who care for them and their children, must be active in developing expanded neighborhood latchkey programs to offer safe and stimulating environments to kids who would otherwise have to go to an empty home at the end of the school day.

People—just neighborhood you-and-me people—have to demand these things themselves, have to figure out ways to get them. Other people have.

The medical fraternity. It is essential to have a multidisciplinary child protection team in every hospital to examine all suspected cases of child abuse. Hospital personnel should be better trained in the detection of abuse and neglect and in the simple procedures for reporting.

Primary preventive services in the form of hospital-based pre- and postnatal education programs and home care services must be designed and publicized in the community to forestall child abuse and neglect. All hospitals should develop parent education programs and a routine of home visits for all new parents. Hospital intake, treatment planning, and discharge procedures should be structured to assure that all new parents are able to take adequate care of their children in terms of their own physical and psychological health as well as their ability to provide the necessities. If necessary, referrals for public assistance must be made.

All states should develop policies officially expanding the child protective role of hospitals regarding the release of newborn babies. Some medical facilities do this already, but it should be standard procedure for all hospitals to screen all newborns for drugs and syphilis; screen all parents of newborns for histories of abuse and neglect; assure that parents, especially teenagers, have made adequate arrangements for the care of their babies before discharge.

To reduce the heavy toll of substance abuse on the next generation, care providers must take a family-centered approach to treatment. It is pointless to treat users of alcohol or drugs and ignore what might be happening to their children. Children's services have to be incorporated into the treatment setting, involving the entire family in the process and paying special attention to the possibility of child maltreatment by substance-abusing parents. Two outcomes can be expected of effective approaches. Treatment programs can reach children who have suffered physical or psychological damage from their parents' addiction and provide early interventions to mitigate the long-term consequences of their early drug exposure. And treatment programs can teach recovering abusers better parenting skills than they might have learned in their own childhood.

Auxiliary health care planning. I have tried to present a plan for a hospital-based program for prenatal and postnatal care that I think can be valuable in every state. What I believe needs extra emphasis is the *pre*-prenatal state. In other words, we must *get to them in school.* Get them while they're young, both the boys and the girls; get to them in the human sexuality and family development classes and teach them the health basics of pre-birth mothering. School nurses and counselors and social workers must be ready to lend support and advice whenever it becomes apparent that it is needed. The consequences of sexual encounters and youthful pregnancy must be hammered home at every opportunity; and if prevention fails, practical advice and counsel have to be available.

If this seems intrusive, so be it. It is part of contemporary education—a sorry part, reflective of our times—but we are wading in murk and we must get out of it. Let us not produce one generation after another of abusable children for want of teaching today's kids, at all ages, what is right and what is wrong and what is smart and what is stupid and what leads to happiness and what leads to a dead end. It must be brought home, preferably with the help of parents, but even if necessary without it. It is never too early to start, but it can be too late. Even hospital- or clinic-based prenatal programs can be too late. We must hope that schooldays are not too late.

The city: child protective services. In New York as in some other cities, our crisis intervention services are themselves in a state of crisis. They are in desperate need of being streamlined and strengthened. Our first priority must be the creation of an autonomous local Department of Children and Family Services. The next is to insist that it develop a coherent, integrated system of child protection that will enhance its credibility and performance.

A city's child protective agency is the children's emergency service. It must be geared to respond with all possible immediacy to calls for help, no matter where they come from: a sanitation worker hearing the cry of a newborn infant coming from a garbage can; a student telling a school nurse that she is being sexually molested at home; a hospital physician examining a badly bruised baby and finding indications of brain hemorrhage; a grandmother reporting that her son-in-law is beating her grandson; a cop answering a call about a domestic disturbance and observing a cruelly neglected child. All their calls go directly to the state's central child abuse hotline, whose intake workers quickly set the wheels in motion for the dispatch of caseworkers to the places where they are needed.

The caseworkers on the spot interview the people concerned and attempt to ascertain the facts. If there is a determination that maltreatment has taken place, they must then take on the awesome and difficult responsibility of treating the entire family: rescuing the maltreated child, protecting other children in the household, and rehabilitating the abusers.

As we know, the agency for which they work is in a state of chaos, and we know that the caseworkers are for the most part undertrained, overworked, underpaid, underappreciated, and drowning in paperwork. We must find ways of streamlining the paperwork and speeding up the flow of information. We must attract the most qualified workers by offering appropriate salary incentives and financial rewards for work particularly well done. We must create a "career ladder" in the field of child protective services to ensure that supervisors and program directors have adequate experience in the sensitive and difficult work of protecting endangered children.

In short, child protective workers on all levels must be uptrained and upgraded, so that not only do they do a more effective job but they are perceived as skilled professionals by other professionals with whom they must interact, as well as by their clients and the public at large.

Next, in those communities in which it has not already been done, let us separate the investigatory from the rehabilitative functions of the child protective caseworkers. It is simply not very smart to expect those who must dig out the facts and finger the probable perpetrators then to provide protective services to the children with one hand and rehabilitative services to abusive parents with the other. Finally, every child protective agency must have a multidisciplinary team for internal review, so that no decision is made on the basis of a single person's bias or perception.

This may sound difficult and complicated. It isn't. Like street directions to a stranger's house, the whole thing seems impossible when you first hear it, but the fact is that once you're on the road all things are recognizable and all instructions start making sense— as long as somebody has been paying attention.

To make all this work requires the establishment of a central department for children and family services in every city, distinct unto itself and responsible directly to the mayor or city manager; as well as a one-stop multidisciplinary family support service in every community, linked by computer to a central data storage and retrieval system so that all pertinent information on the families seeking service is available in one location.

The police department and domestic violence. There is a need for clearer policies and procedures for the protection of children in households that present a pattern of domestic violence. Police officers coming into contact with situations of domestic violence have not understood the impact on children in the household. Studies have demonstrated very clearly that when there is violence between husband and wife there is, sooner or later, likely to be violence against a child. In a violent household, *all* the kids are in danger, and the police must be trained to deal with these ugly domestic situations instead of walking away from them after a man-to-man chat with Dad. I believe that a more protective approach can be worked out in consultation between the police department, the district attorney's office, the child protective agency, a hospital child abuse team, and the victims' services agency; and I'm astounded that this has not been done already in every municipality in the nation.

The business community. Whenever possible, employers should try to provide day care or a day care plan, and extended leave policies for new parents.

The media. Public awareness of abuse and neglect is no longer an issue. Everybody who can read or watch television knows about child abuse. Now we need *responsibility awareness.* We need regular media campaigns to persuade people to report suspicious cases. We need to persuade the victims to come forward, before their pain and fear get worse. And we need to galvanize communities and politicians into action. We have gone beyond the stage of saying, This is child abuse and this is terrible. We are saying, This is how it hurts *you.* This is how you fight it. We are down to the core issues now. We must move on from the TV dramas to real life. Real life is worse, and we are living it.

Charitable contributions. Where are the very, very rich when we really need them? What does it take to persuade American philanthropists that there is no more important cause than the salvation of children? Than the cleansing of the polluted human environment? That no disease is more devastating to our national health, our environment, our work force and our battle against crime than the disease of child abuse? I wonder what their priorities really are.

The law and the community. Our judicial system, from the local family courts to the highest court in the land, must educate and revitalize itself in order to address the problem effectively. Every community should have a multidisciplinary panel, preferably hospital-located, to do two things: examine and assess allegedly abused children in connection with their appearance on the stand as witnesses in cases of abuse, sexual and otherwise; and assess the potential harm or benefit to the child when criminal prosecution is recommended for the perpetrator of the abuse.

Further, judges must realize that a crime against a child is just as serious and even more of an abomination than a crime against an adult. Sentences for child murder have often been outright travesties, making it horribly clear to any sadistic killer of the young and helpless that he or she need only expect a slap on the wrist. We are not discussing salvageable parents here, but brutal killers.

The state, part one. Coordination of efforts requires the establishment in each state of a computerized registry or data base to keep track of all child abuse reports until they are *proved to be unfounded.* But the state should take initiatives as well.

In addition to community programs for the prevention and treatment of child abuse, we must expand and replicate throughout all states programs that have passed the test of time and proven effective in treating abused and neglected children. Some of them deserve attention on a nationwide scale.

Consider Hawaii. The nation's newest state has been the first to develop a program aimed at identifying and aiding every newborn believed to be at risk of maltreatment by a parent. Hawaii's Project Healthy Start, begun in 1984 in an economically depressed area with a mere $400,000 allocated by the state legislature, has recently been expanded across the state and given a bankroll of $7 million to reach all new parents who appear to be headed for a dysfunctional family lifestyle. Early support and counseling are keynote themes.

Dr. Calvin Sia, past president of the Hawaiian chapter of the American Academy of Pediatrics and cofounder of the program, explains that the idea was born in about 1980 when it became apparent to him and his colleagues that school screening programs identifying youngsters in trouble were spotting them when they were already too damaged by family conflict to benefit greatly from treatment programs. There was virtually no intervention in the neonatal and toddler period. At the same time, the health care providers associated with children's protective services were burning out and breaking under the straining of ever-increasing caseloads.

The purpose of Project Healthy Start is to identify babies at risk for poor parental care. Hospital personnel scan the charts of all new mothers for indications of risk factors, such as single-parenthood, lack of housing, or lack of financial support. Women whose records suggest a possible need for help receive a visit from a family support worker, who uses what Dr. Sia calls "a kind of Welcome

Wagon approach" in offering services ranging from "grandmothering" to lining up better housing and adequate food supplies for the family. Through a series of home visits and the backup support of the primary care physician when necessary, these lay therapists routinely shepherd their charges through the maze of existing resources and match them up with the social programs they need.

In one early study of the program, 241 families defined as being at high risk were followed for a number of years. Only 5 infants were removed from their homes after having been deemed "in imminent danger." Four cases of neglect were identified; no cases of abuse occurred.

The state, part two. Here is an excellent observation by Minnesota's Lieutenant Governor Marlene Johnson on February 21, 1990, as part of a rundown on "The State of Minnesota's Children":

> It makes more sense to invest about $2,600 to keep a child in Head Start today than to spend almost $45,000 for a year in a juvenile correctional facility. It makes more sense to invest $400 a year in nutrition for a pregnant woman than to spend the hundreds of thousands of dollars it can take to treat health and developmental delays that are the result of poor nutrition.
>
> From an economic standpoint, the conclusion is unmistakable. We pay now. Or we pay more later.
>
> Take child abuse as an example. A recent study comparing the cost of prevention to the cost of no prevention is profound. Over the lifetime of one abused child, the cost to the individual, and the cost to society, of physical injuries, chronic health problems, learning disabilities, emotional difficulties, drug and alcohol abuse . . . the costs of foster care, court actions and loss of future earnings . . . amount to $2.3 million dollars—*$2.3 million dollars.* And the cost of preventing the abuse of that child, including parent education, counseling, intervention, child care, is less than $4,000 per family.
>
> Four thousand dollars to prevent the problem . . . or $2.3 million dollars to deal with the problem. We pay now. Or we pay much more tomorrow.

The federal government. I would expect the government to recognize the importance of children—not just through rhetoric but through action. Within the last decade, children and families have not been well served by our nation's leaders. One might have thought that the people's representatives' first concern would be for the well-being of the people, but this has not been the case. Politicians play their macho games there in Washington, but I see no improvement in the quality of life down here at street level. Indeed, it is worse now than it has ever been and I believe it's going to get worse yet before we turn the tide. In large part it is up to us, adult American citizens, to push our elective officials into getting their priorities in order. As Representative Pat Schroeder has pointed out, kids don't vote, but we do.

Let us remind our elected officials that we, the voters, are aware of the link between poverty, ignorance, crime, substance abuse, and child abuse. One begets the other. All problems must be approached with equal commitment. Why is it so difficult for those in power to recognize the fact that the root cause of many of our society's problems is child abuse?

There should be a citizens' demand for the development of a federal agency, headed by a "czar" or cabinet member responsible for making policy and coordinating nationwide efforts to prevent and treat child abuse. This should be our new national defense program, our environmental issue. A department for children is a must. Such an agency has to be appropriately funded to implement and coordinate national child care programs on a selective, coherent basis.

In the past government has not been totally indifferent to problems of child abuse and neglect, teenage pregnancies, substance abuse, street crime, poverty, domestic violence, juvenile delinquency, boarder babies, and the other everyday circumstances of our society, but government has attempted to cope with these problems by throwing money and services into crisis intervention services, by acting only in a reactive manner in an attempt to patch up troubled youngsters and their families *after* great damage has been done—and then making savage cutbacks in the most desperately needed areas because they don't see results.

These reactive efforts will never solve our social problems. They will only increase the costs of government by treating the symptoms of a social problem rather than attacking the causes. Proactive efforts, however, providing sufficient and effective human family support systems *before* the family explosion and deterioration occurs, can prevent much of the enormous burden of cost and effort currently weighing down our monetary and social agencies, as well as an enormity of human agony. In the midst of great need, we are throwing our money away. If government-sponsored programs do not work—and every day we see costly programs around us that are failing—let us trim them down and revamp them so that they do work or let us ruthlessly do away with them.

Of primary importance is to assess all child- and family-related programs in this country and weigh those that don't work against those that are helping to keep individuals intact and salvageable families together. Those that are not working should be eliminated. All monies should then be reallocated so that effective programs can be expanded and supported.

We must establish a *national* research and data base network, computerized to the state of the art. The 1988 amendments to the Child Abuse and Treatment Act of 1974 mandate the establishment of a national data collection and analysis program for the reporting of child abuse and neglect. Does this not suggest a central, national computer? It does to me. And we must make it clear to defenders of civil liberties that it is our civic duty to protect our children as well as the Bill of Rights.

And I would expect our national leader to do more than talk; I would expect him or her to present and pursue specific, well-researched proposals for dealing with child abuse.

Specifically, the President of the United States should:

• Provide leadership by committing major resources to research and to model programs that demonstrate ways to prevent child abuse in different kinds of communities. He should use his persuasive powers to enlist the support of volunteers and paraprofessionals, who can be startlingly effective in prevention programs. There are, in fact, many more than one thousand points of light; there are tens of thousands. But let our President not think that even deeply dedicated and brilliant amateurs can solve national problems by volunteering their time and goodwill or their cash contributions. This is not how national problems can or should be solved; commitment on a leadership level is the key.

• Acquaint himself with the provisions of the Act of 1974, which established the National Center on Child Abuse and Neglect (NCCAN) as a focal point for federal efforts to address the problem. From the outset, NCCAN was intended to offer leadership in establishing child abuse as a national concern and a federal priority. It has succeeded admirably in gathering and distributing invaluable data, and in funding certain community-based research and demonstration projects, but it has never enjoyed the status of a federally empowered force given a presidential directive to fight child maltreatment with all its might. It hasn't been given any "might." NCCAN must be strengthened with the staff necessary to accomplish its statutory mission, given the status of a government department serving under a cabinet-level department head, as suggested earlier, and equipped with funding adequate to support state and local efforts.

• Urge and direct the development of a national policy that encourages day care at the workplace. When children are cared for in close proximity to their working parents, who may drop in to visit at any time, they will benefit in two ways: they are much less likely to feel separation anxiety; and there is a greatly reduced likelihood of abuse in the day care arena.

• Be concerned about the lack of affordable housing for low-income and temporarily unemployed citizens. Growing up in substandard, crime-infected apartments or welfare hotel/motel rooms is devastating to children. How can they ever learn from these disgraceful situations what home and family can and should be like? These living quarters are an example of child abuse and neglect in its most insidious form. Federal funding, with additions by the states, must be forthcoming so that affordable housing can be made available to homeless families and bring them back into the community.

• Be aware of suggested agendas for guiding federal, state, and local policymakers in addressing the immediate and long-term needs of children and families. His own NCCAN can spell it all out for him. Let me, herewith, supply the shorthand version of what his own people would urge him to support—if they could get his ear:

• Public awareness programs about positive parenting and positive family support

• Prenatal health care and parenting education and support programs for all new parents, including home health visits, that reinforce parental responsibility for the children

• Support services for parents under stress, such as child care, respite care, crisis nurseries, helplines, self-help and other groups in a community network that provides a linked system of family care running a service gamut from housing to job training

• School-based, age-specific prevention education programs for all school-age children

• Coordination between child protective services and law enforcement in domestic violence situations

• Therapeutic care for victims and perpetrators of abuse, and follow-up services for the whole family

• Parenting education programs that include projects for the prevention of alcohol- and drug-related child abuse and neglect— for example, teaching about the dangers of substance abuse.

I would add that basic health care services must be expanded to the hundreds of thousands of families that do not have health coverage. If, for political and economic reasons, it is not possible to enact National Health Insurance for the entire population of the United States, it would seem sound policy to take an intermediate step with the enactment of a universal health program for all children and pregnant women. This would be analogous to the provision of medical care for the elderly under Medicare.

Under the leadership of some form of national health system, we should develop innovative ways and means of encouraging all pregnant women to use prenatal and postnatal health services. We must develop formalized outreach, systematically aimed at those who need it most and are most reluctant to seek help. In France, for example, financial incentives are used to encourage the full use of prenatal and postnatal health services. Under its family allowance system, prenatal allowances are paid to all expectant mothers when they register their pregnancy, consult a public health nurse or private physician, and follow the physician's medical, nutritional, and other instructions. After a child's birth, similar financial incentives encourage parents to take their infants for regular periodic medical checkups and immunizations. Human support services are provided if the need is apparent after an assessment of mother and child. Pregnant women are required *by law* to make four prenatal care visits to their doctor. Children also have a series of compulsory examinations—at eight days old, at nine months, and at two years old. The school health service picks up at subsequent stages of development, checking the children at the ages of four, seven, ten, and fourteen. Is this too hard for us to do?

The United States has neither a family allowance system nor a comprehensive prenatal and postnatal health system for mothers and infants nor a system of compulsory examination. We might think about these things. Meanwhile, Americans can and should employ financial or other incentives in a reaching-out approach in order to achieve the fuller and more effective use of *existing* health and social services until such time as we have a national plan. These efforts could have a major impact in reducing our national incidence of child abuse and neglect.

Studies in thirteen low-income counties in California and in South Carolina, and in the city of Baltimore, have shown that comprehensive and supportive prenatal care reduces the proportion of low-birth-weight babies; other studies have shown that intensive family support, nurse home-visiting, and child care programs have resulted in fewer children removed from home and lower rates of child abuse and welfare dependence in New York State, Washington State, and the city of New Haven, Connecticut.

A major area of national endeavor in the prevention of child abuse should be the increasing impact of drug and alcohol abuse on the maltreatment of children. Every year, more children are born addicted to drugs; and every year, child protective services receive more and more reports of abuse and serious neglect coming from families where one or both parents are using drugs. An expansion in prenatal care to all pregnant women would help improve the chances of children born to mothers addicted to drugs or abusing alcohol.

Let us talk more about home visitors and child health: the history of using professional and paraprofessional home visitors goes back to the late nineteenth century, when public health nurses and social workers routinely called upon the homes of the mostly urban poor to provide services to new mothers and young children. We in the United States have cut down drastically on public health home-visiting services because of budget slashes, but it is clear that we are making a very grave mistake. I resent the fact that we trail so far behind other industrialized nations in our primary care for kids.

Some form of visiting nurse program has been in effect in

England for close to 130 years and has been virtually universal since the beginning of this century, when we Americans commenced the programs that we subsequently dropped. Under British law the local health visitor, a registered nurse with special training in public health, is notified of every birth in her area and calls on each family with a new baby to offer advice and make a risk assessment. Visits continue throughout the first year of the new baby's life and, on a less intense schedule, through the preschool years. The visiting nurse program is part of the national health service, and salaries are paid by the government. The service applies to all families in England and Wales regardless of means—a health visitor called on the Princess of Wales after the births of Prince William and Prince Harry—so that no stigma is attached. We in America scorn "socialized medicine," but I think we have a great deal to learn.

When I get discouraged by government inertia, as I often do, I remind myself of how much has been accomplished and how much can be taught by private citizens. After thirty years of trying, child advocates have not persuaded government on any level to develop a coherent program of child abuse prevention and treatment. We are fortunate, therefore, to have a great many do-it-yourselfers—gutsy, determined civilians—who develop their own programs to fight the fight that should be led by government.

One such program fills in gaps the government never even thought of, I suppose because it may be too visionary.

The VisionQuest approach to breaking the cycle of abuse in families is the vision of a man named R. Ledger Burton, an administrator in Arizona's juvenile corrections system in the late 1960s and early 1970s. In 1973 he made the choice to get out of the corrections system and develop a new and more positive way to deal with maltreated and exploited kids and their families. This was the beginning of VisionQuest, a program started in Tucson, Arizona, on the premise that children and their families needed help and reunification, not punishment and alienation.

VisionQuest takes its inspiration from the culture of the American Plains Indians. Those early Americans sent adolescents of their tribes into the wilderness to seek a vision and learn self-sufficiency, and upon the youngsters' successful return rewarded them with tribal recognition of their adulthood. VisionQuest carries on this tradition in the realization that the quest is a rite of passage and that adolescence and its conflicts conclude only with the discovery of a pathway to maturity.

Today's version of this venerable tradition is a licensed child welfare program providing an alternative to institutionalization of children damaged by their abuse. Centers are located in Arizona, California, and Pennsylvania, and the quests operate in camps, on wagon trains, and aboard tall ships along the Eastern Seaboard. The children seen at VisionQuest are troubled youngsters caught in a downward spiral of failure and considered hopeless, beyond the help of conventional services and supposedly destined to become disturbed, destructive adults. But this has not proved inevitable. Independent studies have demonstrated the effectiveness of VisionQuest programs in salvaging scarred and troubled youngsters, which suggests the need for more such programs throughout the United States.

Another novel enterprise was born some years ago in Ohio.

Crisis nurseries and respite centers are not a new idea. What is new, and desperately needed, is a service that operates on weekends when so many vital services are turned off for want of full-time help. A crisis intervention program called Turning Point, developed by the North Side Development Center in collaboration with the League Against Child Abuse, both based in Columbus, Ohio, has shown the way to plug this gap by operating a weekend crisis assistance and child care program that is available to all stressed mothers from 6 P.M. each Friday until 7 A.M. the following Monday. Children up to twelve are accepted, although the primary focus is on children five years or younger. This was the first such program in the state of Ohio to offer relief from parental responsibilities to parents experiencing a crisis, without requiring them to risk legal entanglements.

The benefits of programs such as this have been cited extensively in child-abuse-prevention literature. Young parents are especially vulnerable on weekends, when all possible entertainments are open and available but all helping services, such as the preschool program, the doctor's office, the clinic, the family support group, and the baby-sitter's answering machine, are locked up as tight as Sunday in the Bible Belt. And usually there's not even a relative to help out in a time of trouble.

The National Center for the Prevention of Child Abuse and

Neglect has included crisis nurseries as part of its Community Plan for Preventing Child Abuse. It has indicated that such facilities can give parents support to alleviate the stresses of a particular situation and can provide assistance in locating long-term human support services. Every community, every neighborhood, should have a respite crisis nursery for the stressed and troubled parent who is at risk of harming a child.

If the government still needs a model, there are many more in the private community, some of them on a scale to shame a democracy into realizing that it has allowed its citizens to do by default the work that its leaders are paid to do. But committed people don't waste themselves on small resentments. They look to leaders, find nothing there, and build their own national programs.

One such program, Childhelp USA, has given severely neglected and abused children a second chance at a better life in an unusual residential treatment center: the Village of Childhelp in Beaumont, California, just outside Los Angeles. Childhelp USA is a self-contained, full-service community in itself, as innovative and comprehensive a program of treatment as any devised anywhere in the world. A twenty-four-hour-a-day hotline—1-800-4-A-CHILD—is manned by twenty-two counselors who answer some 175,000 calls for help per year. Tireless, dedicated therapists and counselors at the Village have given new life and hope to the children who are among the worst child abuse victims ever to be rescued. After an average of eighteen months of therapy these fixed-up kids move back into the community via adoption, foster care, or a return to their rehabilitated parents.

This model village, opened in 1978, was the vision of two remarkable women, Sara O'Meara and Yvonne Fedderson. At Childhelp, children are given a home filled with a spirit of caring and love in an environment conducive to a child's learning and caring. It is a home also for a whole barnyard of animals, from lambs, goats, ducks, cats, rabbits, cows, and ponies to a potbellied Vietnamese pig. I have been impressed with this remarkable place since my first visit back in 1985, not only because it is a fine treatment center but because it is also a temporary home infused with a sense of family. The animals gave it something special that I have not seen at other therapeutic centers: a kind of earthiness, and also something warm and playful. It has been said that as long as a child cares for his animal, he can be assured of unquestioned devotion and companionship, which is something that the child of neglect has never known before. From the uncomplicated emotional tie with a favorite animal, he learns rapidly that there is a very simple cause and effect: love and care beget love and care.

The Village has room for eighty kids at a time, ages two to twelve, in a complex of eight homy cottages plus treatment buildings. They are not easy cases. Here are children who have been sexually abused since babyhood, locked in closets for days on end, seared with red-hot pokers in every part of the body. Here is quiet, obedient little Cynda, whose habit of holding her dolly underwater was hard to understand until caseworkers learned that she had seen her mother drown her baby sister in the bathtub. Here is Rick, the child of drug-abusing satanic cultists, so afraid of adults that only now is he able to raise his head to them without flinching. And Frances, no longer here, who came to Childhelp at the age of seven after having been viciously abused by her stepfather in a variety of ways, mostly sexual, and then bounced from one foster home to another because of her bizarre behavior. She spent three and a half years in the Village of Childhelp, and on her discharge was viewed as a leader in her cottage unit. She is now in a stable placement with a loving family and doing very well.

Most of the stories that come out of this place are success stories, but they are nearly all success stories with something missing. It would be wonderful to say that, at the end of the abuse and the rehabilitation, a happy Mommy and Daddy and their carefree little children walk together into a new sunrise, but it doesn't happen that way. This is the village of second chance, but it can't give back the family's first shot at life or turn it into something that never was.

Virginia, for example, was three and a half years old when she was admitted, unconscious, to a hospital intensive care unit after the latest of her father's beatings and burnings. He, loathsome to the last, had ordered his wife to tell the paramedics and authorities that she was the one who had hurt the child. In her misery and guilt, the woman did shoulder some of the blame, but it became clear that she was a loving mother who had herself been victimized. The father went to jail, but she did not.

After three months of treatment for the array of injuries to her entire body, from belt marks to a brain hemorrhage, Virginia was discharged to Childhelp. For a while she continued to have terrible nightmares from which she awakened screaming with terror; and during the days she was moody and negative and subject to temper tantrums. But as time went by, the good-natured yet intensive therapy she was getting at Childhelp began to reveal the real little girl hidden by the wounds. There was a day when she began playing with the animals and another when she showed her first genuine interest in romping with her peers. She began to show enjoyment in singing and riding her bike; she developed a sense of fun and even of humor, for she was—and still is—a bright little kid.

There is an early childhood development program at Childhelp, and Virginia did well in it. Then it was on to kindergarten, and there again she did well both behaviorally and academically. Meanwhile, she continued to receive therapy on a weekly basis. At the same time, Virginia's mother, who had been an abused child herself, was also receiving individual therapy in addition to an indepth course in parenting. By the time the little girl was ready to leave Childhelp, her mother was ready to take her home and love her unconditionally.

The Childhelp Aftercare Unit has been keeping a familial eye on mother and daughter since then. Virginia and her mother still get individual and family therapy. One year later both of them are happy and doing well.

Clearly, this is no fairy-tale ending, but at least two people have been salvaged from the tragedy of three, and Virginia and her mother are their own intact family. If ever again they need help, they know where to turn.

The full services of Childhelp include research into all issues of child welfare and service delivery systems; prevention by means of public education; multidisciplinary treatment services; aftercare family support; a foster family program in which potential foster parents are strictly screened, trained, and provided with ongoing support; and a family evaluation program that provides one service—among others—that probably deserves the overused word "unique." This has to do with family court.

Most family courts in this country, as we all know by now, are effectually buried under an avalanche of child abuse and dependency cases. Childhelp's core evaluation team of psychologists works with public child welfare agencies and judges in reaching critical decisions regarding *the best interest of the individual child* in terms of therapy, family reunification, and placement. What this boils down to is that the child has a battery of experts on his side at a traumatic time of his life that is usually made worse by the processes supposedly designed to save him. Foster care placements are chosen with extreme care; families are reunified only when genuinely rehabilitated. Yes, occasionally things do go wrong after a time; but an 87 percent success rate is not bad at all.

The total Childhelp program is truly admirable. It is also exceptional, and it shouldn't be. It can be replicated on an official basis, but it hasn't been.

Why, I wonder, can't public facilities for children be anything like this? Why can't the government of the people lead the people into a better future, instead of leaving the action to a scattered band of civilian pioneers?

Many of my recommendations have been made in the past. This doesn't mean that they don't or won't work. It means that they haven't been tried. That the problems I have talked about are still with us, virtually unchanged, and that children continue to die under virtually unchanged circumstances suggests that there is something terribly wrong with a system that is failing to correct its own obvious shortcomings. The magnitude and complexity of this country's child abuse problem demand that we redesign the institutions responsible for responding to the needs of the children they are meant to serve. The time has come to stop the hurting and start the healing. If we continue to fail our maltreated children and their families, we will be starting the twenty-first century with a grim legacy: one generation after another of disturbed, violent, hollow young men and women.

Epilogue: What Is a Child to Do?

What is left untold, unresolved, is what a child can do when he or she is being abused or molested. Only the victim truly knows—without always understanding—what is happening, where it hurts, and how much it hurts. Adult victims of child abuse remember and keep hurting. They, of all people, could help the abused kids of today—if only they knew where and how to reach them.

For adults with unhappy pasts, talking is easier these days. Airing the family's dirty linen in public is no longer a shame. There is a growing awareness that it is the healthy and necessary thing to do. We know now that many show business personalities and other public figures suffered painful and tormented childhoods. We discover, through them or their authors and the multiplicity of stories told in our daily newspapers, that what we thought was a unique and shameful little secret is a common, everyday practice. I hope that readers of these pages will recognize themselves or people close to them, will identify, will empathize, will *speak*. There is plenty of company out there. This is dubious consolation in terms of what it says about the American way of life, but the abuse victim need not feel singled out and lonely. About one out of four men and women, by the time they reach adulthood, will have experienced at least one episode of abuse during childhood. Most of those whose secretly unhappy lives I have uncovered would seem to be less hurt than those who wind up on the streets or in jail, but I am not sure they are. Something has been done to their personality, to their well of happiness, and there is no knowing when what they have turned inside upon themselves may be turned outward again to inflict their hurt on others. Besides, it is enough that they themselves are hurt.

Yet—there may be a way they can exorcise their demons. Maybe they can listen as well as talk. Better than anyone, they know that it is inconceivably difficult for a child to open up to someone about the things that disturb him or her the most. Who can she trust, if not those closest to her, the very people who are doing the disturbing things? Furthermore, young victims are reluctant to believe that the parent or other loved one is actually doing something wrong; in our formative years we assume that the older person knows and does what's best for us. If we doubt that, we hurt, but still we have our loyalties: the world must not know that Daddy or Mommy or Uncle Joe is acting funny or ugly—and anyway, we may be mistaken.

Well, chances are we're not. Kiddy "badness" does not merit relentless, irrational abuse. Physical punishment of a child is wrong in itself; a pattern of self-indulgent outbursts in the guise of discipline is a crime against childhood and against the terrified, defenseless child. And the sexual abuse of a child is truly an abomination. Most children sense that what is done in secret to their most private selves is not normal; they may be told it is love and they may think it is supposed to be love, but when they feel it is wrong, it *is* wrong.

The question is, who can abused youngsters talk to when they want to talk? If they are lucky, they may have an understanding cousin or aunt. But usually the best listener is not another member of the family, who may tend to be unwilling to believe the shameful secret; it is easier to assume the child is lying or fantasizing. An outsider is in the best position to be objective. But what outsider? Conventional wisdom says: a trusted older friend, or a guidance counselor at school.

But how many kids have a trusted older friend? Who would this this person be? Perhaps a friend's mother, or a neighbor, or a favorite teacher. These are all possibilities, but it takes a very tuned-in youngster to choose a confidant with the wisdom to know what to do. There are some excellent guidance counselors around, but in my experience the average counselor is a better basketball coach. How about the pastor or physician or school nurse? These are possibilities in certain cases, but they are not the answer; they are authority figures, much like the parent, and from the child's point of view there is no knowing whose side they will take. And certainly a little kid, a three- or four-year-old, is not going to have an idea in the world where to turn.

What, then?

I urge all individuals in all families to be alert and responsible. We are our brothers' and our sisters' keepers, and we are the keepers of their kids, and we could at least look as though we can listen and care.

I urge teachers in appropriate classes—those relating to human behavior and family studies—to talk candidly about the oddities of human nature and indicate what is normal and permissible and what is not. If this requires a curriculum change, so be it.

And I urge guidance counselors and those who appoint them to inform themselves about the range of child abuses and how best to help the children. Special skills and special training are a must. Reporting, by itself, is not enough and may even be unwise in some cases. The child needs an ear and the family needs help that may be a touch more individualized and sophisticated than the intervention afforded by the lumbering welfare services.

This still does not fully address the question of what the aware preadolescent child can do when he or she must find someone who will not only listen but be able to take appropriate action. This is it: *There are helpline and hotline numbers to call.* These numbers are proliferating and are posted in public places, including bus stations and subway cars, and can be found in telephone books and community notices. They should be present on every school and library bulletin board in the nation. I have known one or two people to sneer at this solution as a copout—"Oh, sure, wrap up the whole problem with the Hotline!"—but they are clearly unaware of the very positive advantages. Helpline and hotline numbers, and the services available through them, offer total anonymity and confidentiality to the caller. A child who is afraid or ashamed need not feel shame or fear when talking to a total stranger whose sole function is to help whoever calls.

And the little kids? Some very little ones are sophisticated enough to call a helpline. But we can't count on that. And we certainly can't expect babies to act like adults. We—especially men and women who were themselves abused as children—have to be there for them. If we suspect unhappiness, we must encourage them to speak. We have to use our eyes, our ears, and our instinct.

There are children out there crying for help, and we are still not listening to them.

When are we going to hear them?

How about right now?

RESOURCES FOR PARENTS

Lifelines

Parents Anonymous
For information and referral to
regional resources   1-800-421-0353

Childhelp USA
Child-abuse hotline; crisis counseling
for abused youth and stressed parents; referrals to local programs and
help in reporting abuse to state
agencies   1-800-4-A-CHILD
                                                      (1-800-422-4453)

Domestic Violence Shelter Aid Hotline
Referrals for victims of domestic
violence   1-800-333-SAFE

Cocaine Hotline
Information and referrals on substance
abuse   1-800-COCAINE

Covenant House Nineline
Crisis intervention for kids in trouble
and parents having trouble with
their children; referrals to community
resources   1-800-999-9999

Runaway Hotline   1-800-621-4000

All areas: See the front pages of your local telephone directory.
Under the general heading of Community Services Numbers,
find specific listings for Children's Services, Crime Victims Hotlines, Domestic Violence Hotline, Drug Abuse, and Family and
Children's Services.

Coping With Stress—How Not to Fly off the Handle

The National Committee for the Prevention of Child Abuse suggests a list of *Twelve Alternatives to Whacking Your Kid*:

1. Stop in your tracks. Step back. Sit down.

2. Take five deep breaths. Inhale. Slowly, slowly.

3. Count to ten. Better yet, twenty. Or say the alphabet out loud.

4. Phone a friend. A relative. Even the weather.

5. Still mad? Punch a pillow. Or munch an apple.

6. Thumb through a magazine, book, newspaper, photo album.

7. Do some situps.

8. Pick up a pencil and write down your thoughts.

9. Take a hot bath. Or a cold shower.

10. Lie down on the floor, or just put your feet up.

11. Put on your favorite record.

12. Water your plants.

How to Help a Stressed-out Parent Let off Steam

1. Encourage your friend, relative, or neighbor to talk about her situation. Lend a sympathetic ear.

2. Empathize with the difficulty of coping with active children in the home, the supermarket, or the playground. Smile and show friendly interest rather than disapproval.

3. Volunteer to do some of the parent's shopping or other chores.

4. Offer to stay with the children when Mother needs a break at the coffee shop or the manicurist's.

5. Find out about specific support systems available in the neighborhood—mothers' groups, respite centers, Parents Anonymous—and refer her to them.

Rules for Preventing the Risk of Child Abduction and Molestation

1. Know where your young children are at all times and let them know of your whereabouts. Urge them to phone you, as a matter of habit, when they reach their destination.

2. Never leave a child alone in one area of a mall or store while shopping in another.

3. Do not allow a child to go to a public restroom alone.

4. Never leave a child alone in a car while you shop no matter how soon you expect to return.

5. Never allow young children to play outdoors in secluded places without adult supervision.

6. Make arrangements for your children's schools authorizing who picks them up after school other than yourself.

7. Teach children how to use a phone in case of an emergency. Make sure they know how to call the operator and the police for assistance. They should know where they live. They should be taught their own phone number, including the area code.

8. Always choose a responsible, trustworthy, well-recommended baby-sitter for your children. Listen carefully to what your children say about their baby-sitter.

9. Instruct your children that when they are away from home, they should never take a present or a ride without your permission.

10. Give clear directions to your children that it is *OK* to say *NO* to any adult asking for assistance, offering gifts, rides, or asking to take the child's picture. Instruct the child to say no, and then to come and tell you what happened!

APPENDIX

Mandated Reporters

Mandated reporters are those individuals who must report, or cause a report to be made, whenever they have reasonable cause to suspect that a child coming before them in their professional or official capacity is abused or maltreated, or when they have reasonable cause to suspect that a child is an abused or maltreated child where the parent, guardian, or custodian or the person legally responsible for the child comes before them in their professional or official capacity and states from personal knowledge, facts, conditions, or circumstances which, if correct, would render the child an abused or maltreated child . . .

If you suspect child abuse or maltreatment while acting as a staff member of a medical or other public or private institution, school, facility or agency, you must immediately notify the person in charge of such institution, school, facility, or agency or his or her designee. That person also becomes responsible for reporting or causing a report to be made to the SCR [State Central Register]. . . .

The purpose of the mandatory reporting statute is to identify suspected abused and maltreated children as soon as possible, so that such children determined to be abused or maltreated can be protected from further harm and, where appropriate, can be offered services to assist their families. The intervention of the appropriate local child protective service cannot begin until a report is made. Consequently, as a mandated reporter you play a critical role in preventing any future abuse or maltreatment to a child.

The preceding paragraphs constitute the official—if abbreviated—word of New York's State Department of Social Services with regard to the function of mandated reporters. Following is an essential piece of information that, incredibly, seems little known to the appropriate professionals:

PERSONS MANDATED TO REPORT

Physicians
Surgeons
Medical examiners
Coroners
Dentists
Osteopaths
Optometrists
Chiropractors
Podiatrists
Social service workers
Day care center workers
Child care workers
Family or group family day care providers
Peace officers
School officials
Employees or volunteers in residential care facilities
Residents
Interns
Registered nurses
Hospital personnel engaged in admission, examination, care, or
    treatment
Christian Science practitioners
Foster care workers
Mental health professionals
Psychologists
Police officers
Other law enforcement officials
District attorney or assistant district attorney
Investigators employed in the office of district attorney

In New York, reports can be made seven days a week, at any time of the day or night, to the state's Central Register of Child abuse or Maltreatment (or SCR).

One final note here, on legal liability and obligation, drived from the state child abuse laws:

Any persons, officials, or institutions who in good faith make a report, take photographs, and/or take protective custody, have immunity from any liability, civil or criminal, that might be a result of such actions. All persons, officials, or institutions who are required to report suspected child abuse or maltreatment are presumed to have done so in good faith as long as they were acting in the discharge of their official duties and within the scope of their employment and so long as their actions did not result from the willful misconduct or gross negligence of such a person.

Any person, official, or institution required by the law to report a case of suspected child abuse or maltreatment, who willfully fails to do so, may be guilty of a Class A misdemeanor. Furthermore, any person, official or institution required by the law to report a case of suspected child abuse or maltreatment who knowingly and willfully fails to do so may be civilly liable for damages caused by the failure to report.

INDEX